# THE LIFE AND TIMES

# OF

# HOWARD H HIGGINSON

*with*

*Beverly Higginson*

ISBN 978-0-9831191-1-1

Published in the United States by
Blue Jay Ink
451 A East Ojai Ave.
Ojai, California 93023

bluejayink.com

BLUE JAY INK

# THE LIFE AND TIMES

## OF

# HOWARD H. HIGGINSON

*Dedicated to My Family*

*In memory of My Parents*
*My Brother and My Sister Lizzie*

*With Love and Appreciation to My Wife Bev*

# Table of Contents

**Introduction**      9

**Preface**      10

***Part 1 – 1947-1965   Early Days***      12
Arrival • About Arthur & Flora • 6-1-6      13
Old Lady Lybrook • St. Malachy's      25
Don't Smoke • A Taste of Rich • Changes      34
Goat Soup • Summers • Trip to the Docks      42
Early $$ • Extra Extra! • Boxing • Bishops Band      54
Bess 2 • Cornbread Days • Church Stuff      66
Cousin Albert • School Again • Texas Christmas      77
Teen at Last • Hawking for Mr. Cooper      92
What I Knew by Age 14 • Salesian • Pius X      101
Getting My Wheels • Senior Year      111
Watts Riot • More than a Notion      117

***Part 2 – 1966-1979   Guns and Badges***      129
You're in the Air Force Now • At the 'Berg      130
Desire vs Common Sense • Vietnam • TET      138
Short Timer • Homecoming • Back to Life      153
Apartment • Going to the Chapel • Docks      163
Marshal Years • Dad • Academy • Belshaw      174
JON • West LA • Compton/Long Beach      184
One Hot Item • Whose Bentley? • Moving Again      196
Skywood • LANCE • Max Burgers      207
Six Year Itch • Hub City Car Wash • Vermont      213

*Part 3 – 1980-Present   Down to Business*                    256
Switching Gears • Taco Truck #1 • Azusa                        257
The Thing • Manchester • Slow Going                            262
Taco Truck #2 • Movin' & Shakin' • Sinnreit                    273
Riot • Long Neck Long Shot • Hacienda Days                     286
Weathering Storms • Obstacles                                  296
Azusa Sale • L'Arthur • Leaving Skywood • Paris                300
Unit 534 • To the Beach • Muhtha-Lizzie                        312
Turning 60 • No Longer a Tenant • Epilogue                     319

# Introduction

This story is
  true
  feel-good
  smile inducing
  a love story

This story is NOT
  a tragedy
  a how to
  a thriller
  a mystery

This story is not about
  abuse
  addiction
  drugs
  dysfunction

This is Howard's story
told his way
with no frills or fluff.
That was our mission
(nearly mission impossible)
I hope you will decide that it is
"mission accomplished."

  *~ Beverly*

# ~ Preface ~

"Always start with an outline!" I remembered that rule from Mr. Finney's English class at Harbor Junior College in 1971. It came back to me when I began looking back on my life.

Why did I want to tell my life story? Several reasons, one of them being my age. Time passes so quickly in this fast-paced life we live, I found myself talking more and more about the good old days, the *Leave It to Beaver* days, when life was like the lyric in *Summertime...the living was easy*. I'd almost describe my childhood as carefree. And there was another reason that was prompted by a friend after I had related some crazy incident from my kid days. He said, "Wow. You should write a book." I thought, *maybe I will.*

I had fun growing up in Los Angeles in the '50's and '60's, and I experienced unforgettable moments in history as one of seventy-five million baby boomers who came of age against a backdrop of tragedy and uplift: assassinations, riots, war, and the civil rights movement. Thank goodness for '60's music that helped bring our spirits up during those crucial times.

Now as a senior citizen, I'm proud of my life and what I've accomplished, and I've wanted to share the story of how I made it through, from then to now. I didn't start out with much, but I had a need to rock my own boat. Early on without realizing it, I was thinking "outside the box" about the life I wanted to live. This "scrapbook" tells how that life came to be.

I miss those days of thirteen-inch tv's with only seven channels, watching shows like *Father Knows Best* and *Stoney Burke* and the *Little Rascals*, playing in the street until dark, and riding my bike all over the neighborhood. Those simple days are gone, never to be seen again. I'm grateful and happy to have been a kid then, and even more grateful that I'm able to share those times, and the years that followed with anyone who cares to read this book.

Not every famous person has a biography written about them, and some biographies are about non-famous people who had a desire to see their story in print. This is one of those. I hope you enjoy it.

# PART ONE

## 1947 - 1965

## Early Days

# ~ Arrival ~

South Hoover Hospital, Los Angeles is where life started for me. I got the spank at 8:05 in the morning, March 11, 1947, the third and biggest baby of Arthur Wade Higginson and Flora Bell Navy-Higginson, weighing in at eight pounds, nine ounces, and 20 inches long. My siblings were my sister Gwen, the studious one, my brother L'Arthur, the enterprising one, and my baby sister Lizzie, the one who always tried to get along. In temperament, and appearance, I was the one most like my dad. I had his deep brown skin and wavy hair. I was a prankster as a kid, hard-headed at times, but easy going and single-minded once my mind was made up. A boy of few words who grew up to be a man who didn't always bite his tongue.

But I'm getting ahead of myself.

My dad named me after millionaire Howard Hughes. If there was a memorable story behind that decision, I never heard it. I'm guessing it was a spur of the moment idea sparked by something in the news about Hughes and his money and dad thought naming me after someone with big money might be lucky.

I think my dad believed in luck, though he never had much of it. His idea of good luck would have been picking the right horse at the race track and "winning a hatful." I think he had high hopes for me, his second son, and for all of his kids, and dreams for himself that never came true. But he was always trying.

I have memories that go back to when I was four years old. We lived in the Willowbrook area of Los Angeles, on 119<sup>th</sup> and Holmes Avenue. Like my parents, most of our neighbors were southern Negroes from Oklahoma or Alabama or Texas, country folks raised on farms. As late as 1951 nearly every house on Holmes including ours had some type of farm animal. A goat, a cow, pigs, or chickens, animals for food and some profit, all of us living on farms in the city of the Angels.

Our house was old, probably built in the 1920's. We had neighbors on both sides, a long back yard, patchy grass, rough wood floors full of splinters, and two small bedrooms. We had a double bed that hardly fit in our room, and Gwen, L'Arthur, Lizzie and I all slept in it together. Many mornings I'd wake up with somebody's foot in my face.

A lot of memories are tied closely to Flora Bell, my mother, though we never called her "mother." Or ma, mama, mommy, or ma-dear. She was just Muhtha, round and plump. She had a shy smile and easy way about her, but she could be tough too. I remember her marching Gwen, L'Arthur and me around the living room making us repeat our address over and over, 11902 Holmes, 11902 Holmes.

I remember her expression, so intent, holding a burnt tipped needle like a scalpel to dig splinters out of my feet from those floors, and how she bribed me to make butter in an old wooden churn my dad had made that was kept on the back porch.

"Turn the crank, make that butter, and I'll give you a piece of chocolate." That was the promise, and the prize was tucked inside her apron pocket. I cranked that handle with a smile on my face. It didn't seem like work because I was going to get a reward, a piece of chocolate.

Muhta had planted a vegetable garden in the backyard, and we had to help pick the crop—collard greens, tomatoes off the vine, and string beans. When Gwen and L'Arthur were away at school, my special job was gathering the eggs from the chicken coop. Some were for us to eat and some Muhtha would sell to neighbors who came to the back door. She sold hunks of butter wrapped in wax paper, and milk from our cow Bess to neighbors who didn't have a cow. She had a little pouch where she kept the money, and at the end of a week, she and daddy would stack each denomination of coins on the kitchen table and add them up. It made me think of the nursery rhyme about the king and queen counting the money in the parlor and eating bread and honey. The rhyme didn't apply to my folks, but it came to mind anyway.

We didn't have a refrigerator, just an ice box not much taller than Muhtha, and it was thirsty for a five-pound block of ice every few days. We had to be on the lookout for the iceman. He came through the neighborhood in a steel gray truck calling out "*iiiiiiiiiiiiiiiice for sayaaaaaaaal.*" One of us would run outside and flag him down. He'd haul the block in on a dolly through the back door, use his giant tongs to lift it, then drop it into the bottom of the box. Muhtha would pay him with coins out of the pouch.

With me tagging along, she and I fed the chickens every morning. To me it was fun, not a chore. I liked the sound of clucking all around my feet, watching them scramble to get the seed. I didn't understand the chickens weren't pets because when a new chick was born, we'd bring it inside and play with it like it was a kitten.

I hadn't yet made the connection between the

chickens in the yard, and the fried chicken on our plates for Sunday dinners. Not until I heard the squawk of death one morning. Muhtha had grabbed a chicken and chopped off the head. She was so quick with that ax it was a wonder she hadn't cut her own hand. The headless bird with its wings flapping ran around the yard. I didn't want to watch, but I couldn't look away. Muhtha was a one-woman band after the kill. She caught the bird by a wing and dropped it into boiling water in a pot already on the stove. After the bird cooled, she plucked out all those feathers and then separated the wings from the breasts and the legs from the thighs, dropped the pieces into a bag of flour, salt, pepper, and spices, shook it up, and then slipped each piece into a skillet of poppin' hot grease.

For the rest of the day I kept seeing that bird running around the yard with no head. And then, that night at dinner, there it was on a plate in the middle of the table, golden brown and crispy. Muhtha's delicious fried chicken, long before KFC and Popeye's.

Besides chickens and one bad tempered rooster that chased us around the yard, Dad had fenced off an area next to the coop and stocked it with turkeys that he sold at Thanksgiving. I don't remember how successful that was, but that was the plan. We had a lean-to ramshackle put-together barn with one stall for our Holstein Bess. Dad milked her every morning. I'd watch him from a distance do that dance with his hands—pull squirt pull squirt—sitting on an upturned bucket. He'd call to me.

"Come over here boy, she ain't gonna hurt you." She was big, and I was afraid of her. He knew I was afraid but still, he tried to get me to milk her. I tried, but I didn't like the sticky feel of those teats. He'd get a whole bucket of milk out of her, then walk her across the street to the vacant lot where the grass grew tall and wild, and where Muhtha had a clear view through the kitchen window to watch her. Free grazing across the street. That was a big part of why he bought the house.

While Watts and Willowbrook were experiencing an influx of Negro residents, there were Caucasians like the Dobbins, our next-door neighbors, still living in the area. One of their four kids was a teenage girl who would pick me up and press her cheek to mine and tell me how cute I was. I think her name was Marilyn, or I might be confusing her with a later famous blond.

She once told Muhtha that she knew all about babies from her little brother and sisters, hoping that Muhtha would let her babysit us, but Muhtha didn't trust her. My most vivid recollection of this light-haired "Marilyn" is of the time I watched her milking their goat. She turned the teat in my direction, and squirted milk right into my face. I ran into the house not knowing if I should laugh or cry. I may have liked being babysat by mischievous "Marilyn," but it never happened.

Our babysitting neighbors were Mr. and Mrs. Polowitz, German refugees who were the first to welcome us to the neighborhood just before I was born. Muhtha and Mrs. Polowitz became as close as two women could in those days, being of different races and one not working for the other. She would come to our side door and call out, "Yoo hoo, Higgins," and they would have coffee and chat like neighbors in a tv show.

She once found me at the table with peanut butter and jelly on my face. "Oh, you little swine eagle," she said laughing. She wet a towel and wiped my face like any grandma would.

I had never heard the words "swine eagle" but I've never forgotten them. It may not have been the nicest thing to say. May have been a flat-out insult. But Muhtha didn't seem offended, and I was too young to get my feelings hurt.

The day L'Arthur started first grade at St. Leo's Catholic School, Mrs. Polowitz came right over to watch Lizzie and me while Muhtha walked L'Arthur to school. Gwen had been at St. Leo's for two years and was already down the steps raring to go. She actually liked school. Mrs. Polowitz stood with Lizzie and me at our front door, and we waved goodbye to L'Arthur like he was never coming back.

Muhtha told us Mr. and Mrs. Polowitz were good people. They empathized with their Negro neighbors who had their own history of suffering and discrimination. They liked the neighborhood, and the people who lived here because we didn't judge them. Muhtha never questioned or doubted their kindness. She took them at face value and by example, we did too. We gave to them what they had given to us—colorblind friendship.

St. Leo's was our parish, Gwen and L'Arthur attended school there, and the priest, Father McNulty had christened me. But Leo's had no kindergarten class. In the fall of 1952, when it was time for me to start school, Muhtha walked me to Lincoln Elementary, a public school at 118th and Compton Avenue, and turned me over to my teacher, Miss Segal who took me by the hand. Holding her other hand was a little girl who looked at me and said, "Hi pretty boy." She was my first girlfriend.

After the first few days, I was a five-year old on my own. If Muhtha had any concerns about me walking to and from school by myself, she didn't show it. It was a three-block trek, and I was to take the same route every day, no detours, no lollygagging. I don't remember being afraid walking by myself even after being chased by a dog. After that ambush, my eyes were like searchlights to see everything around me as I walked, not just what was right in front of me.

Some days, I'd come out of school and Muhtha and Lizzie would be across the street waiting for me. I'd feel such a relief a big smile would overtake my face.

Near the end of the school year, Miss Segal walked me home and came right into our backyard to see our farm animals. I do believe if all my teachers had been like her, I may have become a better student.

## ~ About Arthur and Flora ~

My folks were never very forthcoming about their early lives, except to say they grew up poor and were raised on farms. What I know came in bits and pieces, some from them, some from relatives.

Arthur (Dad) was born in August of 1912 in Texas, in a place that would never be found on a map called Reisel. It was fifteen miles from the larger city of Waco. His father, a light-skinned bootlegger named Frazier Higginson had the misfortune of being killed in a car crash at the age of twenty-four. Arthur was a three-year old toddler deprived of ever really knowing his father. His mother Sofia, a dark-skinned Negro woman was made a widow at the age of twenty-three.

Frazier's father was said to be the white owner of the general store in Waco. His Negro customers called him "Mista Man." The unspoken secret was that Arthur was Mista Man's grandson, but it wasn't really a secret at all. As the story goes, anytime Arthur came into the store with Sofia, Mista Man would give him hard candy from the candy jar on the counter.

The only role model Arthur had growing up was the man Sofia married a year after Frazier's death. Stepfather Rufus was fifteen years older than Sofia. She bore him five more children. By the time Arthur was sixteen he had four half-sisters and a half-brother named Joe. As Arthur got older, in addition to his farm chores, Rufus charged him with taking care of his siblings, almost before he knew how to take care of himself. He and Rufus clashed. Step relations between fathers and sons are hard. Theirs was no different.

Arthur left home at seventeen with his good friend Cal. They hopped a convenient freight train, one that came through Reisel at the Harrison Switch Junction. The two became train-hopping hobos through Oklahoma and Kansas. Ten years passed before Arthur came back to Texas and wound up in Houston where he met Flora Bell Navy. She lived with her parents and five brothers and sisters and was originally from Baldwin Louisiana.

When Arthur began showing up at Flora's door, her family did not approve. They had several reasons, and one in particular. Arthur had no religious affiliation and did not attend church. Ever. Her parents and siblings were devout go-to-Mass-every-Sunday Catholics. They thought Arthur was a heathen. However, he prevailed. The two were married by a justice of the peace in March of 1942. Less than a month later, the two were formally married in a ceremony at St. Nicholas Catholic Church in Waco.

Arthur was tweny-nine, barrel-chested, and handsome. He didn't have many skills, but he did know how to drive. He had a job as a chauffeur. At twenty-three, Flora was demure and shy. She had been cooking and cleaning in other people's homes since she was fourteen. Neither of them had more than a sixth-grade education.

When daughter Gwendolyn was born on Halloween of the following year, Arthur thought it was the right time to move out of the home of his in-laws where they had lived since the wedding, and make a major change. He'd heard about the opportunities in Los Angeles and was ready to go. He had a contact, Frazier's half-brother Ben Cooper. Arthur left Flora and Gwen temporarily with her family and caught a train that brought him to Los Angeles.

Mr. Ben Cooper, "Uncle Ben" was in his late 40's and had been living on 41$^{st}$ and Hooper for three years, a few blocks from Central Avenue. For Negroes coming to Los Angeles in the 1940's and early '50's, Central Avenue and 41$^{st}$ was the hub of Negro nightlife, "the main drag" complete with black owned small businesses, and the Negro-owned hotel, the Dunbar.

Ben got Arthur hired at the ice plant where Ben had worked for over a year, but soon Arthur got a better paying job working for Pacific Pipeline digging underground trenches for the city.

Nearing the end of World War ll, a government project was initiated to construct housing complexes for low income families. The complexes themselves became known as "The Projects."

One of the first complexes was constructed on 120th Street between Central Avenue and Wilmington. It was called Palm Lane and consisted of three-hundred brand new bungalows. Arthur rented a one-bedroom and sent train fare for Flora and Gwen. The three of them lived in the little bungalow for eight months but Arthur had been looking for something better when they spotted the house on Holmes Avenue a block away, that was up for sale. He had saved enough to make a down payment on the $3000 cost, and after paying it, they moved.

In December of 1944, my brother was born. They named him Arthur Jr. Muhtha's older sister Elizabeth came on the train from Houston to help with the baby. She called him Little Arthur. Saying the two words together sounded like L'Arthur, and that's what everyone called him even after he started school. Two years later, I came along, and two years after my birth, my baby sister was born in April of 1949.

Aunt Elizabeth came again to help just as she had with my brother and me. Muhtha had named her fourth child Elizabeth in honor of her sister. But when Auntie arrived and saw her newest baby niece, she shortened the baby's name. After that, only the nuns called my little sister Elizabeth. To everyone else she was Lizzie.

Dad had become a longshoreman before I was born. That was his job for more than twenty years. He was lucky to have it. Racial discrimination had excluded black men for any longshore jobs, even men able-bodied enough to do the hard, physical manual labor of working on the docks.

In those days, other blue-collar jobs such as janitors, cooks, assembly-line and day workers were held primarily by Negro men and women. Like my parents, people from the south came to Los Angeles for a better life. They came looking to work. They had a strong work ethic, and beyond that, they had their pride. They were not looking for a handout. My folks and many of their generation fell short of even a sixth-grade education. They took whatever jobs they could find and stayed with them. At that time, welfare did not exist for black folks. People worked, and families helped each other. Dad did his part to help his siblings still living in Waco.

After moving in and getting settled on Holmes, he contacted his siblings and urged them to save enough for train fare and come to Los Angeles.

One by one his sisters, Louise, Dorothy, Beulah, Ruth and his brother Joe made the journey from Waco to Los Angeles. Each stayed with us for a short time in our little house on Holmes. They enrolled in school, found jobs, met their spouses, and started their families here. They couldn't say enough good things about their big brother Arthur.

## ~ 6-1-6 ~

The decision to move from Holmes Avenue in the summer of 1953 was already decided, but the four of us kids didn't know anything about it until dad parked in front of an olive-green house on 84th Place and Avalon.

"This is it," he said. "The new house."

It was hardly new, just new to us. The numbers 6-1-6 were tacked on a wood railing over the porch.

L'Arthur and I jumped out of the car. We ran to the top of the front yard, laid out flat on the grass and rolled down to the sidewalk, a practice tumble for future cowboy and Indian shootouts.

Compared to Holmes, this house was BIG. It had a dining room, a breakfast room, and three bedrooms! The wood floors didn't have splinters and a heater was under the floor in the hallway. The bathroom had something we'd never seen before, a stall shower. Gwen and Lizzie would share the second bedroom which meant the third bedroom was for L'Arthur and me. That made the two of us so happy, we'd have slapped palms right then if high fives had been invented.

Two fruit trees were in the backyard, but they were nothing compared to the tree in the neighbor's yard. The branches of it spread out like a fan over the roof of our garage. Muhtha said it was an avocado tree. I wondered how she knew that. We had never had avocados, and here were bunches of them hanging like grenades from the biggest tree I had ever seen. I liked this new house. By the end of summer, we had made the move to 84th Place.

Leaving Holmes Avenue after six years meant leaving the farm, the barn, the chickens, the vacant field, and our good old cow Bess. She had borne Dad three calves and he hated to sell her but he had to. Muhtha wouldn't let us forget her though. Unintentionally, she came up with something that repeatedly put Bess on our minds. When Uncle Ben finally got around to visiting, she said, "Ben, we haven't seen you since Bess had a calf." That's what we started saying to anyone we hadn't seen in a while. "We ain't seen you since Bess had a calf," and we'd say it with a southern accent.

84th Place was only four miles northwest of Holmes Avenue but seemed much farther away. Every move my dad had made was to make life better for us. One family friend jokingly called us "big shots." We knew we weren't big shots but the move to 84th Place was a sea change. Different environment, a new church and school, new friends, and new discoveries including avocados.

Holmes Avenue and 84th Place were in fact outside of Watts, the area my dad was adamant about leaving, which is funny because all our lives we thought we lived IN Watts when really, we had skirted Watts with both moves.

Technically, the Watts boundaries were 92nd Street north, Alameda on the east, Imperial Highway on the south and Central Avenue on the west. Those boundaries were only street names on a map that didn't identify the area as the section in LA, the inner city, where poor, low income black people lived. In the minds of those farther west or north, east or south, and by our own belief, we were residents of Watts, and already the area was beginning to have a negative stigma attached to it.

## ~ Old Lady Lybrook ~

Nearly half the families on 84th Place were either Spanish or Caucasian, including Mary Lybrook, the previous owner of the house. Dad called her Old Lady Lybrook, a nickname that always put a self-satisfied smile on his face. After selling the house to us, she had moved east to Huntington Park which was all white.

In the early fifties, Negroes were restricted from buying property in Huntington Park and discouraged from shopping there even if they could afford to. Some restrictions were written into law. Were Arthur and Flora aware of those restrictions? I don't know. But there seemed to be unwritten laws that Negroes instinctively knew applied to them, i.e. stay out of areas where neither you or your business are welcome. After a time, a self-defense mechanism grew inside the Negro head and heart. *Why would I want to go there? It's all white.*

Even so, Dad had two reasons to go to Huntington Park. Weatherby's Sporting Goods Store, and Old Lady Lybrook.

We went with him and Muhtha one Friday night, the four of us kids in the back seat of his old Chrysler going east down Manchester. Once the street name changed to Firestone Blvd, we had crossed the invisible boundary into Huntington Park.

We stopped first at Weatherby's. Once inside those walls, you needed at least an hour to see everything. It was stocked to the ceiling. Fishing gear, camping equipment, rifles, guns, stuffed animal heads all along the wall, and at the end of one row, a ten-foot stuffed bear that looked so real you expected it to growl.

Dad was there to buy a pair of Frys boots, the one luxury he afforded himself. He and Muhtha would never be described as folks who indulged in the nightlife, but these were Dad's dress boots, worn on special occasions, with a $40 price tag that he would pay in installments. That night, he put five dollars down, and watched the clerk tag them and put them on the layaway rack behind the counter. By the end of the month, he would pay the balance, and the boots would truly be his.

After Weatherby's, we drove deeper into the residential section of Huntington Park. Dad parked in front of Miss Lybrook's house and we waited in the car as he went up the front walkway. The porch light came on, the screen door was pushed open by a cane, and a voice said, "Come in Arthur." Dad disappeared inside.

*What I learned later was this: 84th Place cost $12,000 dollars, four times what the house on Holmes cost. Dad had gotten a mortgage from Great Western for $7500. He had sold Holmes to his half-brother Joe for $3000 and used $1250 of that for the down payment on 84th. The $3250 balance was owed to "Old Lady Lybrook" on a second mortgage. He paid on it for what seemed like the rest of his life, $25 a month, manually recorded in a payment book that he took in with him.*

When the door opened again, he followed behind a woman walking with two canes coming toward our car. She waved one of the canes and called to us. "Hi kids."

There she was, Old Lady Lybrook. I tried to picture her tottering around our kitchen or washing her face in our bathroom sink, but I couldn't see her there. She smiled at us and we smiled back. Muhtha, was never impolite. She rolled down her window.

"Hello Miz Lybrook."

"Hello Flora," the woman said. She turned to dad. "Arthur, you have a beautiful family."

We made that drive to HP every month and turned the minor aggravation of its purpose into smiles. It became our Friday night dinner outing. We looked forward to it. Most often we wound up at Smith's Barbecue on 108th and Wilmington, Dad's favorite spot. Their weekend special was famous: barbecued beef tips drowning in a warm secret sauce, piled onto a fresh soft hamburger bun, twenty-five cents each. He would spring for ten of them, and six red soda waters, and in no time the car was steamy with the smell of barbeque. We'd sit right there in the parking lot eating dinner and look out the front window of the car at the dim outline of the Watts Towers, unaware that we were looking at a future historical monument right in our own neighborhood.

## ~ St. Malachy's ~

Catholicism lulls you into your faith by its rituals. Swiftly and with ease, the responses become engrained and automatic, the symbols reverential and sacred. The crucifix, the rosary beads, the sign of the cross, the stations of the cross, the thumping of the chest, and bowing of our heads at the sound of the chime. Muhtha was a devout Catholic, born, christened and raised in the church, and there was never any question regardless of the tuition, that her children would be raised in the religion and go to Catholic school.

St. Malachy's was a small church, unadorned, no stained glass windows or marble pillars. Just dark wood pews and heavy doors, a modest altar with one carving of Jesus on the Cross. Even before Lizzie could walk, Muhtha took the four of us to early mass every Sunday. Dad never went. He had maintained his non-church-going ways. Public school was free and close, but he never opposed her agenda to send us to Catholic school. We never questioned his refusal to attend church, never knew if it bothered her that he didn't go. She would say, "You know how he is," and that was the long and short of it.

Muhtha didn't drive, so when we were older, we

usually walked the eight blocks, her holding Lizzie's hand, the three of us tagging behind down 84th to 82nd, down 82nd a couple of blocks past Central to Naomi. On Sundays that dad didn't work, he'd get behind the wheel and give us a leisurely drive. One Sunday we had gotten a late start. Muhtha looked over at him, agitated. He wasn't driving fast enough. But her "look" wasn't enough to convey her message so finally she said, "Step on it Arthur," as if we were in a getaway car in a gangster movie. We cracked up. Every Sunday after that if dad drove, the four of us were the chorus in the back seat. Late or not, we'd sing out, "*Step on it, Arthur!*"

St. Malachy's school was a single-story row of buildings, all connected around the outer edge of the school playground, one room for each grade, first through eighth. I was taught by nuns with the exception of two "lay" teachers which simply meant they weren't Catholic and they weren't nuns. Seven nuns in full black and white habits taught all subjects at St. Malachy's. They lived together in a little house behind the church. Mother Columba and Mother Lawrence, the two older nuns had been at St. Malachy's for years. The other five Sisters were young, soft-spoken and friendly. Their faces were always framed by those starched white headpieces that looked uncomfortable. I never knew if they had blond hair or black hair or no hair. I wondered sometimes, that if I passed one of them on the street wearing regular clothes, would I even recognize her?

Catholic School was more regimentation than hardcore academics. The emphasis was on discipline, obedience, and rules of conduct. Academic competition was at a minimum, and the work wasn't that hard. From first through eighth grade we were in one classroom all day with the same teacher, and she taught all subjects. School hours were eight to three and walking took about 15 minutes if you didn't mess around. We were to be home by 3:30, a curfew we hit maybe once a week.

Some of the boys I met in first grade and during the years at St. Malachy's, I would know all through high school—Gary, Greg, Alvin, Ramon, Gerald, Tucker, Melvin, Billy. Some have remained in my life through the years, and all hold a place in my overstocked memory.

Gary Desmore was closer to L'Arthur's age, and lived two blocks away. His older sister Connie was best friends with Gwen, and his younger sister Veronica was best friends with Lizzie. Gary's mother was the only grown-up we knew with a nickname. Hers was Lumpy. She didn't know we knew, and after Gary told me, I could hardly look at Mrs. Desmore without grinning.

Greg Vital had two sisters and was the first friend I knew whose parents were divorced. His mother was a nurse, his dad a barber who had his own shop on 86th and Central. I always wondered what that was like, living with just your mother and only seeing your dad every once in a while. Greg didn't talk about it, so we didn't either. Occasionally we'd go by his dad's shop walking home from school, and his dad would give him a hair cut. I looked at it in a practical way. He got his hair cut by a real barber whereas I never got a barber shop haircut until I was in high school. Dad was my barber. In the summer, he gave L'Arthur and me swipe-down jerries, hair shaved off as close as it could get. Dad said he was helping us stay cool during the hot summer months. I don't know where that name came from.

Alvin Hurd loved movies and he knew the names of all the actors. His half-sister Pat was in the 8th grade when Alvin and I met. She was a tomboy and always available to fight anybody if Alvin was getting picked on. But being seven years older than Alvin, the two of them didn't talk much. Besides that, his dad was hard on him. Any time spent at Alvin's, you had to walk on tiptoe and whisper because Mr. Hurd worked nights and got highly upset if his day sleep was interrupted. Years later when Alvin was in the eighth grade, his mother had another baby girl they named Jenny. She idolized her big brother Alvin. But she was so much younger, he didn't have much to say to her either.

Some of us were in the same classes for years, and in and out of each others homes as well. Muhtha knew their parents and we all knew each others brothers and sisters. It was a good feeling having friends around who were close, and it was common for us to to know each other as we did. We were neighbors, and it was a time when you knew who your neighbors were.

I remember those days, all of us innocent Catholic boys walking to school together, wearing our prickly corduroy pants and sky blue shirts, and tennis shoes with thin rubber soles that Muhtha said had to last the whole school year. But mine rarely did. Either a hole wore through on the bottom, or the rubber would pull apart from the top and flap when I walked. Worn out or not, those were my shoes for the year and that was it. I wouldn't be getting another pair. The temporary fix was cardboard cut in the shape of the shoe, and wedged inside. Wasn't comfortable, but I wore them that way until I got a new pair. I didn't think anything about it because I wasn't the only kid on the block wearing shoes with holes and  cardboard soles.

I was seven when I made my first Holy Communion. That special Sunday morning I was dressed in a white button-down shirt and a gray suit. My hair was parted on one side and slicked down with water. Vaseline had been smoothed onto my face and hands to banish the ash, and applied likewise to Gwen, Lizzie and L'Arthur. Muhtha would not have her children looking ashy, especially at church.

When it was time for the communion ceremony, the entire class of second graders marched up to the rail and knelt on the padded step, our hands pressed together, prayerful, waiting to receive the Body of Christ for the first time. What did it all mean? I wasn't sure. But, after the wafer was placed on my tongue, I walked back up the aisle, hands still pressed together, telling myself that even though I didn't *feel* different, I *was* different. That was the start of my faith, a belief that I might not see or fully understand, but a blessing that would stay with me for life, or so I was told.

Two years later, at the end of our Sunday morning mass, our priest announced signups for third and fourth grade boys to become altar boys. L'Arthur hadn't been an altar boy so I was only mildly interested until Alvin became one.

"Look what I got," he said one Sunday after mass. He showed me a ten-dollar bill.

"How'd you get it?"

"I was altar boy at a wedding. The groom gave it to me."

"Ten dollars?!" I said. Alvin was nodding his head

with a grin as wide as his face.

I went back to the sacristy and signed up right then, unaware that there was more to becoming an altar boy than standing next to the priest in a white robe and knowing when to ring the chime. I had to attend special classes after school and memorize the prayers in English and Latin! I had to serve at least twice a month and keep up with the schedule posted in the sacristy.

After serving as an altar boy twice, I surprised myself. I realized I didn't mind the duty. I kept up with the schedule and tried never to miss my turn.

One Sunday I sat next to Muhtha, and she started nudging me and cocking her head, and pointing her eyes in the direction of the priest, Father Mechlor. That's what mothers do. Send messages with their eyes. Without saying a word, she was telling me to go help with communion because there was no altar boy.

If I'd had my druthers, I would have been okay with someone else beating me to the job, but that didn't happen. I didn't really mind. I just wasn't prepared mentally for a command performance.

I inched my way out of the pew, went into the sacristy, and slipped on the one white robe hanging in the closet. Father barely acknowledged me stepping in by his side. We continued as if nothing was amiss. The show must go on.

When it was over and Father was thanking me for stepping in, Muhtha said, "See what you can do when you put your mind to it." I would hear those words often. She was proud of me that day. Not long after though, she said something else I'd hear again. "Wait 'til your daddy gets home."

## ~ Don't Smoke ~

Every student at St. Malachy's was scheduled a work day to do a specific chore. It was a morale builder for the school and the student, but also mandatory like catechism.

My work day was shared with an Italian classmate, Gregory Fassiano. Our job was to collect and bag the trash outside the school grounds. We hadn't been outside more than five minutes when Fassiano showed me the surprise he'd brought to school that day—a magnifying glass. Right off the bat he'd broken a school rule. Do not bring toys to school, or words to that effect. But that was him. Pushing the envelope even in fourth grade. As I was chucking papers into my trash bag, Fassiano was looking around for something and finally found it. A cigarette butt, crumpled, but usable. He wanted to see if he could light it with the magnifying glass the way Porky lit the firecrackers in an episode of the Little Rascals.

He slanted the magnifier this way, that way, trying to get the sunrays to hit the cigarette butt through the glass just so. I was thinking, no way is this gonna work. But it did. The stub began to smolder. Fassiano was beside himself. He sucked on it to keep it lit, then passed it to me, and I took a puff. Neither one of us really knew how to smoke and we didn't even *try* to hide what we were doing. Father Mechlor saw us easily from the window of the rectory. He summoned Mother Marselis, our fourth-grade teacher, and she sent us to the principal's office.

"Woe be tied," the principal said, her favorite recrimination, meant to send us into a frenzy of guilt. *Woe be tied*. What did that even mean? We hung our heads and waited for the lecture.

I decided to keep the incident to myself. Why bother the folks with bad news?

But Muhtha came to school for her scheduled visit a few weeks later, and my teacher asked her if she was aware of the smoking incident that Howard was involved in. Muhtha gave me that look—disbelief and embarrassment. I knew I was in for it. A "whuppin." I could only hope it would come from Muhtha, with a belt. When we got home, that's what happened. Luckily, I was still wearing my corduroy uniform pants, so it didn't hurt much.

Dad came home and hardly had time to pull off his shoes before she called me into the living room to confess. I braced myself, not sure what was coming. But I got a nice surprise. He didn't go off on me. He must have thought Muhtha had handled it. I got to thinking that maybe my dad was more bark than bite, more threat than action. On the other hand, when he was upset, his threats hung heavy over our heads. He had a way of gritting his teeth and talking with just his lips moving that let us know we'd better straighten up.  And his threats weren't always verbal.

I remember him setting his razor strap on the kitchen table to make sure we cleaned our plates, even the vegetables. L'Arthur couldn't stand green beans and sitting at the table staring at them didn't make them go away. He had come up with a solution that was occasionally successful. He'd maneuver the beans into his right hand, lower his hand under the table, and drop the beans into the cuff of his jeans. It worked for a time until Muhtha found beans in the washing machine. Gwen had an issue with peas. She said they made her gag.  She'd start gasping for air after eating just one. Then like magic, the sight of the strap would miraculously help her catch her breath. As for me, I always cleaned my plate. I rarely needed a threat, even when dinner included lima beans which was like eating wax. The strap was present but always returned to the bathroom hook unused, except for its intended use, sharpening dad's straight razor.

Standing in the living room that day, realizing I wasn't going to get a strap from Dad or even a lecture, what a relief. I could tell he wasn't happy to hear I'd been caught smoking at school. But when he closed his eyes to get a little peace before dinner, I disappeared into the hall. L'Arthur had been listening. "You got lucky," he said. "Sort of," I said. *I'd still gotten the belt.*

Dad never mentioned the incident again. I figured he had filed it under the category of boys being boys. I think it's from Dad that later in life, I inherited my laid-back attitude about mid-level crisis. Some things just weren't worth hassling over. Pick your battles. Don't sweat the small stuff. If the cat's out of the bag, no sense getting mad at the dog.

It was different with Muhtha. She told Mrs. Desmore, who commiserated with her. Gary had been caught smoking too. The next time I was at Gary's, Mr. Desmore folded his newspaper and looked over at me.

"What brand you smoking these days Howard? Gary smokes Lucky Strikes."

# ~ A Taste of Rich ~

In fifth grade I was taught for the first time by a lay teacher, Mrs. Johnson, who had been teaching at St. Malachy's for two years.. She was a tall brown-skinned lady who always dressed in suits. What her students liked most about her was that occasionally after lunch, while sitting at her desk, Mrs. Johnson would quietly nod off. Someone seated in the front row would signal the rest of the class— fingers to lips—to keep the noise down. The longer she slept, the less we had to do.

Muhtha got to know her well enough to learn that her husband Mr. Johnson was an attorney, and that they lived in the Pico-Venice area, which was a predominantly white area and very exclusive. She told Muhtha about the birthday party she was giving for her younger son Michael, who was turning eleven. He attended a parochial school, and because his classmates were all Caucasian boys, she thought it would be nice to have some boys outside his immediate circle of friends attend the party, Negro boys who lived in a different part of town and were from a different environment. Catholic boys who perhaps didn't have all the advantages he had, but who were nevertheless, nice, polite, and friendly. And who did she invite? Alvin and me. Not only to the party, we were invited as special guests to spend the whole weekend.

That Friday, straight from school, Mrs. Johnson took Alvin first, then me, home to get our overnight things. Muhtha gave me last minute instructions on manners and behavior, and then we were off to the west side of town, the *real* West Side.

Mrs. Johnson lived on a private street. Two big

arching pillars were at the entrance, and on one was a sign. The exact wording escapes my memory, but it stopped just short of saying, IF YOU DON'T LIVE HERE, DON'T COME IN. Every house on both sides of the street was a two-story on a big lot with a deep front lawn. She turned into the driveway of her home and parked in the two-car garage. We followed her inside.

The house was huge, a mansion. Marble entry, a wide staircase, crystal chandelier. Right then it hit me, something I'd never thought before.

*Mrs. Johnson was rich. Who knew?* I looked up at her out of the corner of my eye and saw her in a whole new light.

We peered into the living room as we walked past. There was a grand piano with the lid up, creamy white sofas, chairs and lamps. I would learn later the furniture was French provincial. The kitchen door swung open, and the smell of roast beef seeped out along with a woman wearing an apron over her dress and carrying a stack of plates. She glanced at us quickly and then began setting the long dining room table. For a split second I thought maybe she was a relative...an aunt maybe. Guess I couldn't wrap my head around what she really was. Their maid. I remember thinking three things: *This is how rich people live. Mr. Johnson must make a lot of money. This is the type of house Muhtha cleans.*

Mrs. Johnson called to Michael and he came down the stairs. We were about the same size. We kind of nodded at each other. It was always kind of awkward meeting new people when a parent was standing there. Seems they always wanted you to become instant friends.

He took us up to his bedroom which was big

enough for four twin beds. He had his own double bed, plus his own bathroom, a desk, and a shelf full of books. His older brother was in college and lived on campus, so it was like Michael was an only child.

At dinner that first night, he was friendly enough, but quiet. When he finished eating, he asked to be excused. Alvin and I exchanged glances. I had never asked to be excused from the table. That night I did.

On Saturday, his mother reminded him that the dog needed a bath, and in a cheerful voice suggested that maybe the three of us could do it together. Michael groaned a little, while Alvin and I said, sure, no problem. They had a separate enclosed back porch with a wash tub, so we put the little dog in it and bathed him and dried him off with a big soft towel until he squirted away from us into the backyard and rolled around on the grass.

On Sunday afternoon, about ten of Michael's school friends trickled in, all boys. There was plenty of food and a huge cake. Alvin and I hadn't brought a gift, hadn't even thought of it until we saw the gifts from his friends. I don't remember his dad talking to us, and I wish I could say we all mingled and got to know each other, and that a friendship was starting to happen. But that's not the case. When the party was over, and Mrs. Johnson brought us back home, I told L'Arthur about it, that I'd gotten to see how rich people live. I had to admit that it might be nice to live in a big two-story house with a long driveway and a swimming pool. Maybe one day.

# ~ Changes ~

From 1957-1960, Caucasian families in the neighborhood began moving away, continuing a trend that would become more noticable in the next few years. As kids, we didn't immediately attach anything racial to those departures, but that's what it was all about.

One family that I really missed was Billy Hopkins. He lived a few houses down the block but his grandmother lived directly across the street from us, and he spent a lot of time there. He and I were the same age and he was my first close Caucasion friend. We rode bikes up and down 84th, and played in each other's yards.

I was at his house one Christmas morning to see his new stuff. They had a big tree, lots of presents. His little brother Jimmy was on the floor playing with his new truck happy as he could be. He stopped for a second holding the truck in the air and blurted out, "I like this truck better than my booty." Billy and I laughed and laughed. Mr. Hopkins was so flustered he didn't know what to say. He tried telling his four-year-old son not to say things like that, especially in front of company. But Jimmy was laughing too.

When Billy moved away to Huntington Park, I hated that we didn't remain friends, but leaving a neighborhood and going to a different school ended most friendships. I don't think I ever saw him again.

Other neighbors with names like Montoya, Cabrera and Rodrigues also moved away. These families emphasized in neighborly conversations that they were second generation Spanish descendants, not Mexican, and proudly stated that their families years before had helped settle many parts of California. When I became acquainted with hard working Mexican people years later, I remembered how the superior attitude of those Spanish people had cast a negative light on Mexicans that I didn't understand at the time.

Moving into those vacated homes were Negro families with names like Austin, and Brown, and Davis. Later the Byrd family moved in. They had four kids like ours, two girls and two boys. In age the eight of us were like stair steps, and the older daughter Debra became my second girlfriend.

Kids our age were part of nearly every new family. We made new friends. We didn't know the real reason the neighborhood was changing, that white people were moving to get away from black people, but maybe we suspected it a little. If Muhtha and Daddy discussed it at all, it was when we weren't around, or not paying attention, mouthing words in whispers, said over our heads.

Muhtha became acquainted with most of the new neighbors, being more sociable than dad, and in turn, they got to know us, the four Higginson kids. Some of the new families were Catholic and attended St. Malachy's, and like Muhtha who always volunteered to help, they would organize the yearly fiesta and bazaars.

One thing I thought was funny. Even though the women were neighborly, they addressed each other formally. "Hello Mrs. Higginson," "Good morning Mrs. Desmore," "How are you Mrs. Emerson," "I'm fine Mrs. Austin." Likewise, Muhtha told us to use their surnames, and remember our manners around the adults. We were not to interrupt when grownups were talking, and we were to be respectful. It was home training, she said, and important to her that the neighbors recognized her children had received it.

## ~ Goat Soup ~

One neighbor who hadn't moved away was Mrs. Alvarez who lived next door. Her house was decorated in a Spanish style—the tile roof was brick red, the house was the color of clay. Her flower gardens were always blooming and she had stacks of pots painted bright colors on her porch and front lawn. It was one of the prettiest houses on the block.

One Easter break we were up for a bike ride. It was a rare event because it wasn't just us kids. Dad was on a bike too. It was L'Arthur, Gary, me, and Bobby, Mrs. Alvarez's visiting grandson on his bike, and Lizzie on the sidewalk on her three-wheel tricycle, all of us racing down 84th. That deep wicked chuckle of my Dad's was egging us on. He was determined to beat us all, even though L'Arthur was in the lead.

Our street got very little traffic, usually, only the cars of people who lived there, and no one in those days parked their cars overnight on the street, or even during the day. That's what garages were for. But suddenly, a car was coming toward us, right down the middle. L'Arthur and I both swerved toward a driveway, but my front wheel clipped his back wheel. It was a pit maneuver, that didn't go well.

My bike spun around, and I was spring-loaded over the front landing face first in the street. I flipped over in serious pain, and I could feel my front teeth dangling. Suddenly Dad was there standing over me. He didn't say anything, just scooped me up in his arms and ran back to the house. Muhtha wasn't home, a good thing because she would have fussed before trying to fix me up. Bobby went for his grandmother.

When I opened my eyes and could focus, Mrs. Alvarez was on the side of my bed grimacing as if she was the one in pain. She slipped out of the room as Dad put ice wrapped in a towel over my mouth to sooth my aching teeth and gums. When she returned she was holding a big bowl of something with a strong meaty smell. In spanish she called it birria. Dad asked her what it was in English.

"Goat soup. Very good," she said, offering it to me. It didn't smell like anything Muhtha had ever made, but dad had barbequed a goat once, and it wasn't half bad. My aching face felt as big as a balloon. I was ready to try anything to feel better, so I took a sip. It was sweet, peppery, and bitter, all at the same time, and I didn't like it at first. She made me drink some more and either the taste got better, or I just got used to it.

Dad and I both drank goat soup that day. I don't know how much the soup helped, but my teeth, gums, and face healed. What I didn't know or even suspect then, was that thirty years later, goat soup would come into my life again.

## ~ Summers ~

Every year just after the short break for Easter, I'd start thinking about the big break: summer vacation. Three whole months without school. Made me smile just thinking about it. Gwen would mark the calendar. Five weeks to go, the longest five weeks in the year.

Summer meant freedom. It was getting up in the morning and knowing there was nothing you absolutely HAD to do, and nowhere you absolutely HAD to be. It was like being let out of a cage after seven months, and finally the chain was unlocked, and the gate was wide open. No teachers, no classrooms, no homework, no scratchy corduroy pants.

In the summer, I wore shorts every day. I went to bed in those shorts, I woke up in those shorts. We played in the streets until dark, and never put on shoes. We made pancakes when we got hungry and scarfed them down in the middle of the day, rode our bikes to the beach, maybe ten or twelve miles, straight down Manchester to Playa del Rey, single file, racing each other for the lead, and spent the day swimming and catching sand crabs, me, L'Arthur, Gary, and sometimes Alvin. We played baseball in the street and hide and seek into the night.

Some days we just stayed in, watching cowboy movies, or old movies with kids in them, sprawled on the floor eating peanut butter and jelly sandwiches, or fried baloney on white bread with mustard, or peanut butter with mayonnaise if we were out of grape jelly. It was relaxing to get all caught up with Tom Sawyer, or the crazy antics of the Little Rascals, and the fights and brawls and New York slum life of the East Side kids. Their lives were so different from ours but seemed so real. There was no way we identified with them, and it didn't have anything to do with race. We watched for the sheer entertainment value, the pure fun of it. The kids in the movies did things we'd never even think to do, but occasionally we'd try, like firecrackers lit by the sun.

The Manchester theater near Broadway, and the Triple AAA theater around the corner were both in walking distance. That was Alvin's favorite thing to do, go to the movies. He knew the names of all the movie stars.

Tickets were nine cents to get in, and a sugar daddy sucker cost a nickel and lasted the whole movie plus a cartoon. Alvin and I went together to see *The 7th Voyage of Sinbad*. The theatre was packed. We hardly talked during the movie, that's how good it was. Better than *King Kong*, almost.

We didn't have a local YMCA or a Boys Club, but South Park Elementary School was just a few blocks from the house and had a game room that was open every day during the summer, except Sundays, and it was free. We'd go there and spend hours playing caroms, cards, dominoes, all kinds of table games, crafts, building balsa wood airplanes, ice creams stick cabins. Stuff to keep us busy.

My friend Melvin lived across the street, one of a few friends who went to public school. We got on a Robin Hood kick one summer and bought bow and arrow kits from JJ Newberry's for a buck. My dad in his off-handed, non-specific way had mentioned once that he'd shot rabbits as a kid, but he never said how he did it. Melvin was game, so we went rabbit hunting one day with our bows and arrows and rode our bikes down to the open fields off Avalon and 180th.

We crept through the overgrown grass and spotted jack rabbits popping up and down and scampering away. We did plenty of pointing and aiming after getting the arrow on the line. But *shooting* a rabbit with an arrow was something else again. The rabbits showed us they were no sitting ducks. We never shot even one.

After a while it was more a game of chasing after rustling grass and trying to find our lost arrows.

Turns out Melvin and I were better at fishing.

Mr. Jessie and Miss Lulu were older neighbors who loved to go fishing and didn't mind taking a few neighborhood kids with them if the parents didn't mind. They lived in an apartment behind Melvin's house. They invited him to go fishing one day, and he invited me. Muhtha didn't know them well and may not have let me go if she'd known we'd be riding in the back of Mr. Jessie's old pickup truck. That's how we got to his special place on the docks in Wilmington near some abandoned oil derricks.

He pointed us to spots where the water wasn't too deep. We climbed down between rocks and logs to where the fish were biting and we sat on big beams of wood with the poles he'd given us, peering into the water to see where the fish were.

Our poles had about five hooks on the line. He'd brought anchovies for bait and showed us how to wrangle a piece onto each hook so that it wouldn't fall off. He dropped pieces of bait into the water. He called it "seasoning." It didn't take long before something was grabbing at my pole. When I pulled it up, a fish the size of my hand was hanging on every hook. "Them's tomcods," Mr. Jessie said. That first time out I must have caught at least a dozen. I took them home and that night we had fried tomcods for dinner.

After that, L'Arthur, Gary, and I were out riding our bikes exploring, and we stumbled onto a spot around Artesia and Vermont, another fishing hole that looked like a swamp. That's what we called it, the swamp. It was really a creek running alongside Vermont, and people were down off the side of the road fishing in it. We parked our bikes and climbed down a steep slope to get a closer look. They had stick poles with string attached, and hooks on the string baited with liver. They were pulling up crawfish. They looked like baby lobsters, orange colored, about the size of two fingers, with snippers and sensors like threads floating off the end. We wanted to get in on that, so we came back the next day with our own stick poles and pieces of baloney. We caught a bunch. L'Arthur had saddlebags strapped to his bike and that's how we got them home. Muhtha couldn't believe how many we had. Gary's mother told her to drop them into a pot of boiling salted water for about five minutes. She said crawfish were the poor man's lobster, and we had scored big because we got them for free.

In the summer, we went swimming nearly every day. I learned how to swim like most kids—trial and error. Once that water gets snorted up your nose, and you feel that discomfort of pinging bubbles up your nostrils, you figure out fast how to hold your breath or hold your nose or both, float on your back or dog paddle. We didn't know anyone with a backyard pool, so aside from the beach, the public pools were our only option, and we knew where they were.

Roosevelt Park on 79th between Compton and Alameda was twelve blocks from home, a long walk just to go for a swim. But we'd make that trek because it was safer than the pool at Will Rogers, on 103rd and Central, a bigger pool, but risky. At Will Rogers, fights had been known to break out for no good reason, especially if you were considered an outsider. It was common knowledge that tough guys and bullies hung around Will Rogers looking for some kid to corner.

"Hey kid, gimme your money," they'd say. Never happened to me. I managed to avoid confrontations of the physical kind. But I saw it happen. For the unsuspecting kid, it was give-up the coins or get punched. Luckily, that was the worst of it—a punch or a bloody nose. Nobody got shot.

Manchester pool, at 88th and Hoover, wasn't exactly around the corner either, but closer to home, and it opened at nine a.m. We'd get there sometimes as early as 9:30, and swim until noon. The manager would close for an hour to take his lunch break. If we wanted to swim again in the afternoon, he'd give us a free pass if we'd pick up trash outside the fence. So, we picked up trash.

After that second swim, I was always starving. Nothing tasted better after gulping pool water than hot popcorn. A guy with a bright yellow cart was "the popcorn man" and he was always there, dependable as the sun, and parked just outside the entrance. You could smell the popcorn in the air, hot and fresh. Ten cents a bag. It was a sad day if I'd have to go home with an empty stomach, so I always made sure I had that dime. The corn was topped off with so much butter, your hand got greasy just holding the bag. So good.

I was lucky to have my brother and friends, even adult neighbors like Mr. Jessie to do stuff with especially in the summer. Dad wasn't the outdoor type, wasn't really into sports which weren't the major attraction that they are today. There was no basketball, football, or baseball on the radio, much less television.

Dad's job as a longshoreman was hard labor, and sporadic. He didn't complain about it, but when he wasn't working, he liked nothing better than doing pretty much nothing. He was content to lay on the couch, watch a little tv, or study the horseracing form. Betting on the horses wasn't a habit, he wasn't addicted to it, he didn't go to Las Vegas and gamble. But betting occasionally put dreams in his head of winning "a hatful." He said it so often, that I hoped he'd win a hatful too.

I loved horses from seeing them on television. Roy Rogers with Trigger, The Lone Ranger with Silver. The closest I'd come to riding a horse was riding Bess, our old cow, when I was little, and dad would hoist L'Arthur and me on her back and we'd ride her around the backyard. I wanted to ride a real horse, maybe even own a horse one day. Dad only wanted to bet on them. "Going to try my luck," he'd say, "See if I can win that hatful." He'd laugh that deep chuckle on his way to Hollywood Park Racetrack. We never knew how much he bet, or how much he lost. But we knew when he won, because he'd give most of his winnings to Muhtha. That made the betting okay, sort of.

Sports on television then was wrestling and roller derby. Friday and Saturday nights, we watched both on our black and white, 13-inch tv, in our bedroom, L'Arthur's and mine, which doubled as a den. Muhtha would either be darning socks, or hemming a skirt or braiding Lizzie's hair, but she'd look up long enough to root for a favorite when the women skaters were on. The four of us would sprawl wherever there was room on the floor, and dad would be on his side on the bed with the racing form nearby, ever hopeful.

Our one real summer vacation trip was when we drove to Yosemite National Park and camped in a tent.

We had a campfire every night, and we'd go exploring in the morning hoping to see a bear or a deer. The more I've learned about bears in the woods, it's probably a good thing we never happened onto one. Most summers we took one short trip, usually to San Diego. Muhtha always wanted to see the swallows come back to Capistrano, so we'd stop and walk through the missions. The summer we were boy scouts, we went on hiking trips with the troop, and then at home, L'Arthur, Gary and I would scrounge up old blankets or sheets, an old broom stick, rocks, anything we could find to make and secure a tent, and the three of us would camp out in the back yard.

We went to Disneyland the year it opened, Knotts Berry Farm, twice, and the LA County Fair when it was all about the animals. Dad's favorite part was strolling through those barns to look at the cows, the horses, and those prize-winning hogs.

## ~ Trip to the Docks ~

Near the end of another summer vacation, I was maybe ten, L'Arthur twelve, out of the blue dad asked if we'd like to go with him to the job. It was a payday he said, and he wanted us to see the docks, see the dispatch hall, and just get a feel for what he did and where he went every day. We got excited. Yeah. We wanted to go.

We drove down Avalon past familiar scenery that we knew from riding our bikes. The closer we got to Wilmington, we couldn't see the ocean, but we could smell it.

The dispatch hall was sprawling, twice the size of St. Malachy's hall. Both doors were flung wide open.

It was noisy and loud. A bunch of men inside, I'm guessing, maybe a hundred talking and laughing, their voices echoing against the walls, numbers being called as men waited to get a job for the day, and everyone in a good mood. It was payday.

We tagged along behind Dad. I think he liked having us there with him. "These my boys," he said, his hands on our shoulders. "Arthur Jr. and Howard." The men smiled and nodded, said we looked just like the old man. And I did look just like him, chocolate brown skin and wavy hair.

Dad called out names of this guy and that guy. They dug into their pockets, handed us loose change. "Put this in your bank," they joked. "Pretty soon ya'll be down here with your old man." It was embarrassing, but also kind of fun, so we laughed too. I liked being there with dad, being around men who were like him and everybody was friendly.

Dad picked up his check, we climbed into the car, and all the way home, L'Arthur and I were smiling. But when we got to the house, Muhtha fussed. She didn't know what went on "down there at the docks" but she was certain being around a bunch of longshoremen was no place for children, especially hers. But her fussing didn't change our mood. L'Arthur and I were happy. We emptied our pockets onto the bed and counted it out. Just being dad's sons had netted us nearly ten bucks each before eight in the morning. Ten whole dollars all at once without doing any work, compared to the quarter we got once a week, or if we were lucky, the couple of dollars, on a good day, for sweating over somebody's lawn.

We went with him a second time after school

started back. Work had been slow. He hadn't caught a job in a week, but he did have a check coming. I never knew how much my dad made, but I knew missing a week of work wasn't good. I had heard him and Muhtha talking in low voices, not really arguing, but close to it, about what bills could be paid, and what bills would have to wait.

L'Arthur and I went along for the ride. He'd get us back in time for school. There was almost no traffic on Avalon, especially early in the morning. Getting to the docks only took about twenty minutes. Quick in and out he said, as he pulled into the parking lot near the dispatch hall. We waited in the car, and when he returned, he was in a hurry. He told us we'd have to ride the bus home. His number had been called for a day job. He couldn't pass it up. He was so matter-of-fact about this turn of events that the panic I was starting to feel began to subside. L'Arthur and I exchanged looks. I didn't know how far we were from home—maybe fifteen miles—but there was no way we'd get back in time for school.

Dad backed out of the lot and drove to the Pacific Coast Highway/Avalon bus stop. He shelled out the fare into our hands, and nodded as if to say, Okay, go on home. To us it was a crisis, but to him, no big deal. I tried to see it that way too. We'd ridden our bikes this far before, and it wasn't like we were virgin bus riders. I'd ridden the bus once a week for a year by myself to Kaiser on La Cienega to get my allergy shot, and I never got lost or stranded. I had no reason to be worried. It wasn't like we were a hundred miles from home.

Dad drove off with a backwards wave. There we stood, craning our necks southward for the bus going north. We waited and waited. No bus came and we didn't see one in the distance. Either the bus wasn't coming, or we were waiting in the wrong place.

Before we had time to consider something drastic like walking, a car pulled up in front of us. The driver yelled out the open passenger window. "You Higginson's boys, ain't ya?"

Without a thought to 'don't speak to strangers,' we said, "Yes." He said he worked with dad and offered us a ride home. Had dad had asked him to come get us? Did the man recognize us from the time before? We didn't know and we didn't ask. In fact, we didn't ask one single question. We didn't run for our lives either, or ask each other what we should do, or hesitate before climbing into the back seat of an old car with a man we'd never seen before. We weren't afraid. We weren't living in a scary world where every stranger was suspect. We took him at his word, and rode silently in the back seat, grateful for the lift. In no time, he pulled up in front of the house. We thanked him, grabbed our books from inside, and headed for school. Late.

A note came home asking why we were late. Muhtha wanted to know too. "How could you leave your two sons stranded nearly twenty miles from home?" she asked dad. "What were you thinking?" She turned to us and fussed some more. "...getting into a stranger's car. Haven't you learned anything?" We'd heard questions like that before, so we did the usual. We buttoned our lips and looked contrite.

## ~ Early $$ ~

L'Arthur and I had been mowing our front and back lawns since forever. Our tools were the push mower, a rake, a broom, a dustpan, and a hand-held edger that was scarcely better than a dull pair of scissors. In the spring my allergies gave me sneezing fits and an itchy throat. In the summer, it didn't take long to work up a sweat, especially mowing our Bermuda grass, which was tantamount to cutting through wire.

Working for the house, aka Muhtha, meant our payment was in the learning experience rather than anything monetary. To achieve some financial return, we offered lawn-cutting deals to our neighbors. L'Arthur did the talking while I stood at his shoulder looking hopeful, hiding my true feelings that were like a double-edged sword. I wanted the reward, but the labor required to get it took fortitude. I had to stay focused. Our objective, after all, was M.O.N.E.Y. Our neighbors who liked doing their own lawns were hard sells. They either gave in out of admiration for two boys trying to make a buck, or soft-heartedness because we looked so needy.

Swattybabe was the nickname L'Arthur had given to our neighbor Mrs. Swartz, a stout middle-aged German lady with gray hair twisted into a ball at the back of her neck. She would never be described as "a babe." But L'Arthur got a kick out of this secret joke. "Let's go see Swattybabe," he'd say, and we'd head in her direction. She always had a smile for us, and we'd follow her into her back yard, dragging the mower behind us.

"What do we have for the boys to do?" she'd say to her husband sitting on the porch. Mr. Swartz would silently turn palms to the sky. He'd sip on his bottle of beer and puff on his filter-less cigarettes and watch us work. Our normal rate was $4.00, front and back, negotiable of course. Her yard rarely needed us, but even so, Swattybabe always found something for us to do that was worth four dollars.

A good Saturday could net us twenty dollars, and we'd split it down the middle. Most of our customers gave a thumb's up on our work, but old Mr. Beamon at the end of 84th was a special case. He would pace the lawn after a job, his hands behind his back as if some big decision had to be made. "Boys," he'd say, drawing the word out in a lilting crescendo, "there's always time to do the job twice, but never enough time to do it right the first time."

He'd point out a couple of spots we'd missed, then look off into the distance, thoughtfully, as if he was trying to decide whether to pay us at all. Slowly he'd peel out $2.00 from a coin purse and tell us to come back in two weeks. After doing some extra hedge trimming, we got $3.00 out of him once. It was our sole remittance for an especially unproductive day, but I splurged with my $1.50. Kites were on sale, ten for a dollar, at one of the first Pic and Saves in the area. It was too good a deal to pass up. I bought ten kites, all different colors, and used five blue ones to decorate our bedroom wall. Made it look like the ocean.

One desperate Saturday, we were flat broke. We had a pigeon coop that needed cleaning but who wanted to do that?

We were saved, so to speak, by Cousin Ethel who called and asked Muhtha if we could cut her lawn. Muhtha suggested we do it for free. That was the craziest idea I'd ever heard. Cousin Ethel and her husband Paul had just bought a new Cadillac. If anyone could afford to pay us, it was cousin Ethel. L'Arthur didn't argue. He was always the voice of reason, which sometimes meant saying nothing at all.

We ended up pushing the mower all the way to 90th Street between San Pedro and Main, more than eight blocks to Ethel's house on a Saturday in the sun. She greeted us with hugs and kisses and called us precious. She was young and pretty. I had a crush on her, which made me feel a little weird, because she was a relative, though I never knew exactly what the connection was.

She sat on the porch and talked to us while we worked, like a big sister, and gave us cookies and milk when we finished. I was almost ready to follow Muhtha's suggestion until good old Cousin Ethel paid us double our rate and wouldn't take no for an answer. Thanks to cousin Ethel, we took the rest of the day off.


## ~ Extra Extra! ~


"We could sell newspapers," L'Arthur said one day as we walked home from school. We had talked about it before and I had envisioned myself wearing one of those newsboy caps and yelling "Extra, extra, read all about it" like the newsboys in old gangster movies. This time we didn't just talk about it. We went to the newspaper office on Broadway and got hired. They told us our street locations, where the papers would be stacked, and gave us each a money belt with pockets to make change.

But no newsboy cap.

My location was the intersection at Manchester

and Main. I rode my bike there after school and chained it to the street pole on the corner where a stack of newspapers was left for me by my boss, a slim dapper white dude named Mr. Dick. He drove a flat-bed Ford Ranchero that was always clean.

Back in those ancient days of yesteryear, before five o'clock traffic increased and became known as "rush hour," there were no left turn arrows or lanes. To remedy the problem of people turning left and holding up traffic, a job had been created to keep the increased traffic moving, especially on a busy street like Manchester, and I watched the guy who had the job.

He happened to be a black man and he was quick, efficient and didn't mess around. He'd pull up at four o'clock driving a city truck, park it at the curb, jump out wearing his khaki uniform, grab the metal sign stationed on the corner telephone pole and wait for the light to change. When traffic in one direction stopped, he'd roll the NO LEFT TURN sign to the center of the intersection, hustle back to his truck and drive to his next location.

The sign was as good as a signal light and traffic kept moving. Like clockwork, the guy would come back at six p.m., roll it out of the street, and stand it near the telephone pole. He didn't chain it or secure it in any way, and in those days, he didn't have to. Nobody graffitied or swiped it for scrap. Nobody messed with it. It was always there.

When traffic stopped, that's when I moved. "Git yer mee-wer pay-per." That was me, trying to sound like the kids in the movies, slipping in and around the cars. If Muhtha had seen me darting around those cars, or if she'd seen L'Arthur doing the same thing farther west at Manchester and Broadway, or Gary at Manchester and

Figueroa, she'd have blown the whistle on us, and advised Mrs. Desmore to do the same.

Three cents off a ten-cent paper was what we were paid. A pitiful return considering the chances we took, but we didn't really think about that. We had a job, so we did the job and occasionally, someone paid with a quarter and said keep the change.

A bigger problem was that by 3:30, lunch was a distant memory, and my stomach would be growling. There was no Mickey D's or Jack in the Box nearby, only one of the first Carl's Jr's. on Avalon, working out of a trailer with a roll-down door and a menu tacked to it. But even on my bike, it was too far from my location.

Much closer was a café, with a counter and stools. I was so hungry one day I took thirty cents of the forty cents in my pocket from selling four papers and ran into the café. I bought a chili dog and gobbled most of it down walking back to my post. With my hunger satisfied I doubled down on my sprints to make the money back. Most days I sold all my papers. I told L'Arthur what I'd done, and he called me a "risk taker." I wasn't really, not yet, but I liked that he thought so.

We left the street papers after a time and began throwing the Examiner, later called the Herald Examiner. L'Arthur got the job and I was his helper. Gary got a route too.

The three of us would ride our bikes to 79th and Broadway at five in the morning to the newspaper dispatch office. The papers for each route were sectioned off. We had to fold them, band them, load them into our canvas bags and onto our bikes, and head out to our routes.

It would still be dark, the streets quiet, empty.

Here and there we'd hear a dog bark when the paper hit the driveway. Eighty-four papers for L'Arthur and me, forty-two each, seven days a week. We dropped them between five and six in the morning to our neighbors between Avalon and Central, on 84$^{th}$ Street, 84$^{th}$ Place, and 85$^{th}$ Street, rain or shine. More work, brutal hours, but a little more money, maybe $20 a month for each of us. Sunday's paper was thicker, heavier. If it rained and dad was home, he'd drive us. L'Arthur on one side in the back seat, me on the other, yawning, dad creeping down the middle of 84$^{th}$ just before daylight.

I remember one morning L'Arthur didn't wake me like usual. I finally woke up at 7:30. A sinking feeling came over me. I jumped out of bed feeling awful. I found my jeans, pulled them on.

"L'Arthur, we missed the paper drop. We're late." I was near tears, sleepy-eyed, frantic. We were going to lose this job and we'd only been at it a few weeks. I rushed toward the door pulling up my jeans. "L'Arthur," I yelled. That's when his arm snaked out from under the covers and he grabbed my leg. "I did it already," he said. When my eyes could focus, I saw he was still in his jeans and old gray sweater that he wore every morning. I was so relieved. I fell back into bed and we drifted back to dreamland still in our street clothes, hobo-sleeping dad called it.

## ~ Boxing ~

L'Arthur's best friend Gwayne was always trying to persuade one of his buddies, usually L'Arthur, to go in with him on some grand enterprise. The latest was Golden

Gloves boxing. Gwayne had hooked up with a trainer who recruited boys ages 12-14 and talked L'Arthur into going with him for free boxing lessons. Gwayne said it wasn't just for fun. There was money to be made. L'Arthur didn't know anything about boxing, but he was stoked by the mention of making some money, so he said yeah. Even though I was eleven, he brought me in on the deal, and I couldn't refuse my brother. The next thing I knew, we were riding our bikes to a house on 74th and Wadsworth to meet the trainer.

Mr. Bell, the trainer reminded me of the Kingfish on the Amos and Andy TV show. He wore a fedora and had a rusty sounding voice. He had a way of cocking his head and squinting his eyes when he looked at you, like he was sizing you up, but in a friendly way. His primary profession, he said, was training 20-25-year-old semi-pro boxers for amateur matches. But he also scouted for youngsters like us who might develop into fighters.

"You boys heard'a Archie Moore, haven't you?" We said yeah, but it was only a vague recollection.

I suspected Mr. Bell had a few schemes up his sleeve. Even though he wore a suit and tie, there was something a tad shady about him. We were kids though, inexperienced, naïve. Mr. Bell wasn't like most of the adults we knew, but still, he was an adult, a businessman of sorts, and being children who had been taught to look up to adults, we looked up to Mr. Bell. He was our mentor and trainer, the man who would turn Gwayne, L'Arthur and me into prizefighters. He was especially taken with my brother who was left-handed.

"A southpaw, yeah, you got an advantage. Southpaws always dangerous," Mr. Bell said, but he didn't explain why. Didn't matter. L'Arthur got a jolt of confidence hearing that. It showed in the big smile on his face. In my head, dollar signs were blinking. Every other thought fell away, including the bigger picture. We would have to punch, get punched and win the match before we'd get paid. That light bulb hadn't come on yet. Cash was our focus. We left our bikes at Mr. Bell's house and rode with him downtown to the training gym on 14th and Wall.

Downtown Los Anegles in 1958 was just beginning to appear a little worn, rundown, and seedy. The training gym was part of that beginning deterioration, with the pileup of trash outside the door, and the smell of sweaty socks and sweatier bodies, an odor that hit like a punch the minute we stepped inside. We just breathed it in, caught up in the excitement of the boxing world, unfazed by the sleaziness around us.

The lockers were dented, the walls streaky. Balled up towels were lying on the floor. We stepped through little puddles of water here and there, and off to one side was the boxing ring. We watched fighters getting busy. Some were in good shape, muscular, others not so much. They were punching the bags, jumping rope, standing in front of filmy mirrors practicing their stance, bobbing and weaving. L'Arthur and I kept eyeing each other. We were in awe.

We trained after school for weeks, sometimes until seven at night, plus Saturdays. Mr. Bell taught us how to wrap our hands, how to stand, legs bent at the knees, how to protect our faces, fists up, shoulders hunched, while we watched ourselves in the mirror. He taught us how to punch the speed bag, three jabs with a left, then one punch with the right, or double punch, right then left. "Keep the bag in motion," he kept saying. I watched Joe Palooka's TV show and practiced until my upper arms ached.

Finally, we were to be in our first exhibition match, the lightweight division, ages 10-14. Muhtha didn't like it at all, but Dad was beside himself. "My boys gon' be prize fighters," he said. He was pumped. We were excited too until Mr. Bell told us the match was to be held for the inmates at the central jail downtown.

*The jail? Guys in black and white stripes with numbers on their backs?*

L'Arthur and I rode with Mr. Bell to the jail. We changed into our boxing trunks and I asked him if he was scared. He just laughed showing all his crooked bottom teeth.

"Nah, we gon' be prizefighters," he said. I laughed too and gulped back the tight feeling in my throat. Scared or not, my attitude about situations like this kicked in: I had come this far, there was no turning back. I started it, and I would see it to the end.

Mr. Bell huddled with us before the fight. Our opponents were Mexican boys. All we had to do was hit them with body shots.

"They eat lots of beans," he said. "Their bodies are soft. Hit them in the gut with body shots, you'll be fine." At that moment it occurred to me that in all this training, we had sparred a little with a trainer, but I hadn't actually *hit* an opponent. Mostly we had hit punching bags. Mr. Bell, obviously not worried about that, attempted to fortify our confidence.

"They eat a lotta beans," he repeated. "They'll fold. Don't worry. Their bodies are soft."

I heard what he was saying, but I was wondering what the Mexican boys had been told about us.

I should say right here, I was never one of those kids who had to be first. First in line, first with a hand up to answer a question, first seat in class. Uh uh. Not me. But in the Golden Gloves arena, the younger boxers got the privilege of stepping into the ring first. Swell.

My opponent had on a tough face. So, I put on a tough face, or tried to. We circled each other, swinging and missing. When one of his punches flattened my nose, most of my training went right out the window, except for the bobbing and weaving which ultimately saved me.

By the time it was over—two rounds felt like six—I had only landed two or three punches. L'Arthur had to sit by helplessly and watch me lose. When his turn came, he didn't do much better. With a cold towel pressed to my nose, I watched him get beaten in the third round, both of us whipped by hard-hitting Mexican boys with solid bodies. Must have missed their beans that day.

We got back to Mr. Bell's house and had to ride our bikes home, bruised, defeated, and depressed, L'Arthur with the beginnings of a black eye, me with a bloody nose. Not a nickel of prize money jingled in our pockets. Adding insult to injury, Gwayne had quit the practices. He didn't even show up to give us moral support.

Muhtha took one look at us and immediately ended Dad's dream of having prizefighter sons.

"That's it. No more boxing for you," she said. No argument from me. I had decided after the first round that my boxing career was over.

## ~ Bishop's Band ~

Much better than boxing, Muhtha decided we needed music in our lives. A neighbor had told her about Bishop's Band, which provided music lessons, instruments, and the excitement of marching down the street in a holiday parade, a 180-degree change from the violent world of fighting.

Bishops's Band was a year-round activity sponsored by the Kiwanis Club, and kids of all ages could become members. We moaned about it at first, but Muhtha signed us up anyway. L'Arthur played the flute, Gwen carried the purple and red Bishop's banner, Lizzie was a pompom girl, and instead of getting beat up, I beat the snare drum.

During the year, we wore our slightly ill-fitting, red, white, and blue band uniforms, and played for every major holiday, strutting our stuff in parades on Manchester, Florence, and Alameda. The spectator numbers would never rival the Rose Parade's turnout, but families did support their kids. High school bands participated, there were riders on horseback and city officials waved from slow moving cars. Dad missed most of the parades but Muhtha came and cheered for us.

After Bishops Band played out, creating music was on my mind. Playing the drum was okay, but I got a hankering to own a guitar and emulate my two favorite guitar guys—Elvis and Ricky Nelson. My taste in music was different than most of my friends. Elvis and Ricky weren't exactly soul singers. But I liked them anyway, and I liked their songs, so I decided to get a guitar.

On 84th and Central was a pawn shop that I

passed anytime I went to Alvin's house, but it wasn't until I decided to get a guitar that I noticed several guitars hanging in the pawn shop window. On one was a tag that said 'Yours for $13.00.' I had half of that saved. I gave it to Muhtha and told her a guitar was what I wanted. For my next birthday a guitar the color of a palomino horse was wrapped up for me, like a surprise.

Every day I practiced my strumming while standing with a leg propped on the bed frame, looking at myself in the mirror. I thought I looked pretty sublime. I imagined the girls screaming over me. I felt I had the look, but the skill, not so much, even after a couple of weeks, leaning over the guitar, trying to make sure I was placing my fingers correctly on the strings. It wasn't easy. I hit a lot of sour notes. I got myself a little pick to strum over the strings, but as hard as I tried to play You Ain't Nothin' But a Hound Dog, I just wasn't getting it.

I admit, I wasn't much for sticking with something for very long, unless I got the hang of it real fast. So, I retired it to the closet, thinking that if my hands grew a little, I might learn to play that guitar after all.

Making some jingle for my pockets was always on my mind, and opportunities were there. Like the avocados, hanging in our yard. I pulled a load in our wagon down the street and sold them three for a quarter. I sold all occasion cards to get a free BB gun from an ad in a comic book. Running errands for neighbors was another way to do it, though it wasn't very lucrative. Miss Emily and Miss Esther Brown, two spinster sisters probably in their 60's, lived a few doors away in the front house, and cared for their invalid father who lived in the smaller house in back. I bought a newspaper for Miss Esther one

Saturday, and she paid me a dime. A second time she gave me money for a few grocery items and when I delivered them, she gave me another dime.

Another Saturday, I overhead Muhtha on the phone talking to one of the sisters.

"You want Howard to go for you?" she asked. I backed out of the room. "All right. I'll send him over."

She called me back into the room and chewed me out.

"I think it's a shame you don't want to help Miz Brown. You know she can't do that much for herself. You should be proud she trusts you to run errands for her. Now you get on over there, and whatever she gives you, you say thank you." That was Muhtha. She was big on extending herself to help others and expected us to do the same.

Miz Brown gave me a five-dollar bill to buy groceries and the Sentinel newspaper. I peddled back to her house balancing the bag on my knee thinking this job was worth 50 cents, if it was worth a dime. Miz Brown greeted me with a smile as I handed her the groceries and change. She rummaged through her coin purse, digging deep. "Thank you, baby," she said, and handed me a dime.

## ~ Bess 2 ~

There were free-fun days, and money-fun days. Money fun was all the things we did with a few dollars in our pockets, or even just a quarter. A quarter plus a few pennies was enough for a ticket into the Manchester or Triple AAA movie theater, and a Sugar Daddy or

Big Hunk that would last through the cartoon and at least one movie of a double feature. With a few dollars, L'Arthur and I would ride our bikes to Red Wing Hatchery on Florence and Alameda, buy two pigeons, rollers or tumblers, cart them home in a makeshift cage, then build a better cage. We'd give them a little time to get used to the new home until we were ready to let them fly. The big lift off was from the driveway. We'd toss them up and watch them do their thing, swoop, dive, tumble and roll, breast up, wings spread, over our house, over the neighbor's, and sometimes fly completely out of sight. But always, they came back.

One money Saturday, we rode down Avalon to Scotchman's Dairy on El Segundo. The dairy was spread out over at least two blocks, and behind the main building were vacant fields, where cows grazed in one section, and horses in another. We parked our bikes under a sign that said CALVES FOR SALE - $6.00. L'Arthur looked at the sign then at me and said, "Let's buy one."

I said, "Buy one what?"

"A calf."

"What for?"

"Just to have it."

He got all excited talking about us having our own calf just like Dad had Bess. I reminded him that Bess wasn't a calf and Dad didn't have her anymore. But L'Arthur was grinning. I could tell his mind was made up to do this crazy thing. The money was in my pocket and the more I thought about it, the idea grew on me. *Yeah. Our own calf. None of our friends owned their own personal cow.*

We each plunked down three dollars of hard-earned lawn-mowing money, pointed to a calf that was

2-weeks old, and named our calf Bess 2. We were given a receipt and I could tell by the grin on L'Arthur's face, he was feeling the same way I was. Pretty proud of myself. Look what we'd done. We started walking away feeling giddy, as if anything happening right then would make us burst into laughter. "Ain't Flora gonna be surprised," we said.

We were on our way out the barn door when one of the ranch guys asked how we were getting the calf home. That stopped us in our tracks. We hadn't even thought about getting it home. He asked where we lived, and when we told him, he offered a free delivery. With us following behind on our bikes, Bess 2 ended up riding in the back seat of a gutted Ford Fairlane.

The man pulled into our driveway and with a rope tied loosely around her neck, we coaxed the calf out of the car and led her into the back yard. Muhtha came outside, circled the critter, but didn't say a word, which was a blessing. We knew Dad was pleased. He circled the calf and started chuckling, shaking his head. I think he was proud of us, his boys, making a move like that. But naturally, Bess 2 couldn't stay at the house.

Dad moved her to a corral at 213th and Avalon, property that spread out behind a Quaker Paint store and was owned by an old cowboy. Cows and horses grazed in his big open field. Dad paid him about six dollars a month. We visited Bess 2, and watched her grow into a full-sized cow. Over the years she gave birth to seven calves, including twins, a male and a female. Dad kept her for about ten years, and we were there for two of the births. He said we had picked a winner.

## ~ Cornbread Days~

By the time Gwen, L'Arthur, Lizzie and I had all been at St. Malachy's for a couple of years, Muhtha was working three to five days a week doing housework in other people's homes. It was called "day work." She rode the bus long distances to neighborhoods whose names we knew but had never been to, including Hancock Park, the Wilshire District, and Glendale. Her clients were well-to-do older white couples who paid her $12 to $15 dollars a day for about six hours of work. I liked calling them "clients" which in my mind made it sound like Muhtha was in charge.

Her wages paid for most of our groceries. We ate a lot of chicken and tuna pot pies, three for a dollar, bread for twenty-five cents a loaf, milk for twenty-six cents a quart, Springfield corn, four cans for a dollar, just a few of the items I can easily recall. Some days I'd wait for her at the corner of Manchester and Avalon. She'd have a grocery bag in each hand as she stepped off the bus and I'd help her carry them home.

I never saw the houses or met the women she worked for. Never saw the areas on the edges of LA where they lived. If I thought of them at all, I imagined they lived in huge fancy homes like Mrs. Johnson's and were very rich. She never talked much about them or described them, so my imaginings may have been greater than the reality. She did mention one "client" more than others, the woman who complimented her hairdo on the days Muhtha was past due for a visit to the beauty shop.

"Oh Flora," the woman would say, "your hair looks so nice today," and on the days Muhtha arrived fresh from her three-dollar press and curl, the woman wouldn't say a word.

She'd chuckle talking about those women who offered her dresses that had gone out of style, or shoes to give to dad, suggesting, "Flora, these might fit your husband...," though they knew nothing about Dad, much less his shoe size. They would give her bags of barely worn socks with holes so small, our toes didn't even punch through them.

Muhtha was proud, but not filled with foolish pride, so she accepted those items she knew we could use. We wore second-hand socks that were like new and we had a drawer full of dress black nylon socks from a man named Mr. Gaskell whom we never met.

Those were the cornbread days, when the four of us had to get clicking in the mornings, with no Muhtha there to make sure we ate breakfast and got to school on time.

Before leaving for work, she would make a tin of cornbread, and while it was baking, she'd sprinkle clothes for ironing or load the ringer washing machine. We could smell the cornbread before we got up, hear her moving from room to room, knew she was gathering together her purse and bus fare, and the cornbread would be on the stove cooling. She'd call to us not to be late, and out the door she went. Gwen was in charge then, honing her bossy skills for later years by hustling Lizzie into the bathroom and telling me and L'Arthur to straighten up our beds.

Our bathroom was hardly big enough for two people, much less four, so we had to take turns. Gwen would help Lizzie with her hair, they'd primp, or do whatever it was that took forever, and didn't improve the overall look. Once L'Arthur and I got in, we'd have a peeing contest to see who could go the longest. I'd use our tiny sink first while he would check his face in the medicine cabinet mirror, hoping to find a hair or two on his upper lip.

Milk didn't last long in our house, so twenty-six cents was left on the kitchen table, and either L'Arthur or I would go the half block past the alley to the corner store to buy a quart of milk. Gwen would give us each a cup full and cut the cornbread into four pieces. We'd break it up into our bowls and pour on the milk. Cold milk over warm cornbread. That was breakfast and we slurped it up. Lizzie rarely finished hers, so I'd finish it for her.

It was okay for us to have cornbread and milk for breakfast, but apparently not okay to tell the nutritionist who came to school periodically to give information about "healthy meals." She came to Gwen's classroom and asked each child what they'd had for breakfast. Gwen spilled the beans. "Cornbread and milk," she said, and later told Muhtha about the visit. "Well you didn't have to tell her cornbread and milk," Muhtha said, slightly annoyed, making us wonder why it had to be a secret. "I just told the truth," said my sister, and Muhtha had nothing more to say about it.

There were no free breakfasts provided by the schools in those days, public or parochial and St. Malachy's had no cafeteria. On the last Thursday of every month though, the school provided lunch, but it wasn't free. It was called Hot Dog Luncheon day. For a quarter, every student got a hot dog, a handful of potato chips, and a cup of Hawaiian punch. Tables were set up in the school yard, and we'd file by holding out our paper plates. If Muhtha wasn't working that day, she would be there to help hand out the hotdogs. It was a small thing, but boy did we look forward to that once a month treat.

Those were the days Muhtha opened our eyes to downtown Los Angeles, taking the four of us on the #49 bus line that we'd catch on San Pedro at Manchester. It was the bus that got her right into downtown, halfway to some of her day jobs, and she saw an opportunity and a way to show us sights outside the neighborhood. To us they were adventures, and Flora Bell was not the adventurous type. But she didn't hesitate.

She took us on Angel's Flight, the ride up that steep rail track in a trolley car when it only cost a nickel. For our birthdays she took us to Clifton's Cafeteria, and we could pick whatever dish we wanted. She took us shopping at Grand Central Market where all the vegetables and fruit were laid out, rows and shelves full, and where we had our first delicious taste of an Orange Julius drink. None of us wanted plain orange juice after tasting an Orange Julius. At Christmas time, she'd usher us onto the bus to see the decorations in the windows at May Co. and Robinson's department stores, elaborate displays of falling snow, electric trains going through tunnels, trees with toys all around them, Christmas carols in the background, and so many lights.

The cornbread days, 1957, '58. With the folks both gone to work, we were responsible for our homework being done. We had to grab the sack lunches left in the refrigerator and get ourselves to school on time. We knew the drill. It was the routine, the pattern, the rhythm of our lives. We slipped a few times, were late occasionally, had to be dragged from bed more than once. We weren't perfect, but we tried hard. Life was what it was.

# ~ Church Stuff ~

Confirmation when I was twelve was the third step toward becoming a full-blown Catholic. By then I had been told like the rest of my classmates, that a Catholic education was the absolute best education a child could receive, and that parents who pay tuition for their children's parochial education, care more about their children than parents who do not, i.e. public-school parents.

I'm not sure I believed that speech completely, but when one-sided carefully designed propaganda is preached year after year, some kids in the Catholic School system—the four of us for example—might begin to believe it. Even if paying tuition is a struggle for the family as it sometimes was for mine, it was hard not to feel slightly superior to kids in public school, based on information for which there was no substantial proof.

But I was a kid. I never questioned that information. I went along with the program, felt I was getting a good education, and believed that along with being taught right and wrong from my parents, my Catholic education kept me on the straight and narrow.

Along with the seven nuns at St. Malachy's, there were two priests. The best liked was Father Flannigan. He was young, a straight talker, devout without being self-righteous. We looked up to him not just because he was young, but because of how he spoke to us, not like a teacher or a priest. More like a youthful uncle that you respected. He made us want to learn and perform our altar boy duties correctly. He even made us believe that becoming a priest might be something to consider, but he never aggressively tried to persuade us to seek the priesthood, although L'Arthur thought about it. Father Flannigan may have put it on his mind after telling us about a retreat he'd attended before becoming a priest.

L'Arthur went on a retreat when he was fourteen at a seminary in Dominguez Hills. Part of the discipline was that for several hours each day, all boys were to remain completely silent. Not say a word. That was a tall order for my brother. He wasn't what you'd call a chatty guy, but he liked to talk and joke, and keep things light. By the time he returned home, he had changed his mind completely. I don't know if keeping silent was the deal breaker or something else, but all he said was, maybe the priesthood wasn't the life for him after all. Boy was I relieved. I think if my brother had become a priest, my life would have changed too.

As to Father Flannigan, he was a positive role model and made us more aware that priests were human beings too, and not that different from anyone else. Around Father Flannigan, I was more attentive when I served mass. I held my hands just so, my gaze always at eye level. No looking off into space or staring down at shoes. No cutting monkey shines when you served mass with him. Flannigan was by-the-book, but he had a sense of humor too. He understood it was tough on us poor altar boys, wearing those robes, and having to hold the wine, and the wafers, and ring the chime too, especially during holiday masses that might last two hours.

One Easter Vigil when Alvin and I were the altar boys for the service, and St. Malachy's pews were packed—standing room only—we were waiting inside the sacristy in our robes, feeling a little nervous as always before a big mass. Father Flannigan came over to us. "All right guys," he said, "I need you to bring the altar into the sacristy."

*Huh*? Alvin looked at me. I looked at him. *Move the altar?* After a split second, we hesitantly stepped toward the door, whispering to each other, "What is he talking about?" We glanced back at Father as if to say, are you sure you want us to do this? He looked at our faces and burst into laughter.

"I'm joking guys." Alvin and I tried hiding our sheepish grins. We should have known Father was trying to put one over on us. He was still chuckling as he nodded for us to begin the procession into the church. I had a lot of respect and admiration for Father Flannigan, but never once did I consider becoming a priest. Altar boy was plenty of sacrifice for me.

Muhtha had some rituals she insisted we do, meant to strengthen our faith and get us through tough times. There was mass every Sunday which we never missed. We said grace over all our meals, made the sign of the cross, made our regular confessions. I sometimes struggled to think of what it was exactly that I needed to confess. None were heavy duty sins, so for penance I'd get off with a few Hail Mary's and a couple of Acts of Contrition.

Muhtha offered up special prayers and candle lightings, called novenas, but not at St. Malachy's. She'd walk or ride the bus to Mother of Sorrows Church on 87th and Main in the early evenings, and Lizzie and I would have to go with her. Not Gwen, not L'Arthur. She would pray to the Mother of Perpetual help on nine Wednesdays in a row during times when money was really tight. Maybe it helped. Muhtha was big on prayers and her faith was strong. Who knows? Without those prayers, our life might have been tougher.

Maybe there wouldn't have been that little extra that allowed her to take us to movies that she wanted to see and felt we shouldn't miss. Dad didn't go, so she took us with her. We saw *The Ten Commandments*, *Three Coins in a Fountain*, and her all-time favorite movie, *Imitation of Life*. What a revelation. To see a black housekeeper as a kind and respected person, in a role that was as important as the star. Muhtha loved that movie and talked about it for days.

I'm almost sure that the year L'Arthur went to the seminary, was the same year I went to one too, but not for a retreat. I went to have fun. It was the last year I served for Father Flannigan. He took the altar boys, about fourteen of us, 7th and 8th graders, on a bus trip to a seminary near Camarillo for the altar boy picnic. About 100 boys our age from a bunch of Catholic parishes were invited. Alvin and I were seatmates for the ride up. It was the first time I had ever been to a seminary or on a field trip this important.

We stepped off the bus after two hours and the scenery was beautiful. Everywhere we looked was green, the landscaping, the lawns. Rows of grape vineyards surrounded the seminary, wide sloping lawns, perfectly cut. One section of grass had a pathway that led to a huge Olympic sized pool. Everyone changed into trunks and went swimming. After swimming, we had lunch, played baseball, volleyball, hiked the grounds. We met guys from parishes in Lynwood, Downey, Huntington Park, El Monte, Monterey Park. You might not think a day at a seminary would be much fun, but it turned out to be the highlight of summer vacation that year.

## ~ Cousin Albert ~

Uncle Ben, the relative my dad stayed with when he first came to LA, had been widowed three times and was living alone until his great-grandson Albert and Albert's mother Bootsy moved into Ben's house after Bootsy's mother died. But Bootsy couldn't handle her bad-acting son Albert. She wanted Ben to "straighten him out" and wanted Albert to be around "nice boys like L'Arthur and Howard who didn't fight and steal and talk back." My brother and I were to be role models before we even knew what a role model was. Albert spent time at our house, playing a little ball, going to movies, sleeping over, and we spent time with him at Uncle Ben's, watching television, and hanging out.

The problem was Ben's neighbors. He called them 'hoods' and they lived right up the street. Ben told Albert to stay away from them, but Albert didn't listen. He idolized those guys, and their fancy cars, and the women that always seemed to be around, and he was only eleven, a year younger than me.

Summer was winding down that day and L'Arthur wasn't with us. Albert and I were at Ascot Park, a few blocks from Ben's house, sitting on rickety bleachers in the hot sun, with pockets empty of even the smallest of small change. Nearby at 42nd and Hooper, less than half a block away, the aroma of pies wafted out of the smokestack of Johnson's Bakery. With our last pennies we'd bought two cartons of milk. Albert's bright idea was to sniff the pies and drink the milk and that would be almost like eating them. We inhaled the smell of apples and cinnamon, sweet potato pies, peach cobblers. We turned our noses up to the air and sniffed like a couple of hound dogs. Albert called it sweet torture. I called it useless. Sniffing was a long way from eating, and not at all filling.

We left the smells and headed half a block down Central to where the bus line ended. An empty bus with its doors wide open was parked in front of Norm's hole in-the-wall donut shop with its greasy windows, and donuts you could see, hanging from hooks. The bus driver was nowhere in sight. I thought we were headed home, but Albert had other ideas. He looked around, then tapped my shoulder as if to say, watch this. He stepped onto the bus, snatched and grabbed something near the money slot, then jumped off and casually walked away, but not his usual walk. He put a little hitch in his step and flashed his take at me when I caught up to him. He'd stolen some transfers. A transfer was like a pass to go from one bus to another without having to pay another fare. "You're asking for trouble," I said.

He kept walking. "I didn't get caught. No big deal."

The minute we got back to the house, he started in on Ben. "Just a dollar Ben, come on, you got it." Albert promised to do some chore that probably never got done. I expected Ben to say no. But he gave in, maybe because I was there. He handed over a dollar and out the door we went.

The bus transfers got us downtown, and fifty cents got us two tickets and two bags of popcorn at the Orpheum Theatre. I spent part of the time in the darkened theatre trying not to feel guilty. I hadn't done anything wrong, exactly, but it felt like I had, and I didn't like the feeling. I'd never stolen anything, never shoplifted. I don't think I was even tempted, though I saw plenty of things I would have liked to have. Miniature cars, games, gadgets, planes, the kind of stuff I used to see at the Rexall Drug store on the ground floor beneath Kaiser La Cienega, when I had to get my allergy shots. So many goodies jammed into a space the size of my bedroom. It would have been easy to walk out of there with something, but stealing, maybe getting caught, having to face my parents afterwards? Uh uh. That wasn't me. Never even thought about it.

After the movie, when we were nearly back at Ben's house, Albert got chummy with some of the hoods sitting on the porch in front of their house. They were some tough looking characters. I couldn't believe they'd take up any time with Albert, he was so little, and young, but he seemed to be on the same vibe with those guys. Albert already had a role model, and it wasn't me or L'Arthur. It was the tall lanky guy wearing flashy chains and rings, the owner of the Cadillac parked on the front grass. Albert said the guy was a pimp, and he wanted to be just like him.

With summer nearly over, I didn't see Albert much after that. He wasn't a full-fledged delinquent, but dad predicted he was well on his way, and he was right. Years later, Albert became the person he had idolized, a pimp with a stable full of girls working for him. Later, when that played out, he was arrested for armed robbery and sent to prison.

The last week of that summer Father Flannigan stepped in and rescued me from a temporary case of the blahs brought on by the unavoidable. School was about to start back. He invited me, Alvin, and a few other altar boys to a Dodgers baseball game at the Coliseum, his treat.

I'd never been to the Coliseum, and never to a live sporting event. Nobody I knew had ever been to a game. I'd never listened to the Dodgers on the radio, didn't even know what radio station to turn to if I wanted to listen. All I knew about baseball came from playing in the street. I couldn't wait to go.

We met Father Flannigan at the church that day, and the five of us rode with him in the church station wagon. Inside the stadium, we had to walk through a long tunnel to get to our seats, and coming out at the end of the tunnel, the sound of the crowd cheering was like a continuous roll of thunder. The stadium was packed. I don't remember who the other team was, or the score, or who won, just that it was a great day and a lot of fun. I wasn't one to save a ticket stub for a souvenir, but I wish I had.

After that game, I started collecting baseball cards. I was buying and chewing bubble gum like crazy, because for pennies, a free card came with a pack of gum. I made a scrapbook out of two pieces of cardboard and pasted the cards on heavy drawing paper for the pages using glue I made from flour and water. I punched holes in the cover and the pages and held the whole thing together with string. My plan was to trade the cards, maybe make some money, but once my scrapbook started filling up, I didn't want to part with any of them. Aside from the ones that came unstuck, or got lost, I kept them all. Sixty years later, I still have my scrapbook.

# ~ School, Again ~

I looked forward to one thing with the start of the school year. New shoes. The rubber smell of a new pair of tennis shoes was addictive. I'd take my new pair to bed with me and fall asleep with that scent in my nose. In a good year, I'd get new shoes for Easter, leather shoes that almost smelled better than the rubber, with shoestrings and hard soles for $7.77 at Hardy's. They felt so good I'd want to wear them all day. But we couldn't. Sunday shoes were for Sunday and might last two years. Even when we outgrew them, we'd squeeze our growing feet into them and wouldn't complain about our toes being pinched.

The year was 1959 and I was in 7th grade. I remember it was a great year for television shows. Every night something good was on. I was heavy into westerns then, and there were a bunch. *Rawhide*, *The Rifleman*, *Cheyenne*, *Bronco Lane*, *Tales of Wells Fargo*, *Have Gun, Will Travel*, and *Wanted Dead or Alive*. By then, Roy Rogers, Gene Autry and Hopalong Cassady were off the air. Cooler westerns were in their prime, and I watched them all. We'd sing the theme songs, especially *Rawhide*. "*...move'em out, ride'em in... Rawhiiiiiiiiiide. Hayah!*"

At the age of twelve, I was moving into my prime too. I was a little on the chubby side, and still shorter than most kids in 7th grade. I was growing out, but not up. Eating had become a favorite pastime, and what I liked most to eat, were the things I should have avoided. Pancakes were high on the list, saturated with syrup. Donuts, Hostess cupcakes, ding dongs, berry pies. For over a year, dad had an old junker of a car parked in front of the house collecting dust and cobwebs. I don't know why he kept it so long and hadn't tried to fix it or sell it. It wasn't worth stealing so it was never locked. I got the brilliant idea to store my secret stash of sweets in the glovebox. I'd hunker down in the front seat when no one was around and scarf down a couple of those Hostess boysenberry pies. I had a sweet tooth that wouldn't quit and a couple of cavities to go along with it.

School started back. L'Arthur had graduated from St. Malachy's so I wouldn't be walking with him anymore. He was a freshman at Salesian High in East LA and rode the bus to school with a couple of friends. He'd become more particular about his school attire now that uniforms for him were a thing of the past. He'd be up some mornings as early as 6:30, waking me up, dressing like he was going to a party. One morning before leaving the bedroom, he flipped open his jacket and showed me the pack of Newport cigarettes in his inside pocket. I grabbed at him just as he did a football move out of my reach. "You smokin' now?" I said. He didn't answer, just gave me that L'Arthur grin and left. I never saw him smoke. I think it was all for show.

At St. Malachy's, some of the faces were familiar, but others were missing. One new face was a transfer student from public school, Gerald Aubry, the "outsider" who immediately became the center of attention, both good and bad.

Meanwhile, old Mother Columba was my seventh-grade teacher. She'd been at St Malachy's forever and she was no joke. In history class when she told us about Russia, the cold war and communism, I sat up and paid attention. She made us fully aware that Russia was our enemy not to be taken lightly, and that its leaders had not only the desire to destroy our country, but also the weapons to do it. Every Friday the horn would sound, the signal for the practice air raid drills, and we would scramble under our too-small desks after the "drop and cover" command. It sounded almost funny the first time I heard it. There was Mother Columba, all decked out in her black and white, her cheeks pale and saggy yelling "Drop! Cover!"

But the more we practiced it, I started thinking we needed to take this maneuver seriously. I don't think any of us walked around preoccupied with the thought of nuclear war, but during the time we were in that class-room listening with eyes open wide, the threat seemed real. There was a country out there that could drop a bomb on us, and our country needed to be ready.

Then one day out of the blue, Mother Columba dropped a bomb on me. While we were in class, she singled me out. Maybe she thought I didn't look serious enough during the drop and cover. She pointed a finger at me and said, "Stop smiling like a Cheshire Cat!" *What was a Cheshire Cat?* I had no idea.

I told Gerald about it. We'd become friends. He had become the undisputed tetherball king. St. Mal-achy's tetherballs had arrived at the end of the previous year. Nobody'd had time to get really good at whacking that ball. Gerald had been playing for two years at public school. It was no contest. He beat the best of the girls and the boys too, and he did it with flair. Nobody seemed to mind losing to "Gerry" which is what everyone started calling him, except me.

It's hard to peg why you become friends with someone, but with Gerald, aside from admiring how he disposed of everybody playing tetherball, including me, we came together over lunches. Mostly his.

Since St. Malachy's didn't have a cafeteria, every one brought a lunch to school. Gerald's lunches were unique, but nowhere near as special or enviable as Arnold Compton's. At least three times a week Arnold's mother would come right into the classroom to bring him his lunch—a hamburger and fries. The juicy aroma would fill up the room like it was just off the grill. That was way beyond anything I could even wish for.

Gerald's lunches were good in a different way. He'd have saltine crackers wrapped in plastic, with ham or baloney and cheese squares wrapped in plastic. He'd make cracker sandwiches. They always looked more appealing than my lunch which by noon would be a soggy squished-up mess. Muhtha would make a sandwich, half baloney, half peanut butter and jelly, and wrap the halves in the same piece of wax paper. The apple she'd put in (gotta have a piece of fruit) would flatten the bread, the grape jelly and peanut butter would turn into a purple blob, and the blob would ooze out onto the baloney. I hated that.

And Gerald understood this. He knew how annoying a ruined lunch could be. Unselfishly, he would share his cracker sandwiches with me, and I'd give him half my pb&j. It followed naturally that we became good friends. It was Gerald who told me what a Cheshire cat was. Unlike me, he knew the story of Alice in Wonderland.

But I soon learned, Gerald was a little crazy. Sensitive, honest, but borderline nuts. He was born with two fingers missing on one of his hands, which may explain the chip on his shoulder. He was ready to fight anybody, anytime, over anything. To his friends, the three-fingered hand was a mystery. How it happened, why it happened.

He never talked about it and neither did we.

The funny thing about Gerald, he was very mild mannered, no temper at all. Just a little touchy. I remember once, I'd spent the night at his house on 58th Drive. To my unsophisticated ear, "Drive" suggested a more upscale neighborhood, one with better looking houses. An address on a "Street" was so common. "Drive" sounded rich, expensive. Boy was I wrong about that. Gerald's house and all the houses on 58th Drive were tiny, older, more run-down. Not that it mattered, it didn't. But it was an eye-opener just the same. It gave me a new perspective on my house, and my neighborhood.

Anyway, I'd spent the night, and the next morning his dad got mad and barked at him for leaving his newspaper rubber bands on the porch. Gerald got very quiet and whispered to me. "Don't you hate it when your father embarrasses you in front of your friends?" He was really hurt, and I felt bad for him. As I helped him pick up the rubber bands, I thought about my dad. He could be tough sometimes, but I knew for sure he would never have said anything about a few loose rubber bands.

Another time, Gerald came out on the losing side of an afterschool fight. I asked him about it the next day. He just shrugged. "He beat me," he said, and his expression was puzzled, as if he couldn't figure out how that had happened. His simple admission of defeat with no lingering anger seemed almost noble. I've never forgotten that.

He'd come over some days after school, and I naturally wanted to give him something tasty in return for all those lunch treats. One time I made a hefty stack of pancakes for us, only to find out we were out of syrup.

Not even a few drops of Karo, the clear syrup Muhtha used in her delicious pecan pies. But Gerald was adaptable. We spread the last of the grape jelly onto the cakes, folded them in half, and ate them like tacos.

All the girls liked Gerald, and he liked them. When he wasn't trying to kiss the prettiest ones, he was teasing them with his natural-born attention getter—a three-fingered hand. He was really into kissing, even chased a few girls home, just for a kiss.

Thinking I was deprived, he set me up for my first kiss. I was pulled into the old dare game, you know, I dare you to do this, I dare you to do that. One of our classmates, a fair-skinned girl named Mona, who was known to be free with her kisses, was crazy about me, according to Gerald.

"She dares you to kiss her," he told me one day after class. The word was out. *Mona dared Howard to kiss her.* Once the dare was spoken, you couldn't back out.

The whole class found their way to the alley after school that day, or maybe it just seemed like thirty kids were looking on. Even Lizzie was in the crowd with Veronica, watching to see the action. And there was Mona separating from the group, coming toward me, looking kind of shy at first. Then she grabbed me. Her arms went around my neck, and she kissed me hard, open mouth. That was a surprise. Did I close my eyes or pull away? I don't remember. I do remember when she was done kissing me, she kissed Gerald too. He said Mona was crazy about me, but I think she was crazy about every boy in $7^{th}$ grade.

In addition to kissing, it was Gerald who talked me into roof-jumping, something that brought me closer than any other to breaking a body part. He told me he did it "all the time," with other friends, and he wanted me to try it.

The trick to roof jumping was simple: don't hit the ground. You could use a fence, a gate, a tall trash can to get from one roof to the next, all the way to the end of a block. Just don't touch the ground.

We climbed up onto his roof and he got zoned in. After staring at it for a few seconds, he jumped to his neighbor's roof, and landed in a crouch. He looked back at me as if to say, See, I told you it was easy.

He sprinted to the other edge and jumped again, then waved me on. I took a breath and jumped. The ground rushed up to meet me, but it didn't. I made it to the next roof, used a fence for one leap, and on and on we jumped to the end of the block. At the end, he slapped me on the back as if it were some great achievement. We must have done it three or four more times over the next few weeks, even raced a couple of his friends who were on roofs across the alley from his house. This is one thing I did without telling my brother. Luckily, nobody got hurt.

Roof jumping wasn't enough of a thrill for Gerald. He'd spent a Friday night at my house, and the next day we were on our way to ABC to buy a watermelon. An overpass bridge had been constructed over Manchester for anyone who wanted to use it, but specifically the for the kids at South Park Elementary School. There was no protective screen over the top of it, and there were at least twenty steps from the sidewalk leading up to the overpass, and as many steps on the other side going down. We had walked across the bridge and were approaching the down steps when Gerald, still at the top decided he was going to jump.

"I can do this," he said.

"Uh uh Gerald. You don't wanna do that." I said. I kept walking down the steps thinking he had to be joking.

"I'm gonna jump," he said. And then he did it. He landed hard on the sidewalk, grabbing his ankle. I helped him up, but I felt like punching him. "Man are you crazy?"

He kind of laughed, trying to pretend he wasn't in agony. He limped into ABC with me, we got the watermelon, and then he limped home. That night, his mother called us from the hospital wanting to know how Gerald had nearly broken his ankle. Muhtha turned to me with that look and said, "What happened to Gerald?" When I told her that he'd jumped off the overpass, she couldn't believe it. "What is wrong with that child?" she said. I wondered too. After his ankle healed, he was at Griffith Park on a hiking trail that ended at the top of a hill. He jumped from the hill down to the trail below and messed up his other ankle. I started thinking, maybe Gerald thought he could fly.

## ~ Texas Christmas ~

We would spend Christmas of 1959 in Houston and meet relatives we'd never met before, except for Aunt Elizabeth. Dad's buddy Cal, the friend he left home with when he was seventeen joined us for part of the journey. He and his wife Ervalee lived in San Francisco and had visited a few times. He looked like Cab Calloway. Every time he visited, he'd bang out some bluesy tunes on the old upright piano we had in the garage and spend at least one night at a club on Central Avenue. He'd say to dad, "Hey man, let's take a cruise down to the 'main drag.' Dad wasn't really a club guy, but when Cal was here, it was a special occasion, so he'd go.

He and Ervalee drove down in his 1955 Buick Roadmaster during Christmas week, and in the wee hours of a Sunday morning, our two-car caravan hit Route 66 headed to Houston. We were in dad's 1959 powder blue Dodge Coronet, his first ever new car. He was anxious to get it out on the open road. He'd padded the floor of the back seat with pillows and blankets to smooth out the hump. Somehow between the back seat and the floor, the four of us managed to fall asleep.

A day and a half later, we crossed the state line into cold, gray Texas. They had true winters, not like LA where the weather was still mild.

Waco was where we met Uncle Ben's brothers, Jut and FluEllen, our cousins. They lived in the woods in the same area where dad grew up. It was isolated, no houses or cabins nearby and only dirt roads leading in and out. Their one-room log cabins were built three feet above the dirt with open space underneath. A rough wooden porch, and high steps led up to the front door. FluEllen, lived in the smaller one behind Jut, both cabins owned by the Cooper family after years of sharecropping.

Jut's cabin was warmed by a pot belly stove. I remember the first thing he said after we sat down. "Y'all done et?" Muhtha was always quick to keep anyone from making a fuss, but she had no chance to protest. Jut produced a slab of bacon from a cold box, cut it into thick slices, put more wood into the stove, and fried the bacon in a skillet on top. The whole room felt like an oven, but it sure smelled good. He cut big hunks of bread, set the bread and bacon in the middle of the table. After he prayed over the food, we all "et."

We'd barely finished eating when L'Arthur let out a yelp and started blowing on his hand. That potbelly stove was like an open flame and he'd accidentally touched it. Jut scooped out some lard and slathered it on the burn and wrapped his hand with a towel. That was sort of the signal for handshakes and goodbyes, so we left soon after and headed for Aunt Elizabeth's house.

The ride was miserable for L'Arthur but he didn't complain until we hit a bump in the road that turned out to be a skunk, a big one. That made all of us groan. The smell filled the car, made us all gag. Nobody had warned us about skunks. We had never smelled anything so awful. We saw the critter from the rear window, a black and white pole cat, dad called it, quivering but flat.

At Aunt Elizabeth's house Dad and Uncle Russell tried to air out the car and wash away the stench. Uncle Russell shook his head. "The smell might be gone by the time you head back to California," he said, "if you're lucky."

Ten miles from Aunt Elizabeth was Muhtha's sister Antoinette. She and Uncle Randolph had five kids, our cousins, Randolph Jr., Lene, who was my age, Howard, Russell, and the baby Patricia, who was a year old. The rest of us were the same ages, nine to fourteen. We hit it off right away.

Muhtha's youngest sister, the baby of the family, was both my aunt and my Godmother. Her name was Teresa but she was called Tuff T because of her swearing and drinking ways, and the rough characters she called friends. Muhtha hadn't seen Teresa's lifestyle up close and personal, but she'd heard enough about it to be worried. Muhtha was a worrier by nature and nothing could change that. Tuff-T was sweet and affectionate to us, so we didn't worry about her. She kept us laughing when she talked about some of her companions and her nighttime exploits.

All of us kids slept in one bedroom. Lene was like my girlfriend without the kisses. We whiled away the daytime hours talking and laughing, comparing life in Houston with life in LA.

All nine of us cousins added ornaments to the Christmas tree in the living room and went to midnight mass on Christmas Eve. In the morning under the tree was the only gift I had begged for that year, an electric football game. I couldn't believe the folks had brought it all the way from home without me knowing. I had searched the house high and low before we left. How did they keep it hidden? I kept an eye on everyone who played with it to make sure it got back to LA unbroken. Not only did it survive the trip from Texas, it's on a shelf in my garage, right now.

We were all together that Christmas in Houston, but I felt homesick. I missed decorating our own tree, buying trinket gifts for each other, getting token gifts from neighbors. I always groaned about having to serve as altar boy for midnight Mass, but I kind of missed that too. At home on Christmas morning Muhtha and Daddy would always tell their sad little stories as we opened our few little gifts, that all they ever got was an apple or an orange. This Christmas those stories went untold. Even the feeling of loss that always crept up on me, the big letdown as the day ended that Christmas was over, didn't happen. Christmas of 1959 was just different.

## ~ A Teen at Last ~

I turned thirteen in 1960. I wasn't expecting any big changes and there weren't any. I was still shorter than most of my classmates, still more round in the face, still chubby. On the good side, my voice had started changing and I wasn't plagued by zits.

I'd become accustomed to having a little money in my pocket, so when L'Arthur got hired as a box boy at ABC market, the paper route was all on me. I bit the early morning bullet and got them delivered, mostly on time. I couldn't decide which was worse, delivering the papers or collecting the monthly payment from customers. The minute I rang the doorbell, whoever opened the door had some excuse as to why they couldn't pay me. I made a lot of double trips just to collect that $1.50.

I'd become friends with a kid named Richard Tucker who lived down the street from us. He called me Hig and I called him Tucker. He was L'Arthur's age and should have been in his class, but Tucker had been held back twice, so we were both in 7<sup>th</sup> grade.

I bring up Tucker because that year, 1960 his dad won the Irish Sweepstakes. The prize was eighteen thousand dollars! EIGHTTEEN THOUSAND! A fortune. Nobody believed it at first. But it was true. Prosperity had come to a poor black man and the news travelled fast all through the neighborhood.

The sweepstakes was like the lottery. Anyone could buy a ticket, and everyone had a chance to win. Dad and Mr. Tucker were not close friends, but they valued some of the same things—farm life, open spaces, country living, cows. When Mr. Tucker decided to use his winnings to build a ranch in Riverside, dad thought that was a fine idea.

Riverside was fifty miles east of Los Angeles, vacant land then, flat and hot like the desert, wide open spaces and no fences. People moved there because the land plots were cheap and country folks like Tucker's father were building their own homes. Dad thought about moving there for those same reasons and even took us all out to look at the area. Fortunately, Muhtha talked him out of it, gently I would guess, as he had his own head and would have done it anyway, if he really wanted to.

The Tuckers continued living in their old house on 84th during the week, but every Friday, Mr. Tucker headed to Riverside to work on the ranch.

Dad, L'Arthur and I drove out to Riverside one weekend to visit. We took Imperial Highway through Orange County, passing rows of orange groves. There was no freeway to get us there, and the San Bernardino 10 freeway was under construction.

Once we arrived, we were surprised to see that even though Mr. Tucker had worked for months on the house, all that was built on the three-acre plot was frame and foundation. The electricity was wired, but there was no plumbing, and no bathrooms. There were doors with hinges that weren't attached to anything, bedrooms without walls, and no floors. The backyard was open field, with a horse in a corral, a couple of hogs, a few hound dogs, and a caretaker who lived in a trailer and watched the place during the week while Mr. Tucker ran his wrecking business in LA.

It didn't appear to be a work in progress. It looked like they had done all they intended to do. Dad would never pry into Mr. Tucker's business, but he suspected the $18,000 might already be gone, and we wondered if Mr. Tucker's dream would ever be completed. If that was the case though, no one seemed worried, least of all Mr. Tucker.

L'Arthur and I took turns riding Tucker's horse Brownie. As the day wore on, his dad told him to take the car to the nearby hog ranch and buy a dozen thin-cut pork chops. Then to the chicken ranch for two dozen eggs and to the country store to buy two loaves of white bread. Mr. Tucker had a 1940 two-door Ford, stick shift on the floor, and Tucker had been driving since he was fourteen.

"We'll go with you!" L'Arthur and I said. I climbed in front, he got in back, and Tucker slid behind the wheel. Mr. Tucker yelled out to be careful. I remember him saying, "Keep clear a them ditches," but by then, Tucker was backing onto the road.

In Riverside in those days, nobody cared if you were fourteen and didn't have a license. There were no speed limits posted, no police or highway patrol anywhere on those narrow, hilly, dusty roads that were punctuated by lots of dips.

Tucker really knew how to drive, no bucking and jerking, and he wasn't afraid. He held the steering wheel with both hands, but low, almost in his lap, and a confident little smile played around his mouth. He took some of those dips at a worrisome speed, maybe 30 miles an hour, just to show us he could do it. No seat belts in a 1940 Ford. Up and down we went like a roller coaster ride into dips so deep you couldn't see over them. Tucker let out a whoop with each one. My stomach was doing flips, but it was cool how smoothly he handled the stick, gearing down, then back up again to pick up speed. I mean he was younger than L'Arthur and driving a stick shift at a time when L'Arthur had barely sat behind a steering wheel. This was a big deal. I stuck my arm out the open window, let it float and dip with the hot air. So much fun. Suddenly, I couldn't wait to learn how to drive.

At the hog ranch we watched a farmer slice the pork chops right in front of us. After buying the bread and eggs, we sped back to the ranch. Mr. Tucker fried them on a hotplate. Smoke rose up from the plate, drifted into the sky just beginning to darken. Everybody made their own sandwich, and while we ate, I was sure I saw a few stars come out in the sky.

Tucker walked us to the car when it was time to leave. "I guess you're gonna tell Pamela I'm driving," he said.

Pamela Cooper, one of the prettiest girls at St. Malachy's had been making Tucker's heart go pitter-pat for two years. His voice suggested he didn't want me to tell her, but I knew he was hoping just the opposite, that I would tell his secret the minute I saw her. Anytime Pamela was around, poor Tucker was struck dumb. Just to mess with him I said, "Don't worry Tuck. I won't say a word."

## ~ Hawking for Mr. Cooper ~

Pamela Cooper's family of four girls and her parents were considered "bigtime" when they lived around the corner from us on 84th and Wadsworth. (No relation to my Uncle Ben) Pamela and her younger sister Debbie were pretty girls—light-skinned, pampered, and unpredictable. You never knew from one day to the next if they would smile and be friendly or ignore you completely. Especially Pamela. I had a crush on her, but even though she had eyes for Tucker, she made him squirm. I was sorry he hadn't seen her eyes light up when I told her he was driving.

Mr. Cooper, an insurance salesman, was a burly Creole with dark wavy hair, and an over the top personality. He was gregarious, freewheeling, a man who wore suits every day to work, carried a leather briefcase, and acted as if money was no object. He was what regular people, maybe even envious people called bourgeois, a class distinction that along with the new car he bought every couple of years, set him apart in every way from his blue-collar neighbors.

He once hired Tucker and me to distribute five hundred of his new business cards. "Saturate the neighborhood boys," he said, and he handed each of us a box.

We gladly took the job. We hit every house and business for blocks, sticking cards in mailboxes, slipping them behind screen doors, dropping them on front porches, Tucker on one side of the street, me on the other, Manchester to 79th and everything in between.

We had distributed a bunch and were ready to call it a day, but we still had cards. Tucker's idea or mine, I don't remember. But together, we dropped the last few cards down the storm drain. I suffered a few guilty moments, but I don't think Mr. Cooper's business suffered. He was a big fish in a small pond, who would eventually move his wife and four daughters to an area more appropriate to his style of living. Paying two boys $15 each to drum up more clients was a minor expense of doing business.

Everyone was impressed by the Coopers, but they

had something that impressed me more than money and new cars. The Coopers had a credit account with the Helms Bakery.

The Helms man was a staple in the neighborhood, everybody's pal. He drove through almost every day in his bright yellow truck, sounding his horn, the call to fresh donuts. All you had to do was flag him down. Inside the truck were pull-out drawers with rows of the most delectable donuts in the world. Chocolate donuts, cake donuts with rainbow frosting and candy sprinkles, strawberry and raspberry filled, lemon-filled, powdered, crumb, cinnamon donuts, bear claws, cream puffs as fluffy as pillows, donuts with so much glaze you could get a tooth ache just looking at them.

Tucker and I were almost home from someplace one day, walking down 84th and there she was, Pamela, stepping inside the bakery truck parked right in front of her house. Her hair was pulled up in a high pony tail and it bounced when she turned and saw us. Casual as you please, she looked over her shoulder. "You want a donut?" she asked. What a line! Tucker hung back but I said, "Yeah." Would I turn down a free donut? No way.

I climbed onto the truck to check out the inventory. I loved watching him pull open that drawer. Air pudding for days. Pamela selected a dozen and a half, an "assortment." She stepped down off the truck and said, "Put it on our account." I glanced at Tucker to see if he'd heard that. She held open the box for us. Not wanting to appear greedy, I took one glaze only. As I bit into it, I considered the power and gravitas of such a priceless convenience. A credit account with the donut man. That was impressive.

When the Coopers left the old neighborhood and moved about six miles away across Normandie, considered then to be the "westside," Debbie and Lizzie who were in the same class remained friends. Lizzie returned home one Sunday with a story to tell after a slumber party for Debbie's eleventh birthday. She raved about the Cooper's huge four-bedroom, three-bath house, their swimming pool, and the birthday party where Mr. Cooper grilled steaks.

"I had my own t-bone steak," she said, as if she couldn't believe it even though she was there. That's when my ears perked up. Everyone had been served their own steak. According to Lizzie, both Pam and Debbie left half of theirs on the plate. I could see Pam pushing hers away, bored, saying, "I'm full."

And what happened to those juicy remaining morsels? Were they at least given for appearances sake to a pet dog? "No," said my little sister. "The housekeeper scraped all the leftovers into a bag and dumped it into the trash." *Housekeeper?* Yup. They had one of those too.

T-bones, barely touched, trashed before the grill had time to get cold. The visual stayed with me for weeks.

I couldn't help comparing that scenario to how often steak was on our table. I had told Muhtha about those pork chop sandwiches, how good they were. "Maybe we could have them sometime," I said. Her answer was, "We'll see." That was the end of that subject. "We'll see," rarely turned into yes.

Pork chops were about as close as I got to steak, except that occasionally, maybe once a month Muhtha would pan fry a steak for dad that he didn't always finish. After eating whatever meager dinner she had prepared for us peasants, dad would give me the rest of his steak. I'd clean that t-bone down to the marrow, and the remains of that bone I'd give to my best dog.

I had always wanted a dog, a special dog, not just any old hound like Tucker's, but a real smart dog, like Lassie. You couldn't watch an episode of Lassie without putting yourself in those situations and thinking how great it would be to have your dog bail you out. One of my first dogs was bad luck.

He had followed me when I left school one day and was hanging with me all the way to Gary's house where I stopped. He and his sister Veronica came outside. They petted the dog, I petted the dog, and when I got home, Lizzie and L'Arthur petted and played with him too. The very next day, the health department showed up at our front door. They confiscated the dog saying he'd been exposed to rabies and had to be quarantined. The house was red-tagged and as a precaution, all five of us, L'Arthur, Gary, Veronica, Lizzie and me, would have to get rabies shots, fourteen of them, in the stomach. Just hearing about the shots made me squirm. For two weeks, dad took us to the health department to get the shots. Everybody was mad at me except L'Arthur. He knew it wasn't my fault, exactly. We got good news after the two weeks. We didn't have rabies and neither did the dog. The bad news, everyone stayed mad for two weeks after.

I was leery after that, even when a boxer followed me home and planted himself on the front porch. I didn't touch him, but I fed him after the second day. I called him King. He'd go along with me on my paper route or he'd be waiting on the step when I came home. He was too smart not to belong to someone, but there was no dog tag around his neck. Every day for two weeks when I got home, he'd be there, wagging his tail. And then one day, he wasn't, and he never came back.

Time passed and word got around that a litter of puppies had been born across the alley in the house behind us. Greyhound pups, eight of them! The neighbor owned the male and the female and the male had been a racing dog at the Caliente track in Mexico. I hardly knew the neighbors, but I would climb the back fence every day to see the pups.

All eight were different shades of grey except for one male that was all black. That's the one I wanted. The owner said I could take him home, if it was okay with my parents. I knew dad wouldn't mind, but Muhtha would have the final say. Tucker was with me nodding his approval of all the things I promised I'd do for the dog.

"You won't have to lift a finger," I said, my closing statement. Muhtha said yes but with a look that said I hope you remember all those promises you made.

I named the pup Cocomo after his father. By the time he was full grown, he could fetch, jump, easily scale the four-foot fence in the backyard, and he was fast. We took him to the vacant fields in Carson at 190th and Del Amo, that were full of jack rabbits. We raced Cocomo and Tucker's greyhounds against a man called 'mailman' who had five greyhounds. Cocomo outran all of them. Racing was in his genes. Not even Lassie could have done better than that.

# ~ What I Knew by the Age of 14 ~

I was expected to do my chores and get along with my sisters. Mass every Sunday was undisputed. In school, I was to do my best, do what I was told, and stay out of trouble. That applied to home as well. If I wanted something that my folks couldn't or wouldn't get for me, I knew I'd have to work for it and buy it myself. This proved to be a good thing. It was motivation. L'Arthur backed me 100% and had the same mindset. He bought his first car when he was in the 11$^{th}$ grade working as a box boy, the first among his friends to have his own wheels.

By age fourteen, I owned a BB gun, six pigeons, and a guitar, all bought with my own money from working my jobs, delivering papers or running errands or selling all occasion cards. It felt great. Felt like those special possessions were really mine. Before my 15$^{th}$ birthday, I'd saved enough to buy a Schwinn bicycle. Eighty-four dollars. That was a lot of money for a bike.

For Arthur and Flora, juggling the monthly bills happened a lot. Money was always an issue and when dad didn't work, some bills went unpaid. He always had a car to get to work, but longshoring wasn't steady. Muhtha took the bus to get to her day jobs. She shopped in the bargain basement, bypassed brand names in the grocery store, and put things on layaway.

Still, we always had a roof over our heads and food on the table. Even when our school uniform pants and shirts had to last two years, all four of us received a parochial school education, and most Christmas mornings, there'd be one special gift for each of us under the tree. We had everything we needed. We were not deprived, and I never felt poor.

One gift my folks gave us that money couldn't buy was an invisible security blanket. Whether it was intentional, or just instinct, they shielded us from the fact that life outside our world was not always fair or good. That "shield" protected our innocence and our mental well-being. It kept us from feeling inferior. Prejudice, poverty, and racism were all around us, but in the pre-civil rights years, we didn't feel oppressed, or impoverished.

We hadn't experienced racism face to face. It had eluded us for most of our young lives. Not having experienced it saved us from feeling like victims. For some LA kids in those years, ignorance was bliss. My parents didn't bad mouth white people. They had experienced both sides of the racial coin, the good and the bad, and like many of their generation, they lived not to agitate, but to survive.

I learned to get along with kids of all races because at school, I was in the minority, and would be until I graduated from high school. That didn't bother me. I never felt the need to separate myself from any of my classmates. I didn't go out of my way to be everybody's pal either, that wasn't my personality, but I never had the desire to alienate myself because of race. Flora and Arthur were disciplinarians and quietly vigilant, and they set down rules that I didn't always like, but those rules helped to keep me on the straight and narrow. I wasn't in the habit of thanking them, but I'm glad they did what they did. I enjoyed my childhood, which at the age of fourteen was beginning to taper off.

## ~ Salesian High ~

I graduated from St. Malachy's in June of 1961, entered 9th grade at Salesian in September where L'Arthur was starting his junior year. The '51 Chevy he'd bought for $200, was a stick shift, and sort of a bucket, but it got us to and from school. He taught me how to drive after I nagged him a little, and I'd drive the few blocks to 83rd and Wadsworth to pick up Gwayne. From there, L'Arthur would slide behind the wheel for the rest of the ride to Salesian on 7th and Soto. On weekend mornings, early, we'd practice in the parking lot of ABC market.

It was great having a car, even though it wasn't mine. L'Arthur liked driving and he was more than willing to share his ride. We'd drive to see friends, drive to the open fields in Carson, to the beach, to the movies. On Thursdays when he got paid, he'd cash his check, pick up Gwen and Lizzie, and me riding shotgun, and we'd cruise to Taco Tia on Manchester and Central, buy a half dozen tacos. Or go to House of Burgers on 94th and Avalon, where you could smell the burgers a block away. We'd always walked there before, but once we had wheels, we also had music, so along with riding, we could listen to our favorite station, a.m. 1110, KRLA.

I almost never had to ride the bus after school unless L'Arthur had football practice. Sometimes I'd watch the practice, but one afternoon I didn't wait. I rode the bus from Salesian to San Pedro and Florence and got my transfer. I was minding my own business sitting on the bench waiting for the next bus. I noticed some guys coming toward me, at least five of them. Big guys dressed in identical long blue jackets. Gang members, coming from the direction of Reese, the school for boys who'd been expelled from every other school in the area. I've already said that I was a slow grower, still smaller than almost everyone in my 9th grade class. No way would I come out on the winning side if I had to tangle with these guys. With gang members you never wanted to look directly at them. Even in those days, a wrong "look" could get a little brother into trouble. I let my gaze fall on something else. They got a little closer, and even though I wasn't looking at them, the guy in front called to me. "Hey man. Is that you cuz?" He turned to the other guys and said, "This my cousin Howard. How you doin' cuz?"

I looked over into the friendly face of Pat Landry. Whew. Was I relieved! I stood up as he draped his muscular arm around my shoulder and told his cohorts how he knew me. We weren't really cousins, but if he had said we were brothers, I wouldn't have denied it. I hadn't seen him in a long time. He and his older brother Malcolm had stayed with us years ago when their mother was ill. We'd gotten into the habit of calling ourselves cousins. Pat hung with the wrong crowd, and Malcolm had tried to keep his younger brother straight. Sometimes, people just don't listen.

After a minute of aimless chit chat, he gave me an up-nod and backed away. "Hey little cuz, stay cool," he said. They moseyed on down the street toward Fremont High, probably looking to harass some kid they didn't know. L'Arthur laughed when I told him about it later. He told me something that I believed about myself. I was lucky.

Salesian's student body was 75% Latino, with a handful of Caucasian boys, and even fewer black students. L'Arthur's grades weren't that great. My folks didn't demand all A's and B's, but barely passing was not acceptable. Muhtha thought it was the school's fault, and when she heard me telling L'Arthur about what had happened in my English class, she was sure of it.

My teacher, Mr. Landry (no relation to Malcolm and Pat) was an older man with a short fuse, who combed all of his thinning gray hair over to the left. We were a bunch of unruly boys, no denying that, some more so than others, but it was all in fun. Teenage pranks were what it amounted to. Old Landry couldn't take it. He turned his back, and the spitballs came flying toward the blackboard. One spitball too many flew in, and he turned around, slammed the textbook closed, and shouted, "Fine then. You can just learn it yourselves!" We nearly fell out of our chairs laughing.

Muhtha didn't think it was funny. She talked to Ramon's mother. She had enrolled both her sons in Pius X after they graduated from St. Malachy's. Her older son Roy was a senior, and Ramon and I had known each other since fifth grade. She told Muhtha she was very pleased with Pius X, and Muhtha was very pleased to hear that. It was too late for her to do anything about L'Arthur, who would soon be graduating, but she got busy looking into a transfer for me.

Earlier in the spring of 1963, before his graduation, L'Arthur told me he was thinking about joining the army. I thought he was kidding. He had registered with the draft board when he turned 18, but his status was not 1-A. It wasn't like he *had* to go. He knew guys who had already enlisted. He saw the military as a big adventure. Join Uncle Sam's army and see the world. He had never planned to go to college like Gwen who had graduated from Bishop Conaty High School and went straight to Cal State LA, planning to become a teacher.

I asked him to wait until summer was over, to give himself time to think about it. I hoped he would change his mind. But he could be stubborn. Bullheaded like dad. We both were.

Within days after his graduation he enlisted. He left for basic training at Fort Ord. No big send off, no fanfare. Just a few quick goodbyes.

That was one of the worst days of my life. I had no time to prepare for him not being here, and he didn't seem sad about leaving. I figured there was something else bothering him, reasons other than just a desire to "see the world."

I felt miserable. What can I say? L'Arthur wasn't a jock. He wasn't "big man on campus." I won't exaggerate my feelings by saying he was my hero. But he was my "big brother" my support, my backup. I looked up to him. I always wanted to hear what he had to say, even if I didn't agree with him. I always felt he was looking out for me, even when he wasn't around. He never got mad at me, or mad at anyone for that matter. We got along better than most brothers. We had different interests. We didn't do everything together, especially after he started working. But when we were together, whatever we did was more fun because he was there. I relied on him, he relied on me too. He helped me to do things I might not have done otherwise, and I probably took him for granted.

I guess we should have been proud that he chose to serve his country, but still, it was a sad day for all of us. Muhtha cried. She was worried about him. Dad was down I could tell. I had the bedroom to myself, but it was empty.

I was lonesome for my brother already. More than that, I was hurt. He hadn't talked to me, hadn't told me what he was really thinking. I probably wouldn't have changed his mind, but he didn't give me a chance to try.

That same week, I went to ABC market thinking I might be able to get his old job as a box boy. Part of the job was collecting all the baskets in the parking lot, stacking them one inside the other, and guiding them like a long, unwieldy snake back to the cart area near the doors. Even baskets that people had left across the street had to be rounded up and brought back.

I was sixteen but still short for my age. The manager at ABC, a big guy named Danny, hired me because I was L'Arthur's brother. He didn't say that exactly, but he made a point of telling me what a good worker L'Arthur was. I strained and struggled with those baskets, trying to show him I was a good worker too. But after three weeks, I was fired. A whole line of baskets had gotten away from me and before I could catch them, some had rolled into the street.

"You're nowhere near as good as your brother," Danny said, not sparing my feelings for a minute. Muhtha wasn't sympathetic either. "It's only been three weeks and you're fired?"

The sting of getting fired didn't last long. I wouldn't let it. It was one little setback, I told myself, and I let it roll off and out of my mind, just like those carts.

I'd get another job, I was confident. "Go to Sears," my sister Gwen said. "They always have summer jobs. I worked there, remember?"

Sears on Slauson hired me. Single page application, no background check. I'd be working part-time in the toy department, twenty hours a week.

A Puncho-Ball was a rainbow-colored rubber ball the size of a basketball, with an elastic strap for one-fist punching. Fifty-nine cents each or two for a buck. It was a Sears "Summer Special" and I was hired to demonstrate them. Playing with the Puncho ball meant mastering proper wrist action and the trick to selling them was making the play look easy. Blowing them up was the hard part, my lips to the air tube. The toy department of Sears had no pump.

Working in the toy department turned out to be fun, and Puncho-Balls sold themselves. Plus, I met a lot of cute girls. The best part about the job was on Saturdays. That's when a check arrived with my name on it. Sixty dollars a week, no deductions, and I'd be out on the front porch waiting for the mailman.

Dependable money was a welcome addition to my life. So, when Sears asked me to stay on after the summer, I did.

## ~ Pius X ~

In September of 1963, the transfer came through. It was good-bye Salesian at the end of the 10th grade, hello junior year at Pius X in Downey. Ramon and I had become better friends over the summer. Louis L'Amour novels, fast cars, and street races were his hobbies. He was one friend who always had money. And he got it the easy way. All he had to do was ask his mother and she'd hand over five bucks without a blink. Money for a burger, a movie, a haircut, whatever. Besides that, at sixteen he was not only driving, but he knew a lot about cars. I caught a ride from him most mornings in his 1952 Chevy, the car that was given to him as a gift when his grandfather died.

Pius X's student body, about three hundred strong, was 90% white students, a sprinkling of Latinos, and in my class, six black students, Ramon, Roger Goins, and me, and three girls that I had no classes with and never really got to know. Still, one perk for a guy from an all-boys school was transferring to a school with girls.

Both Ramon and Roger played on the varsity football team. They wanted me to try out. I liked football well enough, but I wasn't anxious to audition for the team. As already stated, I had not yet reached my full height. In addition, I remembered my brother wincing in pain from a cracked rib after playing his first football game. Still, I made a half-hearted attempt by talking to the coach. He advised me that I was ineligible. You had to have been a student at the school for at least a year. No football for me. I was legitimately spared some unnecessary bruising. Pius' football team was good, whereas the basketball team excelled. Two of their star players went on to the NBA, Rick Adelman and Jim LeCoeur, both seniors when I got there.

Ramon, Roger and I formed our own clique, the three black musketeers. We ate lunch together and kept a low profile. Every day we were surrounded by more well-to-do white kids than we had seen in our lives, and by Latino kids who were Spanish, not Mexican. The distinction was made clear, once again.

If the white kids were unhappy about us being there, if they had any prejudices against us, they were masters at concealing their feelings. I never saw any attitudes or behavior that could be called racist, but then, I wasn't looking for any.

Walking down the hall or passing students on campus, I didn't look away. I looked them straight in the eye, always with a smile. They never knew what I was thinking. I had no reason to be hostile, and I wasn't intimidated by their color or their number. Even after two years being there, Roger and Ramon sometimes seemed uncomfortable. I don't think they disliked the white kids or were afraid of them. It seemed they just didn't trust them. They didn't believe they could truly be friends with these guys, and maybe they didn't want to be. I didn't feel that way, and I didn't spend a lot of time worrying about it. I made a lot of friends, even went to Huntington Beach with a few of the surfers and learned how to surf.

I was ineligible for varsity sports, but there was no restriction to getting into the glee club, unless you couldn't carry a tune. I made it into the alto section of the boys' glee club, the lone brown face in the group. I looked at it as an easy A, and it was fun. I was also in the drama club, and had a classmate named Linda who got in the habit of hugging me every time she saw me. It was a little embarrassing, but I didn't mind.

Ramon and Roger waited for me in the parking lot and saw Linda hug me one day, then wave goodbye. I got into the car and Roger said, "Are you crazy?" Ramon started the car and said, "Man you better stay away from that white girl." It sounded funny except they weren't joking. They acted as if they knew something I didn't know and were worried about something that wasn't worrying me at all. Was I taking a chance? Was this a hostile environment? I didn't think so and it turned out I was right. I just accepted that Linda liked my acting and found me somewhat irresistible.

## ~ Getting My Wheels, November 1963 ~

Every day on the ride home from school with Ramon, we passed three long blocks of car dealerships on both sides of Long Beach Blvd. One day we stopped at one of the lots because the dark green 1955 Chevy we'd passed twice with a For Sale sign on it was still there. We'd barely stepped onto the lot when a salesman headed our way. I'd gotten my license over the summer. I was anxious to get a car, but I tried to look casual as I walked around the Chevy.

The salesman let us look under the hood. Ramon gave a thumbs up—new hoses, clean engine, fresh oil. I slid behind the wheel slowly as if I was still thinking it over. But my mind was made up. The black headliner was intact, the vinyl seats would have to be covered with something cool, maybe velvet. The stick shift knob felt great in my hand, and the leather covered steering wheel was just the right height. Even the faint smell of tobacco was to my liking. This was the car for me.

"Four hundred," the salesman said. Whoa. I could feel the tendons in my neck relax. I didn't know if $400 was a good price for an eight-year-old car. I didn't know about the Kelly Blue Book. I didn't know about haggling. But I got very happy. I had $500 saved and it was burning a hole in my pocket. I felt such relief knowing I wouldn't have to ask dad for a dime. I put down $200 right then promising to return the next day with my father who would have to sign for me. I was four months short of my 17th birthday.

A lot of things went through my mind on the ride home. I missed L'Arthur not being there, not so much for advice but to be excited with me as I knew he would be. I worried for a minute that the dealer might sell the car out from under me, but that thought passed. I didn't really think the guy was a crook. I wondered if I'd really gotten a good deal but dismissed that too. Papers were signed. Good or bad, this deal was a handshake from being done.

We closed the deal the next day. Dad signed, I paid the balance, and once the key was in my hand, I thought my chest would burst. I couldn't help smiling. It reminded me of the summer I'd bought my Schwinn bicycle. It was called the paperboy special and cost $84. I'd saved like crazy to get that money together, even exchanging soda bottles for pennies. Muhtha was in the front yard that day watering. She watched me all the way, leisurely peddling my new bike down 84th like I was a tourist, coming all the way from Leo's Bike Shop on 74th and Central. She asked what I was going to do now that I had spent all my savings. I said something flip like, "I'll make more."

Driving home in my "new" car I turned my radio to KGFJ, rolled down the window, let my arm hang. Out of the windshield, the world looked a little different. This was my first real act of independence. Ramon had helped, Dad had signed. But the bottom line: *I bought this car with my own money.* I was riding on air.

Only a couple of weeks later, the world seemed even more different, not so safe or carefree. I was in Spanish class when static came over the loudspeaker that brought the principal's voice into every classroom. After a moment, his voice came through asking for attention and he made an announcement. He said President Kennedy had been assassinated. He probably said more, but I didn't really hear it. The room went silent. All of us just sat there, and then we looked at each other as if maybe somebody had an answer. It was hard to process what we'd just heard. It had to be a mistake. Presidents got assassinated in history, not in current times, not in our lifetime. Our teacher looked at each of us, so taken aback, he didn't know what to say. But what could he say?

School was dismissed early. Any other day that would have brought smiles. No one was smiling.

At mass on Sunday Muhtha lighted a dozen candles for the Kennedys. We watched the funeral on television, Dad quiet, Muhtha too, slowly shaking her head. How could this have happened? At the time, there were no answers.

## ~ Senior Year 1965 ~

Dancing wasn't really my thing, and Ramon wasn't much better. But we both got a little excited about dressing up in something other than school duds, taking a couple of cute girls as our dates, and being able to stay out past midnight for the senior prom.

We had flipped a coin to see whose car we'd take and when tails showed, my call, I considered it a win. True, the back seat of any car had an unmistakable allure, but whoever was in the driver's seat was the man in charge, and to my mind, the man in charge was the coolest.

I had enhanced my Chevy's appearance by adding carpet floor mats, velvet seat covers, several wax jobs to bring the forest green to a shiny brilliance, and the best addition of all, the installation of a Vibrasonic sound system. At full volume, my windows shook.

As cool as my Chevy looked and as much as I loved driving it, I did not drive it to the prom. In appreciation for all the rides I had given Gwen and her girlfriends, who considered me their little brother, my sister allowed me to drive her brand new 1965 Plymouth Barracuda, a car that would later be described as one of the ugliest ever produced by Plymouth. However, the unmistakable new car smell gave it the advantage over the musky scent of stale tobacco. I sacrificed cool for new, and away we went.

The dance was at a hotel ballroom in Downey, followed by dinner at the Tail O'The Cock restaurant on La Cienega's restaurant row, the location of some of the most expensive restaurants in Los Angeles. It was a new eye-opening experience for a youngster like me from the southeast end of town, and for my date Geraldine.

After dinner, the four of us left the restaurant and cruised down Sunset Blvd. all the way to the beach. That was the thing to do on prom night, go to the beach, walk along the sand holding hands, look at the moon over the water.

Ramon entertained our dates by telling them about the day I almost drowned at the beach. He was laughing as he told it, but at the time it was anything but funny.

"He got caught in a riptide trying to teach me how to bodysurf." Haha. "Had to be rescued by the lifeguard." Haha. Geraldine's eyes got big. "Really?" she said, looking at me. I finished the story. "Yeah, the tide was pulling me back...anyway, the lifeguard paddled out on a board and threw me a rope and pulled me in. I knew how to swim out of them…you swim parallel with the water, not against it…"

"Not that time," Ramon said, haha. Geraldine seemed impressed, maybe because I was still alive. She was a nice girl and I might have dated her again except for one thing. She had a boyfriend that she hadn't bothered to tell me about. I found out later that the boyfriend broke up with her because of our date. He was a student at Fremont High and his name was Julious Green.

Six years later, my sister Lizzie was married. Her husband, my new brother-in-law, was Julious Green.

By the time graduation rolled around in mid-June 1965, my height had shot up to just under six feet, surprising everyone, including me. I wasn't shaving yet, and I still had a chubby face, but at least I was on eye level with most of my graduating classmates. Would have been nice if my grades like my height had gone up. I was short in several areas important to future resumes. I held no class office, had no distinguishing remarks made about me in the yearbook, except from classmates. Despite Muhtha's admonition to "be twice as good" as the Caucasian students, I hadn't put forth the effort, and did not receive any special honors upon graduation.

Still, when I walked across the stage in my red cap and gown, the high school diploma they placed in my hand was as important to me as the honored diplomas received by some of my classmates. I accepted it with excitement and relief, mostly relief. School was over. I had graduated. My last year of high school was done.

Summer started off with a beach party at Playa del Rey given by Washington High School friends of my co-worker Sam Hooper. Sam was the younger brother of Stix Hooper, the leader of the Jazz Crusaders, a trio that was becoming very hot in the world of jazz. We partied until the sun went down. Sand, surf, and music, plus lots of girls in two-piece bathing suits. A great day turned into an even better night, and there would be a few more like that before the summer was over.

Twenty hours a week in the toy department had become something it wasn't in the beginning—work. Couldn't complain though. If I uttered any words that sounded remotely like quitting, Muhtha would be on me. "Don't you quit that job."

Flora and Arthur shared a vision of the future that amounted to a very basic formula: *get a job, work the job, keep the job.* Had I followed that mantra I would have worked in the toy department for thirty years.

I had been giving Muhtha a portion of my paycheck since my paper-throwing days and was still doing it. I griped about it when I was eleven, and I still griped.

"Why do I have to give up my hard-earned money?"

"You should want to help your mother. What about what I do for you?" she'd say.

"Yeah, but this is my money."

"But who cooks for you and does your laundry and buys groceries."

Back and forth we'd go, but she always had a smile on her face. It was sort of our monthly squabble that never got out of hand. She was still doing day work two to three times a week, so in truth, I was glad to help out. I still had my eyes open for a better job and better pay. The question was, doing what?

By the end of July, I began to feel squeezed. I

really didn't know what I wanted to do, except I knew I didn't want to stay at Sears. Like L'Arthur, I had never seriously considered going to college, and hadn't applied to any. My folks didn't knock a college education, but they didn't advocate for it either. They couldn't afford to send me, even if I had applied and been accepted, and in my heart, the idea of more school was a turnoff. I believed that unless the long-term goal was doctor, attorney, or professor, a four-year college for someone who felt as I did would be wasted time and money.

Still, after talking more to Sam, I decided to enroll at Harbor Junior College in Wilmington. Other junior college options were LA City College and El Camino in Redondo Beach. Sam was taking summer classes at Harbor along with a few guys we both knew. The campus was new, he said, there were a lot of cute girls (always an incentive) and the on-campus hangout called Seahawk Center was too cool for words. What finally convinced me was the cost. Only six dollars per unit. Four three-unit classes would only cost seventy-two dollars. I could afford that. The worm began to turn. It wasn't much of a plan, but it was my decision. I enrolled in four classes, two of them in the only subject I was interested in, Police Science.

A few days later, Watts was in flames.

## ~ Watts Riot ~

For many people living in Los Angeles, the week of August 11, 1965 would become as unforgettable as November 22nd, the day the president was assassinated. The riot was a nightmare that changed the face of the city forever.

We were spectators seeing flames and smoke from our own backyard. Muhtha kept turning to dad with the same question. "Arthur, you think they're coming closer our way?" Dad answered through tight lips with the same four words:

"Flora I don't know." That was the worst part, not really knowing anything. Where did it start? Why? Who was to blame? What good did it do to burn down your own neighborhood?

Rioting continued for seven days and nights. News reports showed the looters, the burning buildings, and the LAPD and the National Guard patrolling the streets wearing teargas helmets and carrying rifles. Los Angeles had become a war zone. The rioters were the grenades, and the pins had been pulled.

Eventually reports came out explaining how it started, but there were rumors, different versions of the story. We didn't know what to believe, and in the end, it didn't really matter.

When it was over, thirty-four people were dead. Whether they were looters or bystanders, the news didn't say. Hundreds were injured, hundreds more were put in jail. Police cars had been torched, scores of small businesses burned to the ground. Watts entered the history books as the site of one of the worst urban uprisings in the country's history. And things only got worse.

There was more unemployment. Poverty escalated. Young black males began forming gangs, and any whites still living on the outskirts of the affected area sold their homes at an alarming rate. "White Flight" had begun, en masse, as they scurried west and even farther away, more than twenty miles, to "the valley." The word "ghetto" became synonymous with the two square mile area known as Watts, and the area was unofficially renamed South Central.

Nothing could be considered normal for quite a while, but life did go on.

And there I was, signed up for classes in law enforcement at my local junior college. Was I crazy?

Undecided for most of the summer about what I wanted to do, I had finally made up my mind to pursue something I'd thought about since I was eleven. Me, Gary, Alvin, even L'Arthur. We all wanted to be cops. *Dragnet*, *Highway Patrol*, *Adam 12*. Those were our cop shows. Was my timing all wrong?

After the riot, becoming a member of the LAPD was the least desired occupation in the country, especially for black men. White officers were feared and hated, but so were black officers. To black people who felt oppressed and harassed by the police, becoming a cop was joining the enemy. Cops were called pigs. Imagine how hard it would be to protect and serve people who hate your guts? How had the relationship between the police and the people gotten so bad?

I didn't know. I had never had a bad experience with the police. Maybe I was naïve, but I'd been taught the police were the good guys, and if you weren't doing the crime, you probably wouldn't do any time. I still believed that. One story said the riot began because the police had stopped a black man for reckless driving. Was that the truth, or was that harassment? Did the police escalate the situation, or did the mob who gathered around? Would the truth ever come out? And when it did, would it matter?

I tried to stay focused. I was enrolled, my classes were set, and the goal was to graduate with an associate degree in Police Science, which would take two years and put me in a better place to pass any exam to become an officer. I felt confident two years was doable.

## ~ More than a Notion ~

I was wrong.

I carried five classes, thirteen units. History, swimming, music appreciation, and two comprehensive police science classes. Swimming was great exercise. Music appreciation nearly put me to sleep, but it was growing on me. I had never liked history and the dull dry lectures in the police science courses made my eyes glaze over. I had to face the fact that my heart wasn't in any of it. I just was not cut out to be a student.

By the fall of 1965, the war in Vietnam had ramped up and it dominated the news. Ongoing battles straight from the war zone were shown live on television. The draft was in full force. Single males between the ages of 18 and 25 who were not enrolled in school were being drafted into Uncle Sam's Army, the destination for most, Vietnam.

Single males enrolled in college had to carry at least twelve units and maintain a 3.0 or better grade point average to keep a deferment. Guys were sweating it. There was tension in the air. Even when the war wasn't the main topic of conversation, you knew guys were thinking about it. College students were protesting across the country with sit-ins and draft card burnings. I heard and saw all of it. I knew what was going on, but still, the war seemed remote. It was happening 'over there' in a tiny country difficult to locate on a map. No one I knew had been directly affected. No one I knew had gone to Vietnam.

Junior college was like a glorified high school, except, if you missed a class, you didn't have to bring a note from your mother. I attended classes in silent protest wishing I could be almost any place else. I had a fleeting thought that had I gotten into a four-year college, I might have been challenged to become a serious student. But like I said, the thought was fleeting.

Sometime in October on the way to a party with Sam, I told him I was thinking about dropping out. He was a serious student carrying fifteen units. His grades so far were good, but still he was always tense, worried about the draft. He strongly advised me against dropping out. As we pulled up in front of the party house, I decided not to mention it again.

I didn't know anyone there. Most of the kids were high school seniors from an honors club Sam was in before he graduated. He had been big man on campus but was kind of awkward with girls. Most of the girls he'd met at Sears were girls I'd introduced him to. He wanted me to meet the girl he'd taken to his prom. "She's my girlfriend, sort of," he said.

I asked what he meant by "sort of" and if she was his girlfriend, why did he want me to meet her? An hour into the party, he pointed out a girl with long dark hair who danced to every song and seemed to know everyone. The girl was Bev.

When Sam finally introduced us, he said I was his brother. Even if he had said half-brother it would have been more believable. We didn't look anything alike. She looked at Sam then at me and back at him again. It was obvious she didn't believe him. I liked her right away. In fact she was the girl I'd been watching all night. But even a "sort of" girlfriend was "sort of" off limits.

I worked overtime the entire two-week Christmas holiday, Sears busiest time of year. As I was leaving one night through the furniture department, a beautiful Victorian table lamp got my attention. An $85 tag hung on it. Muhtha would never buy it for herself so I put it in layaway for her. On Christmas eve I set it on the octagon table in front of the picture window. Christmas morning, she almost cried when she saw it. I know it's a cliché, but the look on her face made me truly feel it was better to give than receive.

After New Year's, the toy department was like a morgue. I lived to hear the announcement over the loudspeaker: "The store will be closing in fifteen minutes."

School was no better. I was restless. My grades were on a downward spiral. Army recruiters had been on campus since September signing guys left and right. I read the brochures. Age requirement for Army or Marine Police was 21. The Air Force took guys as young as 17. I stood outside the recruiting office daring myself to go in. I hadn't told the folks that I'd been thinking about this because I knew they would try to change my mind, and I didn't want any opposition. L'Arthur was still stationed in Korea, so I couldn't run it by him either. It was all on me, my decision.

I dropped history when my grade sunk to a D. My deferment was revoked. I was no longer carrying the required twelve units. I knew a letter would come advising me I was 1-A, but it made my head spin to see how quickly it arrived. I was to report for a physical, and after the physical, I'd be contacted. I didn't wait for the call.

In February 1966, one month before my 19th birthday, I went to the Air Force recruitment office and enlisted. The recruiter handed me papers to fill out. He called me "future Airman" and welcomed me to the United States Air Force. That was it.

*Christmas 1955, Arthur and Flora, my parents*

*Dad, me and Bess our cow in the backyard at Holmes, 1948*

*Arthur and I, mugging for the camera. How about those slacks?*

*616 E. 84th Place, where I grew up*

> **PAYMENT RECORD BOOKLET**
>
> Original Amount $ 3250 00
>
> Payments Due 25 00
>
> Payor *Arthur Higginson*
> *Flora Higginson*
>
> Address *616 E. 84th Pl*
> *Los Angeles, Calif*
>
> Owner *Mary E Lybrook*
> *3241! A Hill Dr*
>
> Address *Huntington Park*
> *Calif. 90257*
>
> A lost NOTE may necessitate an expensive Corporate Surety Bond. Keep your valuable documents in a Security First National Bank SAFE DEPOSIT BOX.

*Dad's payment book for his note to Old Lady Lybrook,*
*$25.00 a month for 15 years*

*~ with Beverly Higginson ~*

*With L'Arthur, Lizzie and Gwen in the backyard at 84th,
and Trigger our dog*

*Cousin Albert, me peeking over his head, sister Lizzie, L'Arthur,
Gary (standing at ease) on L'Arthur's graduation day
from Salesian High.*

*School photos from St Malachy's and Salesian*

*My 1955 Chevy, pretty cool in its day*

*With Geraldine, Ramon & his date, Pius X prom, May 1965*

# PART TWO

## 1966 - 1986

## Guns and Badges

## ~ You're in the Air Force Now ~

The last week of February 1966, I was on a commercial 747 flight out of Los Angeles International Airport on my way to basic training at Lackland Air Force Base, San Antonio, Texas.

Everything happened fast after I told my parents and a couple of people from school that I'd be leaving. I didn't want to make a big deal out of it, and I guess I felt the same way L'Arthur had, that I wanted to get on with it, find out exactly what I'd gotten myself into. Was I jumping from the frying pan into the fire? I'd know soon enough.

L'Arthur had completed a 13-month tour of duty in Korea, and was stationed at Fort Sam Houston, also in San Antonio. I couldn't believe the good luck. It had been a whole year since I'd seen my brother, and now we'd be stationed about twenty miles from each other.

There were about forty guys on the 747 flight, all of us from California, black guys, white guys, Hispanic guys. We landed in San Antonio after three hours in the air and were immediately hustled onto a bus already loaded with local recruits for the hour-long ride to the base. I remember the sound of southern accents floating above the seats.

It was midnight when we finally arrived at Lackland. We stepped off the bus into a cold night. Everybody was holding their overnight bags and trying to hear the orders being barked at us from a drill sergeant. I missed some of it but heard enough to know I should follow the guy in front of me leading the way to Lackland's mess hall for our first meal. I was starving.

I don't know what I was expecting, but as I shuffled down the chow line pushing my metal tray, I felt like I was back at Salesian, all of us moving like a bunch of junior high kids. I thought about the good old mac and cheese we used to get on Fridays, but as I looked through the glass that separated us from the steaming pans of food, I wondered what the brown and white stuff was being plopped onto the plates. The cook doing the shoveling spoke up before I asked the question.

"Chipped beef and gravy son, hold out your plate." The guy behind me whispered. "SOS." I looked over my shoulder. "What?"

"Shit on a shingle," he said. "SOS."

The cook was waiting, a spoonful of the stuff held in midair. Someone had definitely given it the right name. I was hungry, but I couldn't eat it. To my surprise, I said, "Keep it." I moved down the line to the fruit. He called after me. "Get used to it youngster. You gonna see a lot of this."

From the mess hall we moved to the orientation room that same night. The onslaught of information jarred me back to reality. Lots of instructions thrown at us very quickly. It was as if they were daring us to miss something or make a mistake.

Blankets and pillows were issued, and we were led to the barracks. Inside, rows of unmade cots lined the walls upper and lower. The blankets were like burlap, the sheets so stiff they could stand alone. This would take some getting used to. I was someone who had to first wash a new pair of jeans to soften them up before I could put them on. I must have been bone tired, because even on stiff sheets, that first night, I did sleep.

Reveille the next morning before the sun cracked the horizon was like a Louis Armstrong trumpet blast, and the drill sergeant's voice wasn't much better.

Basic training had begun, and I wondered if I was the only recruit having doubts. I went back in my head and tried to remember why I thought this was a good idea. Or had I even thought that? Was it just an available option that I hoped I would like? Had I hated school that much?

I put the regrets out of my head. I fought them, as I would fight them several more times in the weeks to come. After all, the deed was done. I'd been here before, in this "already there" position. No turning back. That feeling would always come to the forefront. *No turning back.* I was responsible for being here and I would see it through to the end.

After the first week of drills, marching, verbal abuse and bad food, the first day jitters were long gone, and after five more weeks, basic training came to an end. We had a week's break before the start of technical training and during that week I heard from L'Arthur. He was coming from Fort Sam Houston for a visit the next day and bringing a surprise.

My brother's "surprise" was a girl. She was sitting in the passenger seat of his 1959 Volkswagen Bug parked in front of my barracks. He jumped out of the car, came around to meet me, and punched my shoulder, grinning. "Hey lil' brotha." He made me laugh, always trying to be cool.

We headed off base going for "a little ride" he said, and then he introduced his girlfriend. Her name was Lynn, she had red hair, and she was white. She had joined the Army right out of high school, just like L'Arthur. They were both x-ray technicians. They'd been spending a lot of time together he said. I sat in the back seat my knees pressed nearly to my chest, listening to them talk, staring at the back of my brother's head, and Lynn's profile. All kinds of thoughts were going through my head. This wasn't like high school where the cute classmate used to hug me and skip away. L'Arthur had never really had a girlfriend. He had never talked to girls much at all. But he seemed serious about this one.

Suddenly I got a little tremor in my gut. I looked out the window at rural Texas passing by, the state where only three years ago our president was assassinated. I looked back at L'Arthur's head and got a bad feeling. We must be crazy!

Here we were, two young black guys driving through the dusty back roads of segregated Texas in a VW Bug that could easily be blown off the road by nature or run off the road "accidentally" by some trucker who takes offense at the sight of a white girl in a car with two black guys. Wouldn't matter that we were in uniform, that we were serving our country. It was 1966, the height of the civil rights movement, and here we were unprotected, riding around in the state that was so careless, it couldn't protect the president of the United States. How vulnerable did that make us? I didn't relax until we got to our aunt Antoinette's house, which was about two hundred miles from Lackland. L'Arthur had already driven there one weekend to visit our aunts and introduce Lynn. I would have loved being a fly on the wall for that visit.

Antoinette greeted us with a big smile and offered me a beer. I hadn't become a drinker yet, so I politely declined. We visited for a couple of hours looking out at the field across the street where cows were grazing, just like they were in 1959 when we had come for Christmas.

I reminded my auntie that the creek in front of her house was still full of horny toads. She laughed and gave me a hug for remembering those frogs. If she felt apprehensive about L'Arthur's girlfriend, it didn't show.

Back at Lackland, L'Arthur and I had only a few minutes to talk. He told me he really cared for Lynn, that they were thinking about getting married. "What d'ya think?" he asked. I couldn't believe it.

"Is it that serious?" I tried to sound neutral, but I'm sure he heard the doubt in my voice. L'Arthur was impulsive, we both were. I asked him if he was sure, and he said yes. Even if he had doubts, I got the feeling his mind was made up.

The folks knew of Lynn only through Aunt Elizabeth. They tried talking L'Arthur out of the relationship. They were concerned about his safety, and the problems the two of them would face if they stayed together. It was nothing personal against Lynn. They had never met her. But interracial marriages were taboo, and in some states, still illegal. They were just worried about their son.

L'Arthur and Lynn drove away and I watched the VW until it was out of sight, not knowing for sure what my brother was going to do. But I couldn't worry about that. In a couple of days, I'd start technical training. Eight more weeks of school, and I wasn't looking forward to it.

The following Monday we were moved to a different barracks for the tech training. The food was better, and the atmosphere more relaxed. No one was in our faces barking orders, and we were learning specifics pertaining to air force policing. In one of the classes, I met Ron Goodridge, a New Yorker with a broad accent, a crooner's voice, and a ladies' man to hear him tell it. We became buddies and helped each other with the classes.

Eight weeks later, after a total of fifteen weeks of training, I graduated at the rank of Airman 3rd Class-Air Police. At the same time I received my new assignment, Vandenberg Air Force Base, and I had a 30-day leave. I couldn't wait to get home.

## ~ At the 'Berg ~

They say time flies when you're having fun. Very true of my month off at home. I managed to hook up with some old friends, guys and girls, especially Bev who was no longer Sam's "sort of" girlfriend.

In mid-August, it was off to Vandenberg also known as "the Berg" just north of Santa Barbara, and only a couple of hours from LA. I'd heard that guys didn't always get their requested assignments, but I was lucky again and got mine, along with permission to have my '55 Chevy on base. Goodridge, also assigned to the Berg, had flown home to New York, and then to LA, and rode up with me.

By this time, I felt comfortable about military life. I liked the discipline. I liked that I was taking pride in being orderly, in looking sharp when in uniform, in having specific tasks and carrying them out to the best of my ability, and the importance of the job of a military policeman. I didn't love the work, but it was a routine that suited me, and I felt better about this than being in school.

I was in a squadron of 75 air policemen. Our days were divided into three shifts: days, swings, mids. Everyone worked each of the three shifts for three days, with

24 hours off between each shift. Days were from 8 a.m.to
3 p.m., swings from 3 p.m. to 11 p.m., mids from 11 p.m. to
7 a.m. In the beginning, the shifts wreaked havoc on my
sleep, kind of like jet lag that lasted for days.

Guard duty 24/7, of missile silos, aircraft carriers, main gate posts where we checked for unauthorized
personnel coming onto the base. I used to wish someone
unauthorized would drive up to the main gate and I could
lower my weapon and ask a few questions. Vandenberg
was basically a missile launch testing ground. We guarded
launch sites where missiles including the Atlas missile
were housed in huge steel structures that were called gantries, and the gantries supported the missiles before being
launched. Gantries were twenty to thirty stories tall. Ele-
vators carried guards straight up to the top in full gear,
M16, a gas mask, and a list of authorized personnel.

Vandenberg was huge, more than 20 square miles.
The base was the major attraction of the city of Lompoc,
a rustic little town with touristy gift shops and cozy little
eateries. Nice as it was the charm faded after a few months.
I worried about piling up miles on my old Chevy, but still,
every three-day break, I'd drive the 125 miles to LA and see
the family and visit a few friends, Bev in particular. We
were getting to know each other better. Not only did we
like each other, she liked to dance to my vibrasonic music
while sitting in the front seat of my Chevy.

My car made me popular on base as well. After my
first solo trip to LA, three guys rode with me the next time
around. Goodridge, the New Yorker, was one, Elam, a
sharp brother from New Jersey was another, and Johnson,
a big gregarious country brother from Oklahoma was the
third. I was the youngest, so they called me "The Kid."

They pitched in a few bucks for gas, and once in LA, l turned them on to the Blue Room on 88th and Avalon while l went to visit Bev. Elam had a cousin in LA who didn't mind him sleeping over, and Johnson had a girlfriend. Goodridge would spend the night at my house, a scenario that repeated itself more than once. That was a bad idea. He was the partier of the group and would go to places I'd never heard of, and then come tapping on my window at 3 a.m. That didn't go over well with Arthur and Flora.

The months at the 'Berg dragged on. The summer of 1967 marked almost a year in service for me. Since the nature of military life was not fun and games, if you weren't in battle, you had to find something to occupy your time. Off-duty hours found us sitting around talking about abated love lives, old girlfriends, times we'd gotten drunk. Except me. l wasn't into drinking yet. We would listen to music, and a few guys who thought they could dance would break out with a few moves. There was a day room where pool tables were set up, and tables for cards and dominoes. l got interested in working out and had started going a couple of times a week to the weight room. l liked that drained feeling after a good workout and the ache in my biceps after doing curls with the free weights.

After the first year of a four-year stint, the second year was usually an assignment to a base outside of the US. I talked to guys who were applying for assignments in Thailand, the Philippines, and Formosa, destinations that had two-and-three month waiting lists. Thailand and the Philippines were most often chosen for the second or third year.

Vietnam, the only destination with no waiting list

added an incentive for those who signed up. An additional seventy-five dollars a month, hazardous duty pay. The talk from 'Nam returnees was that an airman could get a part-time job on base and earn another $200 dollars a month at the Non-Commissioned Officer's Club (NCOC). I kept that piece of information in the back of my mind and signed on for Formosa.

Muhtha wrote to me that L'Arthur and Lynn were married in Texas by a justice of the peace. Days later, on a weekend that I was stuck at Vandenberg, they'd gotten a pass to come to LA and were married again in St. Malachy's church. Typical of my brother, he told me not to feel bad that I missed seeing him tie the knot. Muhtha and Dad gave them a reception at the house, and despite their concerns about the marriage and misgivings about Lynn and L'Arthur's future, the folks welcomed Lynn into the family, though her own family had stayed away.

Shortly after the ceremony in Texas, Lynn was honorably discharged from the Army. It was Uncle Sam's rule then, that female soldiers who married while on active duty be discharged. For the brief time until L'Arthur's discharge, she lived on 84th Place with her new in-laws—Muhtha, Dad, Gwen and Lizzie. According to Muhtha, she became acquainted with the neighbors and they welcomed her as well.

## ~ Desire vs Common Sense ~

When the copy of Motor Trend magazine caught my eye in the barracks one day, I had already seen a lieutenant on base driving the 1968 forest green Dodge RT pictured on the cover.

The thought of buying a new car hadn't kept me awake at night, but it had been on my mind. I still loved my '55 Chevy, but it was getting older every day with all my trips south to LA. Suddenly, I had a goal in mind. I wanted that Dodge RT. The cost was about $3500. In minutes, I went from casually thinking about a new car, to figuring in my head how to do it.

Hazardous duty-pay plus a few hundred more a month would cover it. If I went to Vietnam, I'd earn enough money to buy that car, if I lived. But at the time, the thought of not living never entered my mind. I'd talked to other guys who'd gone to Vietnam and come back. Why not me? In the space of 24-hours I went from looking at a photo of a car, to going to the staff office and putting my name on the Vietnam list.

I broke the news to Goodridge, Elam and Johnson. They thought it was a very unfunny joke. They soon learned it wasn't a joke, though it seemed crazy. But I wasn't crazy either. Reckless, and yes, impulsive, but I did have a plan. And I was "the kid." Nothing bad was going to happen to me. They were concerned and I appreciated it, but I couldn't let them rattle me. I just believed I'd be okay. I don't think it was a religious thing going on in my head, although I had said a lot of prayers during my twelve years in Catholic School. There was just no room for me to worry about something going wrong, despite what I knew was happening over there, and what I saw on the news.

My plan was this: I would get that part-time job. I would save my money. I'd be vigilant on my job as an air policeman and watch my back. In a year, I'd return, and buy that Dodge RT. I didn't think of it then, but it was a selfish decision, and on the face of it, not a patriotic one. But once I got over there, I would be a patriot, and do my duty, and when I returned home, I'd be dutiful unto myself, and get that car.

The folks hit the roof when I told them my plan after coming home for my 30-day leave, standard procedure for anyone going into a war zone. That sounded frightening—war zone. *Why would I take such a risk for a car*, they wanted to know. *Why would any sane person do that?*

At the time, I didn't understand why I didn't feel afraid. Maybe I was in denial. Maybe I'd convinced myself that my job over there would be like my job here at Vandenberg, but slightly different. I was focused only on the result, not the process, and I was only thinking about myself and what I wanted, and not the strain I'd put on my parents who might worry themselves sick. And Bev too.Those considerations would come later. The decision was made. I tried very hard to stay positive which wasn't easy in the face of so many glum expressions including Bev's. We were officially girlfriend and boyfriend by then and had spent almost every day together during my leave.

I was scheduled to depart from Norton Air Force Base in San Bernardino the first week of August, 1967. Mentally I was prepared to leave, but not prepared for a delay. The plane was full. Not one extra seat. They sent me home with a new departure date. On the ride back to LA were those same inviting signs I had noticed on the way up, pointing to wineries off the freeway. We were all together, Muhtha, Dad, Gwen, Lizzie, Bev and me in Dad's car. What the heck? I asked dad to pull off the road, let's go to a winery. We took the nearest offramp, got out of the car, and stretched our legs. We didn't buy anything, didn't drink any wine. We just walked around for a couple of hours, taking in the town. We had been so wound up about me leaving, this break put it out of our minds, at least for a few hours.

The second trip to Norton was August 8th, 1967. This time, a seat was waiting for me.

I boarded a C141 cargo carrier, a huge hunk of metal that resembled a blimp with wings. Its intended use was to transport rations, uniforms, blankets and artillery. Not people. But as the war had escalated, these carriers had been reconditioned to run large numbers of troops to Vietnam. Comfort was not a priority. Hard metal benches folded along the sides of the aircraft were unfolded by us, eight to ten across separated by a narrow aisle. Nothing but c-rations were provided for food, and the aircraft had no windows. There wasn't one empty space. Close cropped heads were all I could see around me, maybe two hundred guys trying to settle in for the long flight ahead.

The sound of the engines starting up began to drown out the raucous conversations, and guys reconnecting from past tours. I saw a guy whip out a deck of cards, and others already writing letters, propping sheets of paper against their knees. Cigarettes were lit, passed around, the air got hazy with smoke. Guys joked and laughed, trying to create a party atmosphere, trying to keep the mood light. We were soldiers, marines, airmen. Some younger new guys like me were quiet. Others had been there before, their experiences spilling out in snippets. I listened to the voices around me, but mainly I was thinking about my family, and Bev. It would be a whole year before I'd see any of them again.

Outside I had already said my goodbyes to them. I could still feel the grip Bev had on my hand, her eyes filling with tears. I held her right up to the last minute before boarding. Muhtha had cried a box of tissues. Gwen kept talking about all the things we would do once I got back. I had to give it to my big sis. She was good at keeping a positive attitude. Lizzie looked at me as if she'd never see me again. Dad was all business, making sure I had my ticket and that we were at the right gate. It was hard to make eye contact, and he didn't say much, but that was okay. He was there.

My back was pressed against the hard back of my seat, and I was wishing I had held Bev a little longer. I wanted to catch one last glimpse of her, but I couldn't. No windows. The doors slammed shut, and it was then that I got a cold clammy feeling in the back of my neck. It was like being locked in a vault. No escape. This was it. I was on my way to spend a whole year in a place I couldn't even imagine. A knot rose up from the pit of my stomach to my throat, hard and painful, and I couldn't swallow. All I could do was sit there, hold on to my duffel. I closed my eyes hoping the feeling would pass. I cleared my mind, made it a blank. *Don't think about anything, just stay strong.* It was going to be a long flight.

## ~ Vietnam ~

We landed in Techikawa, Japan eleven hours later to refuel, a rough landing that woke everyone up. Not enough time to do anything but de-plane, walk around, stretch our legs. It was horrendously hot, a heatwave, with humidity over a hundred and temperatures in the high nineties. I couldn't imagine Vietnam being any worse, but four hours later, I knew I was wrong.

Stepping off the plane in Vietnam was literally entering another world. A steam room with no walls. Simmering, immobilizing heat, and humidity more stifling than anything in Japan. Guys from the south described it as a new kind of heat, a heat that made breathing torture. An indescribable stench permeated the air, and in the distance, the sound of bombs reminding us constantly, there was a war going on.

We boarded a bus that took us into the northern section of South Vietnam to the military base at DaNang. It was like a small city. The base was five square miles, housing over 10,000 military personnel of all four branches. When the war escalated in 1965, China Beach was the first place US Marines landed. DaNang Air Base was about twenty miles from there. The city of DaNang was the second largest in Vietnam, but I didn't expect to see much of the city while I was there.

We waited for a second bus that would take us to our squadron, so we had time to look around. The base was right in the middle of several small villages where the people lived, in little shanty huts with tin roofs. Dirt roads were narrow, clothes or rags, hard to tell the difference, were hanging on lines between huts, flames and smoke billowed up from holes in the ground. The smell in the air was terrible. Boarding the bus didn't give us much relief.

I was assigned to the 365th gun fighter squadron. Each squadron was about 400 airmen total and was divided into flights. All of us would be living in Quonset huts for the next year, and each hut held about one hundred guys.

The Quonsets were 30 feet high made of corrugated steel. Around every Quonset along the outside walls were fifty-pound sandbags, stacked four to five feet high.

The Quonset huts were divided into cubicles, maybe ten by ten, large enough for two guys. Each guy had his own bunk bed and his own locker. It was tight, it was small, it wasn't like home. But it would be home for a year, and if you and your bunkmate got along, the setup wasn't so bad.

A concrete path led to the latrine about a hundred feet away. Inside the latrine, right down the middle, was what they called a "universal urinal" a trench about 20 feet long with a trickle of water running through it. Forty toilets and twenty showers were on each side of the urinal. There were no doors, and no privacy. It was a true test to prove that if you hadn't already gotten over certain inhibitions, you'd get over them now.

I was part of the 75-man Cobra Flight. We worked the swing shift, three in the afternoon to eleven at night, guarding the main gate, rear gate, flight lines, ammo dump, bomb dump, base perimeter. Two other flights were Tiger, the midnight shift, and Cougar, morning shift. Two guards manned most posts every shift, while three specially trained airmen manned M-60 machine guns positioned on tripods attached to open air Jeeps. They patrolled the periphery.

The posts were bunkers, and bunkers were about five feet square surrounded by 50-pound sandbags stacked four feet high. Most had wooden awnings. Duties were alternated and every other day, you had a new post. Every military policeman had an M-16, so named because the gun weighed sixteen pounds. Over the shoulder is how we were ordered to carry them, and within a couple of weeks, we were so used to them, sore shoulders from the weight just went away.

Guys in Cobra flight were from all over, but not many from California. Airmen were constantly coming in as others were shipping out. Once the work started, part of the routine was getting to know the guys in your flight. Turnover was constant, so you never really got to know anyone very well, which was probably a good thing.

My worst day came barely two weeks after I arrived. It felt like I'd been there for months. I was on my post, half in the bunker, half out, on an open road traveled by trucks all day bringing in rations, equipment, incoming troops. It was always dusty, humid, there was a constant grimy feeling of grit and sweat on my skin, and relentless heat that I would never get used to.

I stepped outside the bunker for a moment and looked to the sky toward the sound I was hearing. It was a Pan Am Airline 707 taking off. The nose of it pointed straight up then leveled off heading west carrying a bunch of happy GI's back to the world.

I had watched that scene before, but something about it that day got to me. Here I was eight thousand miles from home with a whole year staring me in the face before I'd be on a plane headed back. A miserable feeling came over me, like a heavy weight just bringing me down. I didn't feel sick, I just felt dread. I couldn't stop thinking about it—a year. I still had nearly a whole year, three hundred and fifty days more, give or take a day.

It was a near fatal case of homesickness something no training can prepare you for. Sometimes it felt worse than fear. And there was nothing I could do about it, just suck it up, do my job and hope it didn't last.

In the barracks after my shift some weeks later, amid the loud talk and clunky lockers, an airman nearby was changing into regular clothes getting ready to go out. I'd seen him before but didn't really know him. I asked him where he was going.

"Going to work at the NCO club," he said. He shot a finger gun at me and left.

A bell went off in my head. I had been so down in the dumps, almost depressed, that I had forgotten my plan. I had abandoned my big idea of getting that second job.

The guy was Gary Norman and the next day I told him I'd like to get a job at the NCO club. He was cool about it. He told me Sgt. Brewer was in charge and that he'd see about getting me in to talk to him. A few days later, I met with the sergeant. There was normally a crew of four guys prepping the food at night for breakfast in the morning. One of the guys would be shipping out in a couple of weeks. If I could pick up the duties from him, I could take his place.

That's what I wanted to hear. Right then, I felt better. A week later I met with the sarge again and he hired me. I'd be working every other day, 10:30 p.m. to 6:00 a.m. Along with two other airmen, I was a chef's assistant working with Gary, who'd been a chef in New York "in another life" he joked, and Brewer was our supervisor.

My job started, and I took to it right away. I cracked dozens of eggs into dozens of bowls, stewed pounds of prunes in huge vats, poured gallons of juice into smaller containers. I laid out mounds of bacon and sausage links on huge metal sheets for oven baking, shredded a ton of potatoes for hash browns, and did anything else they told me to do such as cutting a hole in any unopened 50-pound bag of rolled oats and setting it on the warm stove. That allowed the unlisted protein inside the bag—meal bugs—to escape. The sight of those bugs crawling out could turn a person off oatmeal forever.

By daybreak, pounds of breakfast food would be cooked and placed in steam tables for the troops who would start coming in at six. After the prep, but before the troops converged, the help got to eat. Just for the heck of it one morning I treated myself to a dozen scrambled eggs and ate every bite.

After a couple of months one member of the crew transferred out and I was promoted to breakfast short order cook. I was flipping pancakes, cracking eggs three at a time, making hash browns, frying bacon on cookie sheets. When the dinner fare turned gourmet for the visit of a high-ranking officer, steaks would be on the menu. Three of us would cook t-bones on a grill half the size of a dining room table. When the grilling for the brass was done, we grillers were allowed a couple of steaks for ourselves.

There was a juke box in the dining area, and we could hear it in the kitchen while we were working. That's how I first heard Archie Bell and Drells doing the *Tighten Up*, and Procol Harem singing *A Whiter Shade of Pale*. It was music to our ears. Just hearing it made home seem not so far away.

After being in 'Nam nearly four months, I was assigned guard duty at the morgue for the first time. The morgue was a Quonset situated on a tarmac over a mile away from barracks. It was like a warehouse, the doors wide open, with bodies coming in daily. With my M16 over my shoulder, I stood by the caskets knowing the body of a dead soldier was inside every one of them. Most were infantry being loaded for shipment back to the states. The names and destinations were written on the side of each box. Rows of plain wooden caskets, four across and three high were carefully stacked onto a pallet and lifted by forklift into the rear of a C141, the type of cargo plane I came in on. One pallet after another, pushed into the rear of the plane. Maybe a hundred caskets at a time being shipped first to Andrews Air Force Base in Maryland, and then returned to their hometowns for burial.

The birthdates were stamped on each casket. Most were 1945-1947. Guys my age, their lives ended before they had a chance to live. Reading those numbers was physically painful. Guys were dying, I knew that. But seeing the caskets and reading those dates at that moment brought the tragedy of this war to a head. So much waste and loss, so many broken families. And then a thought comes into your head that you can't ignore...it could have been you. Then you buck up, you get a grip, and you might not say it out loud, but the next thing you feel is relief because it's not you. And you remember how you felt before you got here—invincible—and you know some of these guys felt that way too. And then you decide, enough thinking. Just stand guard, do your job, and for a while, you try to stop thinking altogether. That's how I felt.

By Christmas, I had a good routine going. For the twelve to fourteen hours a day that I was awake, I stayed busy. My mind was focused on my jobs, and it made the time go by faster. My routine was a wheel I jumped onto in the morning, jumped off at night. Guard duty, sleep, grilling at the NCO club, sleep, jogging, weight room on my days off, sleep. Then I'd do it all over again. Days and nights folded into each other. The distant sound of bombs became part of the noise of every day. I'd wake sometimes and not know what day it was. Other times I knew I should be tired, but I wasn't. Maybe it was nervous energy, maybe endorphins, whatever they were. Something kept me going even after twelve hours on my feet. The flip side of that were the times I fell dead asleep the minute my head hit the pillow. I once slept twenty-four hours straight, six to six, and never changed positions.

My military pay including the hazardous duty addition amounted to about $325 a month. It was sent in an allotment to Muhtha. She made the deposits into my bank account at Security Pacific, three blocks from the house, an account I'd opened before I started at Sears. The NCO club netted me another $75 a week. That's what I lived on and was able to grow, modestly, by being the loan broker for guys who would lose their entire monthly pay by gambling. They'd bet on a card game, a game of dice, games of chance where they had no chance. The day after payday, they'd be broke. A couple of guys would come to me, knowing I wasn't about to lose my money gambling. I suggested they might want to slow their role. Unfortunately, some guys never learn.

I wouldn't loan more than ten bucks, and only to airmen I could trust to pay me back with interest. Paydays were like mail call with every airman waiting outside the barracks to hear his name and receive his cash in an envelope from Uncle Sam. Anyone with a loan to repay, I'd be right by their side.

Muhtha wrote at least once a week, short letters that always included some little bit of news to keep me up to date, and always ended with her and dad telling me to be careful, and that she was praying for me. I wrote back telling her I was doing fine, eating well and hadn't been sick. I never mentioned bombs or missiles, or the miserable weather. I knew it was pointless to tell her not to worry. What mother wouldn't be worried.

Bev wrote often, letters written on flowery thin airmail paper scented with Ambush cologne. I'd wave the paper under the noses of anyone close by. Before long they were asking me to ask her to write to them, just for the scent. For Christmas, she mailed aftershave lotion, bars of soap, socks, and a photo album, each gift individually wrapped with a little poem, plus a gold ID bracelet engraved with both our names, which I still have.

After New Year's I got reacquainted with two airmen I knew from Vandenberg who were here working in the Arms Room. It was a two-man post and the job was issuing and receiving firearms, keeping an inventory, cleaning weapons, and generally keeping the room in order. It was an inside job. Dust from the road was down to a minimum, and there was activity most of the day. One of the guys, Scully, would be shipping out in a couple of weeks, so he recommended me to the sergeant in charge. I worked with Scully during his last week. He shipped out, a happy man, and I stepped right into his job.

Maybe two weeks had passed when a soldier walked into the arms room during my shift and called out "Hey Cuz." I looked up and saw the smiling face of my real cousin, Howard Jacobs. I hadn't seen him since the Christmas of '59 when we drove to Houston. Here we were, both of us in the Air Force, both in DaNang, connected by the letters between sisters, my mother Flora and his mother, Antoinette. We were in different squadrons, opposite ends of the base, but at least we had a chance to see each other and catch up on old news.

## ~ TET ~

In January of 1968, the semi relaxed atmosphere around the base changed dramatically. All personnel were briefed and put on special alert. Standing in formation outside the barracks we were told that surprise attacks were planned by the Viet Cong to destroy American control centers, control centers of the allied forces, and civilian cities throughout South Vietnam. The action was called the TET offensive, and was set to start January 30th, the first day of the Vietnamese lunar new year. This assault of continuous rocket strikes was meant to be the turning point of the war in favor of the Viet Cong.

After the advisement, normal base operations were suspended. We were put on tactical alert. Only security police squadrons were on the grounds fully armed. Patrols were stepped up and the number of posts were increased. Main gates and rear gates were reinforced with more guards, and more armored vehicles were outfitted with machine guns.

Since September we'd heard rocket attacks in the distance, a sound that was different than the explosion of a bomb. Rockets coming in had a scream and a cracking sound so loud, that for a few seconds after, you couldn't hear anything at all. From the bunkers we could count four or five rocket volleys, one right after the other.

In the first week of February, the continuous foothummm of rocket launches never let up. Ground fighting went on several miles north of us beyond the base perimeter by army and marine infantry. From the base towers, especially those along the flight lines, I saw gunfighter pilots rush from their housing facilities to the planes and    shortly after, watched the planes take off. We could see the air support by F-4C and AC130 aircraft, cargo planes that had been converted to fighter planes. Out of each of the windows was a machine gun, basically a Gatling gun with the power to spew out more than 2000 rounds of ammo per minute. The flames spit out by those guns was like dragon fire. They were killing machines, awesome and terrifying as hell. Rocket attacks from the other side continued for two solid weeks, and then in late February, one month after it began, TET was declared ended. The base remained on tactical alert. We would learn much later that American casualties after TET were in the thousands. Later it was determined that the offensive was not the turning point for the Viet Cong but it made the American military command realize that this war was far from over.

Four months later I was in Thailand on R&R, a week of rest and recuperation, change of scenery, a time to stop thinking about the war, if that was possible. I had arrived with Nick, my closest cohort at the time who'd arrived in Vietnam a month before me. He called me Baby Bru just because he was a year older. We did just about everything any GI does in Bangkok. We stayed at a swanky hotel, swam every day, rode around in a rickshaw sight-seeing, drank to excess, and observed Thailand's sordid, seedy nightlife. In short, as much as we could we enjoyed the time off. I took lots of pictures and bought souvenirs for everyone including a hand-carved mahogany jewelry box for Bev. The week was called R&R, but we needed it more after we got back.

## ~ Short-Timer ~

The makeshift calendar in the middle of the yard didn't lie. I had one month remaining before my year "in country" would be over. I stuck to my routine and packed a little each day.

Everybody did it, and I did too, talk trash about leaving with every passing day. I was a "short-timer" and it was a great feeling.

I was still getting letters from Muhtha, Lizzie and L'Arthur who sent me a picture of his son, Jeffrey, my nephew. Gwen had gotten married and was busy with her new life. Bev's letters had slowed to a trickle.

Finally, the morning came after a sleepless night. I boarded a Pan Am airliner with a bunch of other airmen, everybody smiling, big sighs of relief. It was the same plane I'd seen take off so many times and it was packed. Looking out the window at the base, I was thinking I'd probably never see any of these guys again, and some of them might not be leaving at all. I thought about the lives already lost, and guys my age with injuries that would change their lives forever. I had a lot to be grateful for.

As the plane took off there was a big cheer. I looked out at the rows of rice paddies for the last time and closed my eyes hoping that when I opened them again, I'd be home.

## ~ Homecoming ~

As the plane began its descent into Norton Air Force Base, San Bernardino, I held my breath until it touched down. I grabbed my duffel, and when I stepped off the plane, I was ready to kiss the ground. Free at last, free at last, I was home, back in the world, freer and more grateful than I'd ever felt in my life.

Four guys on the flight were from my squadron, but I was the only one heading back to LA. The others were headed to LAX. One, a very superior acting lieutenant had looked down on us non-coms when we were in that other world, but now needing a ride, he became our new best buddy.

An uncle waiting off base to pick up one of the guys offered a ride to all of us. I had sent a letter to the folks letting them know when I would arrive. Apparently, no one was as anxious to get home as I was. Not one of them objected to stopping at a pool hall in Compton after an hour's ride to chuck a few balls and down a few beers. *Didn't these guys have anyone expecting them, waiting on them, dying for them to get home?*

I hinted to the uncle that I'd catch the bus. But he insisted. A promise was a promise, he said. The game broke up, we climbed back into his car, and a half hour later, he dropped me at the driveway of 616 E. 84th Place. The house never looked so good.

Muhtha came out the front door and down the

steps crying. Mrs. Austin and Mrs. Byrd were right behind her, all of them hugging me, patting me on the back, almost like they'd break into applause. I don't think I cried, but I was close.

They pulled me inside the house and the smell of garlic and pot roast filled the room. The lamp was standing tall on the table. Gwen took my duffel, told me to sit down, relax, my bossy big sister still being bossy. She danced over to the phone and called somebody. "Come on over baby. My brother just got back from Vietnam!"

Lizzie pulled me by the hand out the back door to show me her new Toyota Corolla parked in the driveway. Dad got home a little later, shook my hand and patted my back. "Boy you made it back home." Muhtha and daddy stood there together, looking at me. Could they tell I was thinner? Had I aged in that year? I could see they had, worrying about me. But the worrying was over now.

We were together again. Except for Bev.

I followed Muhtha back into the kitchen. She got busy spooning juice onto the roast. I asked about Bev. She kept basting. She eased the roast back into the oven, washed her hands, dried them, checked a couple of pots on the stove, wouldn't look me in the eye. I asked her again and expected to hear bad news.

"Well..." Her voice trailed off, and then finally she looked at me. "We haven't seen Bev in a couple of months."

That night after dinner I called her. The next day she pulled up in front of the house in her red Mustang. She hadn't changed at all. I didn't want to think too much about why she wasn't part of the welcome home party. She went inside to see Muhtha, then got back in her car. She sat behind the wheel with the door open looking uncomfortable. I knelt next to her, listening as she tried to sound upbeat about school, and the play she was in at Cal State LA. She kept looking off, wouldn't look me in the eye. Something was on her mind, and it wasn't me.

She seemed shy again. I wasn't sure what she was thinking. Had her feelings for me changed? I didn't know and she wasn't talking. I still loved her, but I thought, okay, a year was a long time. Maybe we needed some time to be together again, to pick up where we left off. We'd kind of lost touch during the break in those letters. I had continued to write, but over my last six weeks, her letters had stopped. We needed some time together, but it was up to her.

She finally smiled, said she had things to take care of and promised to call. I said okay.

When she left, my spirits were down but not out. I was an optimist, after all. I went back inside, unpacked my duffel, and got serious about finding my car. I had a thirty-day leave, and I wanted to have my car before it was over. That goal had never changed.

I called around to four Dodge dealerships in the area, and everyone had the same story: all the '68 Dodge RT's in either green or black were gone. All of them. And the '69's wouldn't be out until November.

I wanted to tell those salesmen that the RT was the reason I went to Vietnam. That the dream of buying this car helped me through twelve months in another world. I'd even bought a green shirt to match the color. But I didn't say any of it. Maybe it wasn't meant to be.

My buddy Alvin drove me to Bev's to visit her folks who were relieved to see I'd made it back in one piece. Bev wasn't there. When I told Mr. Cromwell about not getting my car, he suggested 1 call Warren Biggs Chevrolet. He knew one of the salesmen and said 1 should mention his name. 1 wasn't interested in buying another Chevy, but 1 called Biggs anyway.

After speaking to the salesman who convinced me he had something 1 might want to see, Lizzie offered to take me to the dealership on 4$^{th}$ and La Brea. On a back lot was a 1968 Chevelle Super Sport, two-door, black on black, with leather seats, and four speed on the floor, a muscle car and it was hot. The cost was $3600. Right then 1 stopped brooding about the RT.

1 came back the next day, put $2000 down from my savings and financed the balance. The payment was seventy-five a month, which 1 could easily do. 1 had my wheels. 1 was happy again.

Days later after a call from Bev, 1 drove over in the Chevelle to show it to her. The car was gleaming. She was ecstatic, and happy for me. Alvin was with me, and Bev's friend Bettye was at her house. Alvin and Bettye were introduced, and got acquainted in Bev's living room, while Bev and 1 talked in the kitchen. She still loved me she said, and though 1 was somewhat mystified, 1 figured, finally, the girl had come to her senses. The Bev from a year ago was back.

A thirty-day leave was what the Air Force gave me, and Bev and 1 were doing something almost every day. We went to the beach, we sat under the golden arches at the nearby Mickey D's eating Big Macs and fries, we drove to Gwen's and met her husband Errol, and we visited L'Arthur, Lynn and Jeffrey. We went to Bamboo Gardens for Chinese food and went to the movies. 1 saw three performances of the play Bev was in at Cal State, and in quieter moments, we talked about our future.

No one in my family asked me about Vietnam. Maybe they sensed I didn't want to talk about it, and maybe they didn't really want to know. What mattered to them was that I was home, and they didn't have to worry about me anymore. Those first few nights home, I had trouble sleeping. I'd gotten so used to the sound of bombs and screaming rockets that now the nights were just too quiet. I knew it would pass, so I didn't worry about it.

I reported to George Air Force base in Victorville, California, the first week of September 1968. It was about ninety miles north of LA. My four-year commitment to Uncle Sam would end in February 1970, unless what I had heard after arriving at George came true, that my year in Vietnam might get me an "early out." An application for early discharge had to be submitted, so I submitted mine.

My first assignment was working patrol details with a tech sergeant named Roberts, a good guy and a lifer. Everyone called him Robbie and he called me Higgie. He was 34, married, and had two kids. He had been in the service for 10 years, including a one-year stint in Vietnam. He figured he'd do twenty, because as he put it, "It's too late for me to do anything else." We got along well and enjoyed opposing but friendly discussions about the military. The brass was trying to get me to re-enlist, and so was Robbie. No way was I signing up for another four years, but he kept trying to persuade me to do it.

It wasn't that I disliked the Air Force or the military. I didn't. I just knew that military life as a career wasn't for me. It had served a purpose, had helped me find a place to belong at a time when I needed to make a stand and make a change. It showed me how I measured up against others in the same boat. The majority of the guys

I served with were upstanding and serious about the job. They appreciated the requirements and the discipline of military life. I did too, but four years was enough for me. I made that clear to Robbie. We agreed to disagree. I told him about Bev and our plans, and took him for a ride in my Chevelle. It had made the 75-mile drive into LA nearly every weekend with no problem. The joke was that the fire department followed me leaving the base because of the flames I left speeding down the hill to get to LA.

Robbie and I worked together nearly five months while incentives were being offered to persuade me to re-enlist. The one incentive I didn't turn down was the switch from doing patrols with Robbie to the cushier job of the motor pool crew, scheduling maintenance on the air police vehicles.

That's where I was, in the motor pool office, the day Robbie was killed. He had answered a domestic dispute call between a husband and wife, and before he'd even stepped inside the home, the husband pulled a gun and shot Robbie four times. He died on the scene. His partner, waiting by the car, witnessed the whole thing but had no time to react, it happened so fast. If I hadn't switched to the motor pool, I'd have been the partner waiting by the car.

My early out came through. I was officially discharged from the air force on May 8, 1969 at the rank of Staff Sergeant. I had served a total of three years and four months. Once again, and even more permanently, I was free at last. I missed not being able to tell Robbie. He would have been happy for me.

## ~ Back to Life ~

For posterity, I hung one green uniform shirt bearing my name in the corner of my closet. I came back to reality. My bank balance was $500. I needed a job. I never thought I'd go back to Sears, but I did, and my timing was good. They had an opening for someone to be a security guard during the day, and a collector at night to retrieve cash from bad-check writers. I took the job part-time, two day shifts, and three nights a week. I liked being out of the store. Depending on the addresses on the NSF checks, sometimes I'd get by to see Bev. But I wasn't making enough money.

After reading in the newspaper that the Rapid Transit District (RTD) was hiring drivers, I took the written test, passed it, and reported to LA's dry river bed with dozens of other potential new drivers to train behind the wheel. We learned how to steer a city bus around cones, make three point turns over gravel and wide turns around corners. We practiced operating the lift gates, and how to work the automatic doors. I was gritting my teeth the whole time, every fiber in my body telling me "You do not want to be a bus driver."

At the orientation a week later (*why am I here?*) the new hires were told we would work a split shift—four hours driving, followed by a four-hour break, and then a second four-hour shift. They suggested we could go to the library or the park during the break. *What?* Oh no. That was not going to work for me at all. I resigned before I got started. I hung in with Sears and went back to the want ads.

While my job situation was a little iffy, my feelings for Bev were solid. I was in love with someone I knew was the only girl for me, and she was in love with me. What could be better. We had been talking about marriage for weeks, yet I wasn't aware that something was missing until the subject of a proposal came up one night. We were sitting on her mother's vinyl covered brocade sofa, munching on burgers and fries from Mickey D's when she asked me if I was going to propose. I said I thought I already had.

She said, "No, you didn't."

"I didn't?"

"No, not really."

"But we *are* getting married, right?"

"Yes, but you never actually *asked* me."

She wasn't joking. I could tell by the look on her face. The "oh brother" sigh rising in my chest would not be well received, I knew that. I washed it down with my soda. She just sat there with her hands in her lap, waiting.

What's a guy in love to do? I got down on one knee, took her hand in mine. "Will you marry me?"

After all our talk about marriage, and me thinking it was a done deal, her eyes got teary before she was able to choke out a "yes." Then without missing a beat, still holding my hand, she said I needed to ask her dad for permission. She was serious about that too. Mr. Cromwell had been casually grilling me about what I planned to do now that I was out of the service.

"You can ask him now," she said. "He's right here in the den."

Bev's dad was chief technical engineer at Sinclair Paint. He was probably the most professional adult I knew. He worked right under the owner/president Frank Sinclair. I had told him that my return to Sears was just temporary, that I was planning to get something better. He looked surprised and amused when I asked his permission to marry his daughter. I don't remember how I put it but he smiled and said yes, and told me to come into the Sinclair Paint store on Friday and talk to Gersh, the manager about a job.

Sinclair's store on 83$^{rd}$ and Vermont is where I started working after a good word was put in for me by my future father in law. I was hired as a driver to deliver Sinclair paint "the Painter's Choice" to Inglewood, West LA, Beverly Hills, and beautiful Palos Verdes Estates, a part of Los Angeles I'd never seen before.

Palos Verdes overlooked the ocean, a view that gave me a greater appreciation of the beautiful Pacific ocean. I was delivering a palette of five-gallon buckets of paint for the new tract of homes being built. One of the most beautiful of the seven model homes available for viewing was called "The Manchester." It overlooked Marineland and became my dream home.

I worked six days a week, eight hours a day, for $2.25 an hour, plus time and half on Saturdays. I worked fast, and I learned my routes quickly. The workout routine I'd gotten into while in the Air Force was a good thing. I was in great physical condition, I had plenty of energy, and I was, after all, still a youngster, just 22. Keeping the night job at Sears at fifteen hours a week was no problem. With the two jobs, my take home was about $170 a week. Sounds like pittance, doesn't it? But remember, it was 1969. I didn't know what my dream house cost, but I was positive I couldn't afford it...not yet.

Wedding plans were in the works. The date was set. Bev left Cal State LA just short of getting a bachelor's degree in theatre arts, and was hired full-time as a teller at Fireside Thrift and Loan on Wilshire Blvd.

Sinclair's store and Bev's house were minutes apart, so by taking a slight detour to 83$^{rd}$ on her way to work, she'd see me loading paint onto my truck. If the red light caught her, the distance between us was no greater than Romeo's from Juliet on the balcony, except we were both on level ground. Risking life and limb (and maybe job) I'd run to the driver's side and we would kiss. Aaah love. It was great.

Meanwhile, dad had talked to me about working on the docks. The hiring for the Transit Warehouse jobs— TW's—would open soon. Those were part-time entry jobs for workers to eventually become longshoreman with full benefits. The pay was $36 dollars a day for a TW, twice what I was making at Sinclair. Dad could sponsor L'Arthur and me if we wanted it. He would keep me posted.

## ~ Apartment ~

On my way back to the store one afternoon, mid-July, a man was hammering a "For Rent" sign in front of a fourplex on 6$^{th}$ Avenue and Adams. I hung a u-turn, parked my truck, and asked to see the unit. He hesitated for a moment.

"I'm getting married in a month," I blurted out. I practically told him my whole life story, starting with the fact that I'd served a year in Vietnam, and had just been discharged from the air force. He loosened up. He told me he owned the property, and I recognized his German accent. I told him he sounded just like my nice German neighbors Mr. and Mrs. Polowitz, who used to babysit me when I was a kid. I think that little nugget is what sealed the deal.

Herbert Reents unlocked the door and led me into the apartment. It was huge, much larger than Bettye and Alvin's who by the way, had gotten married after a four-month whirlwind courtship. They were living in an apartment complex nearly five miles away, one of many in Baldwin Hills, better known as "The Jungle." It was party central for upwardly mobile blacks and young black couples, but I was looking for something different and I thought this could be it.

This apartment was in a quieter part of the city, and only four units compared to the 50-100-unit buildings in the jungle. This place had French doors, a dining room, hardwood floors, a service porch off the kitchen, and a one car garage. Apartments in the jungle only had car ports and no French doors. Stairs on the side of the garage led to the roof and on the roof was a clothesline. I had never been to New York but standing on the roof, I felt like I was in New York. The rent was $105, about fifteen per month more than the jungle, but I knew Bev would love this place. I handed over all the cash I had as a deposit, thirty bucks, got a receipt from my new landlord, and a week later, I started moving in.

## ~ Going to the Chapel ~

Bev and I were married on Saturday, August 30th, 1969, at St. Malachy's Church in front of 125 people. I guess it was kind of a big wedding—five bridesmaids, five groomsmen, and over one hundred guests. Bev's sister Vicky was her matron of honor, and L'Arthur looking slightly underdressed was my best man. He had misplaced the white collar and bib of his rented tuxedo, which left only the striped tie around his mostly naked neck.

I never liked being the center, or even half of the center of attention. I didn't know most of the people Bev's family had invited, but weddings are a happy time. Like most grooms, my job was to grin and bear it, go with the flow, and know that in a few hours we'd be off on our honeymoon.

Frank Sinclair put a bug in my ear as he shook my hand at the end of the reception line. "You're doing a great job Howard. Good things are in store for you." Behind him Bev's dad gave me that confident Duke nod, the corners of his mouth turned down, which was a thumbs up without the thumb. Would I soon be off the delivery truck and behind the counter in one of the stores? Time would tell.

I had picked Lake Tahoe for our honeymoon, a surprise for Bev. She was so excited, riding the wave of the newlywed high as we walked through Burbank airport heading toward our plane. I turned around to look at her bouncing along slightly behind me, looking around taking in everything. The people, the shops, glimpses of planes through the windows. She looked so young, like a teenager. And suddenly, I had an epiphany. I didn't know to call it that, but that's what it was. An epiphany. It rose up like an open door, and I was stepping through it into a whole new chapter of my life. I was a husband now, with a wife to take care of. A commitment, a new responsibility. Was I ready for it? Was this the right move? Did I really want to be married? It was a heck of a thing to be thinking, after the fact. I thought about my brother and wondered if he'd had second thoughts on his wedding day.

Bev had no idea what was on my mind at that moment, and I was good at putting on a poker face. She slipped her arm through mine pressed her head against my shoulder as we walked. A five-second panic attack washed over me as we boarded the plane and found our seats. Bev closed her eyes tight and held my hand during takeoff. I watched her smiling contentedly, and the tension I was feeling began to slip away. The seven and seven drink I was sipping worked its magic as well.

Tahoe was beautiful, the lake clear, skies bluer than blue, and air so fresh and crisp we wanted to breathe it in all day. We tootled around in a rented VW bug, collected shells and rocks along the lake shore, and visited the Ponderosa ranch where Bonanza was filmed.

Into the casino, we walked around wide-eyed, and tried our luck. For a couple of newlyweds, the clinking sound of nickels and dimes from the slots and the site of three winning cherries was exciting indeed, but feeding those one-armed bandits turned out to be a short-lived addiction. The KENO lounge suited us more. Drinks were free, and the action a little slower. I played several hands. Bev mostly watched. "No sense both of us losing our money," she said.

I went to the pay window after one hand and when I came back, I whispered, "I won." She leaned in, not hearing.

"I won a hundred and twenty-six dollars," I said. She screamed. You'd have thought it was a hundred and twenty-six *thousand* the way she yelled.

The day after we returned from the honeymoon,

after the family helped bring the gifts to our apartment, I looked around at the boxes, the gifts, our new home here on 6th Ave and Adams, and I thought, well, we're in it now. We were officially jumping head first into married life. It was fun, exciting, and a little scary.

Two months later, my dad called. The transit warehouse hiring was open. It's what I'd been waiting for. I felt bad breaking the news to Bev's dad that I was leaving Sinclair. I think he understood, even if he didn't agree with my decision. He wished me good luck and told me I could come back if I needed to. I had high expectations for my new job. Returning to Sinclair wasn't in my plans.

## ~ The Docks ~

My TW number was 611. TW stood for Transit Warehouseman. It meant working three to five days a week to build up hours toward becoming a full-time longshoreman, learning the job as you go. There were a lot of guys starting as TW's, maybe 200, most of them young like me. Dad sponsored me, which was the main requirement, and since L'Arthur didn't want it, I felt obliged to dad to give this job a try.

Once you got your TW number, it was just a matter of showing up and waiting for your number to be called. That's what I was doing one morning, when a big brother came up beside me and started talking. He wasn't much older than me, but he must have weighed 300 pounds. His name was Kelly, he'd been working as a TW for a couple of years, his dad and uncle were longshoremen, and they both knew my dad.

We became friends and partners on jobs. He'd call me some mornings that he'd pulled a job for the two of us, or he'd tell me if things were slow, and save me from coming down. I got called for jobs almost every day, and most were hard, grimy, tiring, and with the heavy crates and cargo hooks we had to use, dangerous. Learning to operate a winch and drive a forklift was done in a couple of days, and after that, it was trial and error.

One of the worst jobs was in refrigeration or "frozen" and any time my number was called for it, I'd seriously consider turning it down. But I never did. Those were the jobs TW's got assigned often. Frozen jobs put us in the hold of the ship. The temperature in some of the cargo lockers was 30 below zero. Twenty minutes in the freezer, 20 minutes out, 20-minute break. We wore insulated thermal gloves, layers of sweaters and jackets, knit caps and earmuffs. In frozen, every worker moved fast trying to keep the body temperature up. We were hauling 250-pound tunas, frozen and hard as a rock, and standing them upright to be lifted out of the ship by a winch to another location on the deck where another crew of guys moved them to their next destination.

As bad as it was, working frozen was better than not working at all. If you'd gotten up at six to get to the docks, you weren't about to turn around and come home with nothing. Sometimes there were no TW jobs left, which was hard to believe. TW's with fewer hours were given jobs over those with more hours, an effort to avoid one TW working more than others; other times there were "short jobs" three to four hours only, usually to finish a job from the day before. The upside to short jobs was that the $36 a day was still guaranteed.

I was a house husband on the days when there was no TW work. I'd have dinner ready when Bev got home. She appreciated it, but she worried when two or three days went by and I wasn't called for a job. I hadn't anticipated not getting enough days. I knew eventually I'd make full time money, but "eventually" was too indefinite. I had to get something else going.

L'Arthur told me about jobs at Bekins called "casual" hiring on Saturdays, $10 an hour. Those were non-scheduled moves or large office moves requiring "helpers." If you called or showed up at the Bekins dispatch office downtown, you might catch a day job and make $80. I landed a few days, but again, it was hit and miss.

Bev's job at the thrift and loan company was solid. At Christmas, she got a $50 bonus plus a $25 coupon for a turkey. In '69 those perks were really appreciated. Our monthly bills totaled about $260. Rent was $105, Chevelle note $75, $20 to Sears for our washer, maybe $50 for utilities and groceries. Things were tight, but we stayed in the black. We saved a little, hit the movies in Westwood now and then, and had enough to buy a new car.

Had we known Bev's red '65 Mustang would one day be a classic, we'd have held onto it instead of letting an oil leak convince us it was time to trade it in. It was barely five years old. But that's what we did.

We'd had so much fun on our honeymoon in the Volkswagen rental, that on a Friday night, we traded in the Mustang and bought a baby blue VW Bug. I remember specifically that it was a Friday because there was one little hitch. Bev didn't know how to drive a stick shift. Over the weekend I had to teach her how to manage that clutch because on Monday's drive to work she would have to get her Bug over a couple of hills. We had a good laugh Monday evening when she got home safe and sound  and told me that driving to and from work she'd done a lot of bucking, jerking and  praying.  After that first day, she was fine.

I began noticing a shady side of working on the docks, specifically drug use among the TW's, and it was out in the open. Guys carrying red pills, yellow pills in their pockets, guys drinking on the job. Guys who'd been in jail were my partners on some jobs, and others were stealing anything they could easily pocket. I didn't like it, and I didn't need to be around it. What I needed was to figure out what I really wanted to do and find it.

Could it be United Parcel Service (UPS)? Brown needed drivers according to the want ads which I checked daily. I applied and was hired full time, five days a week, starting at $7.25 an hour. I rode along as a helper for one week before getting a Hollywood route that included Fairfax to La Cienega, Melrose Avenue and Santa Monica Blvd., areas with lots of houses, and apartment buildings with lots of stairs.

I had approximately 100 stops a day under their incentive program that determined some routes could be done in a certain number of hours, a determination made by an experienced driver who knew the route and the shortcuts. Totally unrealistic for a newbie like me, but I was hustling to make those 100 stops to meet that time frame, sprinting upstairs two at a time and missing a lot of lunches. No time even for a hot dog while I drove. The workdays started at seven a.m. and sometimes it was six at night before I got home. In some ways, working at UPS wore me out more than working on the docks. I soon realized I didn't want to work that hard, at least not for someone else. After six weeks, a supervisor told me I was doing a great job. I thanked him, and after picking up my check for the week, I told him I wouldn't be back.

LAPD was hiring. Back to square one.

LAPD's 77th Precinct offered the written qualifying test to become a police officer every Wednesday night. I decided to take it. My "cousin" Malcolm had recently gotten married and was looking for a different job. I told him about the test, and we went together. That may have been lucky. We both passed.

A week later, I returned for the oral interview. I faced three officers and one civilian, a distinguished looking black man probably in his seventies who was blind. He had been hired by the LAPD to sit in on interviews because of his specialty: voice recognition. His blindness had heightened his sense of hearing and supposedly, he could detect personality types just by the sound of the voice.

I'd been reminded it was important to remember the names of the four people conducting the interview, but as I began answering their questions, and trying to keep those names in my head, I couldn't help wondering what impression the civilian was getting from my voice. Apparently, nothing negative. I passed the interview and was introduced to the man. After shaking hands, he told me I had a strong decisive personality, that I could follow in the footsteps of Tom Bradley, and be a real credit to the force. I hadn't thought that far ahead, but his words were encouraging.

All that remained was the physical. I couldn't wait

to tell L'Arthur. I'd passed the written and the oral. I was about to become a cop! I was excited when I called him, but he stopped me cold. The first words out of his mouth were, "Don't take the job."

*What?*

He ran down a list of reasons. Rookies get the worst shifts, no weekends off, bad partners, and the job was dangerous. None of what he said was news, but one point he made was something I didn't know. If you quit early, any money deducted for retirement was retained by the city. You wouldn't get it back.

My brother had been a marshal for about eight months, a county job, working in the traffic office downtown. He'd met LAPD officers who had told him what he was now telling me.

"Take the marshal's test," L'Arthur said. "Hiring for the Marshal's has just reopened. The job is five days a week, and you'll have weekends off. If you quit, you'll get your retirement money back, and starting pay is $842 a month." Eight-hundred and forty-two a month! That was the clincher. Once again, my brother was giving me a good tip. I followed up.

I scored sixty-seven on the written test, good enough for Sheriff, but you needed at least seventy to become a marshal. I retested in three weeks after studying at the library and surprised myself by scoring 74 out of 75. I had five minutes to call Bev and I heard her telling her co-workers the good news. I hung up and waited to be called in for yet another oral interview.

I was seated in a room facing three officers again, none of them smiling. Almost immediately, one asked about my brother-in-law, Eugene Garrett. I remember shifting in my seat and thinking *Who is he talking about?* I told him I had no brother-in-law named Eugene Garrett, but that my brother Arthur was also a marshal. "No," one officer said, "your brother-in-law." For a few seconds I was literally at a loss for words. Again, I said I didn't know who they were talking about. They moved on to the next question and for the rest of the interview, I was distracted. When it was over, I was certain they had me mixed up with someone else.

Not exactly.

L'Arthur and I talked later that day. He told me his brother in-law had passed the marshal's test and had taken his oral interview that same morning. His brother-in-law was Eugene Garrett, Lynn's brother. I had met the guy only once. "Call me Gene," he'd said. I didn't know my sister-in-law's maiden name was Garrett, and I had no clue her brother had taken the test.

Apparently, my answers hadn't ruled me out because the background check followed soon after. An officer came to the apartment. Again, I was asked about my brother-in-law Eugene. The review board was under the impression that I was distancing myself from him and that there was racial tension between us because of the mixed marriage. "No racial tension," I said, as simply and directly as I could, and I went on to clarify the name mix-up. I decided to bite my tongue on the last point, that technically Gene was L'Arthur's brother-in-law, not mine. In the end it didn't matter. Case closed. I was approved.

I put my TW number on hiatus. It was still active, but I hadn't been to the docks in a while. New deputies were to have no extracurricular activities in the first year, and early on dad had advised me that law enforcement of any kind was not particularly welcome on the docks. The message was clear. The docks were off limits, at least for now.

I reported downtown for indoctrination and to be sworn in with twenty-four other new deputies. We were each given two uniforms, a badge, handcuffs, brass bullets, a leather gun belt, and a 38-caliber revolver, right there on the spot. It was all so immediate. It reminded me of how posses were formed in the old westerns I used to watch. A quick swear in, the deputy gets a badge and just like that, he's the law. But I wasn't headed to Dodge City or Tombstone. I was going to Beverly Hills.

## ~ **Marshal Years – 1970-1979** ~

The Marshal's Department of LA County immersed new hires quickly into the system. We were called Instant Deputies and were paired with experienced marshals in an office environment for evaluation and OJT to see if new recruits would acclimate to office protocols, get along with co-workers, and adjust to being officers of the law while learning desk and field operations. This would be done prior to expending county resources sending them to the academy which consisted of ten-weeks of physical training—Police Officers Standardized Training, POST—followed by five weeks of civil training to learn police procedures.

The marshal's office in beautiful Beverly Hills was

on the first floor of a four-story building at 9355 Burton Way. A dozen deputies split the assignments: lockup, court bailiff, working the desk, evictions and repossessions, and the service of legal papers "in the field" which included small claims actions, civil lawsuits, warrants, unlawful detainers, wage garnishments, and divorce papers. All were being served by the marshal's department.

I was nervous that first day as I entered the building. But the source of greater discomfort was the long-sleeve uniform shirt I was wearing made of 25% wool. Against my skin it felt like tiny pricks of steel wool. I reported to my commander as instructed, but I was thinking *how will I get Bev to sew a cotton lining into these shirts?*

Lieutenant Johnson assigned me to work the desk with three female clerks, and deputy Ted Poltash, who'd been a marshal for about five months. He knew how to work the desk and had already served papers in the field. He'd also been in the academy briefly but had been yanked after two weeks to fulfill a week-long National Guard obligation in the desert. He'd have to start the academy all over again, and he wasn't looking forward to it. "It's a butt kicker," he said. "You'll find out soon enough."

With Poltash instructing and a second desk officer, Sgt. Pattison, observing, I handled much of the paperwork and phone calls all week. During lapses of desk action, I had time to look out the solid bank of windows at the front of the building, a clear view of immaculate Burton Way. Almost any time of day you'd see a Rolls Royce go by, or a clean Mercedes Benz, or a Jag or a Bentley, or a Porsche. Seeing all those beautiful cars nearly every day, and, being a "car person," it wasn't long before I started thinking about buying one.

I was partnered with Poltash serving papers in the field. Riding along in the marshal unit gazing out of the window, it seemed to me that every stretch of sidewalk, every shop, every business, practically every person along those streets—Wilshire Blvd, Canon Drive, Rodeo Drive, Beverly Blvd—all looked like money. Rich area. Rich people. Being in the middle of this affluence, even on the fringes as a deputy, I began to think that maybe I could move in these circles, or at least have some of the riches these people had. Instead of being defeated by thoughts that certain things were out of reach, I was motivated to think these things could be mine. If you didn't know something existed, you didn't want it or miss it. I was now in an environment that exposed me to greater possibilities, and I knew I wanted to make a statement and be part of it. The environment made me believe anything was possible.

I grew up thinking only movie stars lived in Beverly Hills, that they were immune to the problems of regular people. Not so. I served papers on two actors I'd seen on the big screen for back taxes and warrants. I served papers on attorneys, doctors, bankers, business owners, who lived on exclusive streets in mansions with perfect manicured lawns. I learned that anyone can have legal problems and that Beverly Hills was not just for movie stars. Business, not necessarily acting, is what brought people to this high maintenance area.

One day, as we approached the Merrill Lynch office on Rodeo Drive, Poltash said, "Let's get a quote."

"What's a quote?" I said.

He parked the marshal's unit and we walked through the front door of the busy office. Our uniforms got the attention of several people without us saying a word. On the wall above the desks, numbers on small television screens were moving. I had no idea what that was all about. Poltash approached a broker, gave him the name of a stock and asked for "a quote." Ah ha.

His dad had taught him how to trade on the stock market. By the time he was a high school senior, he'd made enough and saved enough to pay much of his college tuition at USC. He still had an open account and still traded. I knew nothing about the stock market, but during the time we worked together, he taught me what the stock market was all about.

## ~ Dad (1970) ~

For more than a few months my dad had been under the weather. Not even Muhtha knew how long he'd been feeling ill. He never liked doctors, wouldn't go for checkups, and he never complained. But when it got so bad that he wasn't well enough to work, he told Muhtha maybe he should see a doctor. After a complete examination he was diagnosed with a malignant inoperable tumor between his nose and throat. He'd been in pain for weeks but had said nothing. He was put on medication for the pain and allowed to come home, but his condition worsened so quickly that Muhtha asked St. Malachy's priest Father Adams to come to the house. At his bedside, Father baptized Dad into the Catholic Church, and if nothing else, knowing he'd been baptized and given last rites, Muhtha felt some comfort in those last days before he was readmitted to the hospital.

On September 12, 1970, I was called in from the

field and told by the lieutenant that my dad had died. At the hospital, L'Arthur, Gwen and Lizzie were already there, holding onto Muhtha who was at his side holding his hand. He looked peaceful, but old before his time. He'd worked twenty-four years on the docks and lived long enough to see three of his four kids grow up and marry. He'd gotten to know his first grandsons, Jeff and Chris, L'Arthur and Lynn's boys, and he was crazy about them. Only last year he'd bought himself a new Chrysler. It still had the new car smell because he hadn't driven it much. I know my dad had more living to do. I hated that he never won that hatful he always talked about, and at 57, he should have had a few more years to try.

## ~ The Academy ~

The police academy was a former Nike Missile site located on a hill three miles above the campus of Rio Hondo College in Whittier. I reported for training in November. It was stress training taught by officers of the sheriff's department. It didn't matter if you'd successfully maxed the evaluations and training in an office environment. If you failed the academy, you were out.

L'Arthur had graduated from class #21. My class, #28 started with eighty-six cadets.

I rode with two of them, Quentin King, who lived close enough that picking me up at 6 a.m. wasn't out of his way, and Gwayne Collins, L'Arthur's buddy who took my brother's tip to take the test. That was L'Arthur. He'd found a good thing and wanted me and his best buds to get in on it too.

Mornings began with a run through the Whittier hills surrounding the campus. We pounded the road three miles to the top of the hill and back. After that it was weight training, stamina and endurance training, marching in formations, performing drills, and target practice. We were put in harassment scenarios, and stress situations to see how well we could keep our cool.

After the ten weeks, which made Christmas that year just a day on the calendar, we went through five weeks of classes learning police procedures. Tests were given weekly and a notebook was required containing all the notes taken in class. Fifteen weeks made as difficult as possible, mentally and physically. If we couldn't manage the stress here, how would we handle it on the job? Fifteen weeks of being on edge, not knowing for sure from one day to the next if you were still "in." You might report one morning and be advised by the end of the day that you were disqualified because of a misstep you didn't know you'd committed.

Every few days the number in our group decreased. Some were eliminated. Others simply dropped out.

I hung in. Of the eighty-six who started, forty-five of us graduated in February of 1971. I was officially a Deputy Marshal. To my great joy I was sent back to the Beverly Hills office. Poltash and Lt. Johnson were still there. Both were glad to see me.

I was assigned a vehicle and went back into the field serving papers. Depending on the number of papers in a day, I worked solo or with Poltash. It was business as usual in familiar surroundings with the occasional unforgettable happening.

I was on my way back to the office waiting at a

stop sign, when a silver Porsche pulled up next to me on the left. The engine was growling. I looked over and there was Steve McQueen behind the wheel. I couldn't get my window down fast enough. He smiled and waved, and then he was gone. McQueen was an actor who would look cool in any vehicle, but that Porsche was so clean, my dream to own one blew up right then.

At some time after my return, a directive came down from the department that regular target practice was now mandatory. I had been going to the range on my own trying to get to "sharpshooter" status and earn an additional twenty dollars a month. The lieutenant rounded up several of us prior to the end of my five to one shift, and we drove to Biscailuz Training Center in east LA. The center housed a jail, a fenced recreation yard, and a shooting range for target practice. Five of us deputies in uniform were walking past the recreation yard where several inmates were playing basketball. One of them called to me.

"Hey Howard!" I looked over as he separated from the group and came to the fence. I recognized him. We had worked together as TW's. He looked me up and down with that homey-head bobbing move. "Man, I ain't seen you on the docks. When you become a PD?"

I made a joke, told him I couldn't hang as a TW, that I thought this would be easier. I asked why he was on the yard. He said the reason was all bogus, that he'd be out soon and back on the docks. I nodded, told him to stay out of trouble. I rejoined my group, who were all ears. "You know that guy?"

Yeah, I knew him, and worse than that, he knew me. Seeing him that day put an official end to me working on the docks.

## ~ Belshaw ~

There was no time table for when a young married couple should buy a house. But I felt two years was long enough to pay rent. We loved our 6th Avenue apartment, but after a year and a half, we went house hunting, though occasionally we were just looky-loos. We started with homes in the Crenshaw district, older homes.   Prices started at $40,000, a little over our budget.

Malcolm, my play cousin and his wife Patricia had bought a new home in a new housing tract in Carson which was about sixteen miles from LA. They told us that more new homes were to be built and models were open on weekends for viewing. "Come take a look," they said. So, we did.

We looked at five different models. The smallest was a single story with three bedrooms, the largest, a two story with five bedrooms. All of them were so beautifully decorated, it was hard not to fall in love with one.

Bev was skittish. She loved the idea of a new home, but $30,000 was big money in 1971. Whichever model we chose, our mortgage payment would almost triple what we were currently paying in rent. How could we afford it, she wanted to know? How would we ever pay it off? I had to make her understand that paying it off wasn't the objective. Becoming homeowners was our plan. More my plan than hers. It wasn't easy, but I convinced her we'd be able to swing it.

We chose the Acapulco model. It had four bedrooms, two baths, a combined kitchen and family room. $29,999. The realtor drove us to the plot where our house would be built.   Construction hadn't begun yet. Even though the entire block was nothing but dirt, the whole idea of seeing our house being built from the ground up was exciting. Our new address would be 20239 Belshaw Avenue.

I was full steam ahead, but the numbers made Bev a little queasy. I calmed her fears. I told her we could do this. We were taking the next step toward achieving the American dream. I was already envisioning the improvements I wanted to make.

The $3000 down payment, 10% of the purchase price, was due in ninety days. We were a tad short. We would pool our monthly checks as usual and give ourselves a meager $10 allowance. Bev's jaw dropped. "Ten dollars for the entire week?"

Nearly every Sunday after mass we'd visit the site. In April Bettye and Alvin were with us when we selected floor tile for the kitchen and family room. We were a month from completion, but we had bigger news to share. Bev was pregnant.

In June 1971, we moved out of the apartment on 6th Avenue. Herbert and Lola our landlords for two years were sorry to see us go. We drove to our new home in Carson, just the two of us with our one moving van. We unlocked our front door for the first time as owners, and standing there in the entry, neither of us said a word.

The inside looked completely different! We had become used to seeing walls covered with flocked paper, and satin drapes on the windows. That was gone. We stared at bare white walls. No cushy pillows or oak bookshelves. No furniture, no decorative plants, no appliances. Outside, no patio, no grass or landscaping, no front walkway! Only dirt and more dirt. We knew none of the staged décor was included, but still, this was an eye-opener. We had a lot of work to do. The brown shag carpet was installed and it was very soft. We slept on it that first night.

Our mortgage payment was $236 a month, not as much as we thought it would be, but double our rent payment. Fortunately, there was a card I had not played.

The GI Bill, Uncle Sam's gift for honorably discharged military, offered financial assistance for a variety of needs. I knew about it, but I hadn't investigated until now. All I had to do was go back to school. Ah, my favorite thing. But I did it. Back to Harbor JC and enrolled in Music Appreciation, Police Science, and English 101, good old Mr. Finney. Three classes gave me nine units. The government would send me a tax-free check for $275 every month. Things were looking up.

Every weekend I looked forward to working on a new project at home. I took one vacation day shortly after the move, and talked my easy-going brother-in-law, Errol, Gwen's husband, into helping me lay the brick for my patio. Neither of us had laid brick before. We had all the tools: string, a balance plane, wooden pegs, mortar, trowel, water, a rough sketch, and a ton of bricks. How hard could it be? With no time to waste, we worked non-stop except for a burger break from Mickey D's.

When Bev got home, the patio floor was done. She was just in time to rub my aching back.

Over the next couple of months, we were steady on the case. I built a trellis over the patio, laid brick for the front walkway, planted grass seed and built a workbench in the garage. I paneled the family room with plywood, burnished the grain with a torch—something I'd learned in Vietnam—and varnished it. Bev papered the baby's nursery and the spare bedroom and hung curtains on the windows and artwork on the walls.

Gold-veined mirrored squares, peel, press, and stick were very popular in the 70's, "to add dimension to any room" according to the description on the box. We put them on the entry wall from the ceiling to the floor. It made a great backdrop behind the four-foot aquarium I built. I filled it with neon tetras, angel fish, and tiger barbs, the same fish I had when I was a kid. I finished it off with a water-proof light. It looked like a Sea World exhibit.

Meanwhile, I was loaned out to the Culver City office to serve papers for three weeks filling in for deputies on vacation. The marshal's office was near Venice and Marina Del Rey, and the whole area was being developed. Instead of completing my service log in the office, I'd complete it while sitting in my vehicle on Washington Avenue, a mile from the beach, and watch birds, ducks, and cranes in the nature water reserve. It was just opposite the property that would later be the Marina City Club, a complex I would later become acquainted with.

Six months after I returned to Beverly Hills, I was transferred to the West LA marshal's office.

## ~ JON ~

Bev took her maternity leave from the Gas Company two days after Christmas 1971. On January 9th, 1972, her friend Bettye hosted a baby shower for her at our house. Both grandmas were there, along with sisters and friends. I made myself scarce until it was over. Just after the last guest left, Bev asked me to take her to the hospital,

Kaiser in Harbor City. She was feeling a little strange she said, and I figured she'd eaten too much. Her due date was still three weeks away.

I held her hand as she was wheeled into the examining room, and after the examination, the doctor said I might as well go home because "there's not much happening here." False labor they called it, but they'd keep her just in case. I stayed anyway until Bev said, "Go home honey. I'm fine." I stayed a little longer, then gave her a kiss thinking I'd come back and get her in the morning.

At three a.m. the hospital called. I was still in my clothes. I grabbed my keys, opened the front door, and in front of me was fog so thick I could barely see my car in the driveway. By the time I got to the hospital, Jon was born. There he was asleep in a bassinet, wrapped in a blanket, so little and cute. The nurse put him in my arms. I was almost afraid to hold him, but I did. I had just become a father. I can hardly describe the feeling. Amazed and happy, for sure, but I was feeling something else. Looking down at his little face I felt instant, immediate love. Bev hardly knew I was there she was so knocked out. The hospital kept her for a week, that's how they did it in those days, and everyday after work I went to see her and practiced holding my little boy Jon.

## ~ West LA ~

I was partnered with Deputy Jerry Kiltz who'd been a marshal for four years and had gone through the academy with L'Arthur in 1968. My brother now worked as a bailiff for a municipal court judge downtown. He told me that he and his judge were "tight" and held up two fingers touching to make the point.

Kiltz was a good partner and like others in the department, always looking for a way to make additional money. He invited me to an opportunity meeting at his home to get in on the "ground floor" of an exciting new money-making venture. He invited other guys in the office, but I was the only one who seemed interested. Maybe they already knew what it was about.

A group of maybe fifteen people gathered in Kiltz's living room in Woodland Hills for the meeting. I was the only black guy. He introduced a speaker, one of the "diamond" achievers, who laid out the "opportunity" in a lengthy presentation. Stacked in a corner behind him were boxes of a product called Holiday Magic.

The program was multi-level marketing but would later be called a pyramid scheme and considered illegal. How it worked was, people would buy the product from someone, in this case Kiltz at the entry level, and then "motivate" others into buying. Each of them would rope in i.e. "motivate" as many people as possible to "buy in" and the ripple effect supposedly made money for everyone.

The buy-in was $135 for a starter kit of Holiday Magic products, but from the number of boxes in the living room, I was sure Kiltz had spent more than that as his "buy in." I'd already been to Sgt. Pattison's house for a meeting pushing a similar product called Bestline. It was the same type of program. Both reminded me of Amway, which I'd gotten lassoed into when I worked at Sears. I was no longer a salesman and it was hard enough to keep myself motivated. But to help Kiltz out, I bought into his "upline" with the understanding that it would begin and end with me. I admired his positive attitude and willingness to stick his neck out. He was going for that extra buck, something other deputies only talked about.

Kiltz and I partnered on the levy crew for several months. The job was repossessions, most often of cars. Most levies were done before dawn, waking people up, or in the case of no owner being present, taking the car and leaving a copy of the writ of execution. We picked up cars in West LA, Culver City, Hollywood, and Marina Del Rey. There were confrontations, not many, but once or twice the police had to be called. Even when the defendants were wrong, most of them got furious when deprived of their wheels.

One repo in particular started out as standard procedure. We located the vehicle, called the tow company who met us at the site, and had the car taken to the marshal's repo storage lot. We turned in the paperwork as usual but were later called into the commander's office. He told us to retrieve the car from the tow yard and return it to the owner. There had been a mistake he said. There should not have been a levy on the car. This was totally bogus. Kiltz knew it and so did I. We learned later that THE Marshal, whose name was Sperl, had put in a call to our commander who, as instructed, told us to return the car to the defendant who was a good friend of the Marshal. That was an order, so we did it.

We had done our job correctly but had inadvertently stepped on somebody's toes. The consequence was that Kiltz and I were taken off the levy crew. Being reassigned was fine with me, but the incident left a bad taste in my mouth.

I went back to my five to one morning shift serving papers until I was pulled from the field to work in court for Judge Johnson. Unlike L'Arthur, my judge and I did not become "tight." I didn't like working in court. The days dragged. Many of the cases were ridiculous. Attorneys were ill prepared. It was 8-5 with a lot of wasted time in between. I shared bailiff duties with another deputy named Mario. He was a Spaniard with a distinction he was proud of. He was from Basque country. Thank goodness for Mario, a real jokester. He made the hours of boring testimony we had to hear almost bearable. He'd whisper comments about some of the good-looking women who came through the court or crack me up with silly sayings like "he who hesitates, hesitates he who" which made absolutely no sense. That's why it was funny.

We alternated bringing the judge his coffee every morning and bringing him his check twice a month. All checks were delivered by courier twice a month on the tenth and the twenty-fifth. Walking down the hall on one of those paydays with the judge's check in my hand, I discreetly held it up to the light. What do you know? I could see numbers. Two-thousand and change. The judge made over $4000 a month, take home. Wow. If I could make that kind of money, I was thinking, I'd be on easy street.

I wanted to get back to serving papers in field and get out of Judge Johnson's court. I put in a transfer request for Long Beach but instead, I was assigned to the Compton office. I said good-bye to Mario, but Bev and I had dinner with him and his wife after I left West LA, and we stayed in touch.

# ~ Compton/Long Beach ~

The Compton office was closer to home than Long Beach, so when the Long Beach transfer didn't come through, I wasn't surprised. By this time, I'd worked Beverly Hills, West LA, Culver City briefly, and now Compton. I was making the rounds.

The office at 212 E. Acacia, less than seven miles from home, was both good and bad news. The good was obvious, only twelve minutes to get to work. The bad? What Compton was known for: gang problems, unemployment, poor housing and a high crime rate. Plus, the office itself was one of the oldest in the county, built in the 1920's.

Twelve deputies and five clerks ran the office, four judges and a commissioner presided over the court. Sgt. Greg Carter and Lt. Howard Trout were the commanding officers. My primary duty was once again serving papers, and once again I was reunited with my buddy Poltash. I hadn't seen him in over six months. We fell right back into the camaraderie we'd had at Beverly Hills, talking about skiing, stocks, cool cars, and now marriage. Since I last saw him, he'd gotten hitched.

One day we had papers to serve on a small business called WaxStax, makers of candles and unusual novelty items. The owners were two 24-year-old entrepreneur college grads from USC, Poltash's alma mater. Their parents financed the enterprise setting them up in a shop on 154th and Broadway that was the size of a two-car garage. I had served hundreds of papers by this time and had seen stony expressions on the faces of people who were happy to see me leave. Not these guys. They accepted the papers with a smile, and the nonchalance of people who knew someone else would handle the problem. They invited us to look around.

Their inventory besides candles was inexpensive art pieces, table décor, candelabras, wall knick knacks, and trendy "units" inspired by collectibles seen in their own homes and the homes of friends. Walk-in traffic was one third of their income, they told us. Most sales came from craft fairs, home shows, trade shows, anywhere they could rent a booth, display their wares, and take orders from other merchants.

They would showcase one item. "Very important," they said. "You have to have one hot item." As they handed us flyers for an upcoming show, I noticed two 1971 Porsche Targas, one black, one a metallic silver parked in the lot outside their back door. Both needed to be washed. "Yours?" I asked. They nodded yes.

Poltash and I exchanged glances. I don't know what he was thinking, but I was thinking how great to be in business making so much money you have no time to clean your $5000 Porsche.


Another deputy that I partnered with for a while, not by choice, was Jim Allen, a tall, hard-nosed gruff brother who was probably in his late thirties. He'd been a security guard before becoming a marshal and he liked working alone. That was fine with other deputies who didn't much care for him. He may not have liked working with me either, but we managed to get along.

Allen was from the south, called himself a cowboy, and he had a horse. He lived in one of the older sections of Carson and boarded his horse at the Circle D Ranch on

Artesia and Western for $60 a month.

I'd always wanted a horse. It was kind of a fleeting dream, not one I ever thought would come true. When you watch cowboy movies as a kid, having a horse seems like it would be fun, but you don't figure it'll ever really happen. Or maybe I did.

L'Arthur, Gary and I used to ride our bikes to a stable on El Segundo and Figueroa just to see the horses. And one summer with my cousin Albert, we got ourselves to Griffith Park and for $2 bucks, we got to ride for an hour.

I met Jim Allen at the Circle D several times and watched him ride his horse, Jamal. On one of those visits I spoke to a man who had his two-year-old Sorrel colt stabled there, a quarter-horse with papers, that he was looking to sell for $500. Allen went with me to see the horse with the owner. The horse was gentle, he looked strong, and Allen said it was a fair price. Even better, it was a price I could afford. The horse had been named Much Too Soon. I didn't think about it too long or I might have changed my mind. A day later, I bought Much Too Soon.

I changed his name to Yago after the Sangria I had recently enjoyed at a favorite Mexican restaurant. My first ride on him was bareback, and he didn't flinch when I climbed on. I bought a saddle and bridle, soon after, stabled him at the Circle D for $50 a month, and rode him often. Bev brought Jon to watch, and I hoisted Jon onto the saddle in front of me for a ride around the corral together. Every outing on the back of Yago I'd think about my dad. I knew he'd get a kick out of seeing what I'd gotten into since returning from Vietnam. He would have loved it all.

I was hardly settled in at Compton when the Long Beach transfer came through. Every office was different in various ways. Personnel, style, racial makeup, the office atmosphere. Being around money in beautiful Beverly Hills, even though the marshals weren't making the big bucks, the office environment was casual and stress-free. Eight white and four black deputies including me and Terry Black, who had gone through the academy with L'Arthur, worked well together, all of us handling our duties without any noticeable personality clashes. We were competent and confident, and everybody got along.

In Long Beach, the deputies were older. Most had been on well over ten years. The vibe was not unfriendly, but response to me was indifference when I reported for work. Out of twelve deputies, only one of them was black. That would be me. I was happy to continue serving papers in the field, alone, five in the morning to one in the afternoon. I didn't even mind the added shift on Thursday nights working traffic court, from 6-9 pm.

Judge John Carroll presided over traffic court. He was about 35, married with two young kids, and a ladies' man according to the rumors floating around. He took a liking to me, his bailiff and I soon learned the judge had a roving eye, which gave truth to some of those rumors. More than once, right in the middle of a hearing he would call to me from the bench.

"Uh Mr. Bailiff, please approach." I'd vault the two steps up from my place on his left.

"Yes, your honor?"

He'd whisper something like, "Do you think that woman in the green is good looking?" I wouldn't dare look around. I'd just nod in the affirmative and try to keep a straight face.

Over time, the judge invited me to the "after night

court watering hole" a restaurant a block from the court-house. Ten or twelve deputies, sheriffs or clerks would show up. Everyone knew Carroll. He made a big deal about introducing me. "This is my new bailiff Howard." He always wanted to buy me a drink, and in those days, I wasn't really a drinker. I'd order rum and coke and sip on it, and watch co-workers who were usually serious and unsmiling, drop their guards and get loose. Those were fun nights, a cool way to top off three hours of traffic court.

I struck up a conversation one day with one of the court clerks who was creating and designing toys. He did it primarily as a hobby, but he had sold a couple of his ideas to Schaper, a major toy company in the 70's. Don't Spill the Beans was one of his creations.

I'd had a few ideas of my own that I had been trying to create ever since working in the toy department at Sears. I had made six or seven models of games out of wood. They weren't state of the art models, but the ideas were sound. I made catalog sheets and explanations of the game/toy, and mailed them out with photos to Whammo, Mattel, and Schaper, but I didn't have much luck. I was an unknown. No one was interested enough to give me shot.

I kept all my designs. I knew I would eventually come up with something of my own that would sell.

I'd been in the office a few months when I was given a new deputy to train in the field serving papers. His name was Bob Tukua. He was quiet, observant, and newly married. He and Poltash happened to be friends. We got along well and had no problems during the training. In fact, the incident that stands out in memory had nothing to do with serving papers. We had finished for the day and were on our way back to the office when we passed three clerks in the hallway on their way to lunch. One of them had a big smile on her face. I didn't know them, and Bob walked by as if they weren't there. I asked if he knew them. He said, "The one in the middle was my wife."

I looked at him. "You didn't even stop to say hi to your wife?" He had no expression when he said, "I'll see her soon enough." Remembering that day and what he said still makes me laugh. Working with Poltash and Tukua was the beginning of a long friendship.

I hadn't given up the Porsche dream. Every weekend I'd check the want ads. Bev didn't really "get" my desire to have this car, but she knew I wanted it, and as it turned out, she was the one who found the ad in the paper that said: "1968 Porsche for Sale - LIKE NEW." The 19-year old owner, Charles Goodrum, had enlisted in the Army and had to sell the car before reporting for duty. Sounded familiar.

I drove to his house on a Sunday to see it and drive it. The ad didn't lie. I had looked at other Porsches, but this one really was like new. Nearly five years old, it had less than a thousand miles on it. The color was Baby S—T Brown. I gave him a $200 deposit, came home and got Bev. She strapped our boy Jon into his car seat and then drove me back to pay the seller the $1600 balance. Monday morning I eased onto the 405 freeway at 4:30 a.m. on my way to work in my new Porsche. The lanes were wide open, and no one except me was on the road. The speedometer's top speed was 160. I cranked it up to 100 and I was flying. I felt like a race car driver until I had to slow down for my offramp. I parked in the lot adjacent to the building, climbed out, and reappraised my new hot motor car. My Porsche. Another dream had come true.

I heard later that one of the female clerks on the third floor saw me get into the car at the end of the day. She was able to get the license plate and ran it through the DMV. The next day she asked around the marshal's office, "Who's Charles Goodrum, the deputy with the Porsche?"

I put an ad in the paper to sell the Chevelle. I'd make back more than half the cost of the Porsche if I got my price. Bev couldn't believe it. "You're selling the Chevelle? I thought you loved that car? How can you just get rid of it like that?"

True, I still loved my Chevelle. I'd risked my life to get it. I'd even raced it at Lions Racetrack and gotten it up to 100 mph. So, it wasn't an easy decision, but this was no time to be sentimental. I'd outgrown "the muscle car." I wanted something more upscale, a car I'd only use for special occasions, not drive to work every day. The Chevelle had already been stolen once and taken on a joyride. And the one time Bev drove it to her job at the Gas Company in Compton, some juvenile delinquent nearly stole it out of the parking lot. No. It was time for the Chevelle to go.

One inquiry resulted in a co-ed showing up with her father. They came ready to buy, and after a quick inspection and a spin around the block, they paid my $1400 asking price in cash and the co-ed drove away smiling. I had a lump in my throat seeing my Chevelle for the last time.

I never intended the Porsche to be my everyday car, so realizing I needed something to drive to work, Ramon suggested I call Ronald Kyles, a friend from the old neighborhood who was really into cars. Turned out, his wife's 1964 Ford Falcon had been parked for a year and he was ready to sell it. The paint was oxidized, and the rear fender had a dent. For sure I wouldn't have to worry about it being stolen. Ronald vouched for the engine, so I felt okay paying his price, $300. I drove it to work the day after I bought it. Tukua was still my partner. He named the Falcon, Old Blue.

## ~ One Hot Item ~

I was reassigned to the Marshal's office in Compton early in 1973, back with Poltash, Tukua, Sgt. Carter, and other deputies like Jay Zuanich, John Durkin, Jay Wright, Don Wilson, all important as co-workers during my marshal years and beyond those years, as friends.

I drove those streets every day, served twenty to forty papers in my eight-hour shift. It left time in the afternoon to go by the ranch and ride Yago. My schedule and duties in Compton were the same as in West LA and Long Beach. The elephant in the room was my new environment, Compton itself. The job and the place invited distracted thinking, and boy was I distracted. I knew there was something else out there I could be doing, something that would turn some dollars.

I thought about my toy inventions, all of them passed over, sitting in my garage collecting dust. I recalled the words in the book *Think and Grow Rich* that was included with the Holiday Magic kit I'd bought from Kiltz. I hadn't read many books, but that one had a real message, that if you can envision your goal, actually imagine your-self in the place you hope to be financially, and take that thought to bed at night, the sub-conscience will begin working on the idea that can help make those imaginings come true. Also I recalled what the WaxStax guys emphasized, that in any retail business it was important to have one hot item...*one hot item.*

While waiting for the light to change, I was still in my marshal's vehicle trying to figure out personalized license plates when something else got my attention. Stickers on car bumpers. Chevron-shaped decals with the word AFRO printed on them in red, black, and green, the national colors of Africa. It wasn't the first time I'd seen them. All over the hub city, not only on bumpers, but on windows and windshields. Black people were identifying, signifying and sporting their African pride with these little stickers.

A light came on in my head. Why have them only on cars? Why not create another way to show black pride? Why not create something people could *wear,* around their necks maybe, or better yet, on their *wrists,* like the POW and MIA bracelets so popular a few years earlier to raise awareness during the war.

Bingo! Why not make a *bracelet* with the word AFRO in red, black and green. It wouldn't be something sold at Tiffany's, but it would be something new, something different.

Very quickly, step by step, the how-to of this idea took shape in my head. I'd make the bracelet out of stainless steel. I had to find a company that worked with steel, polishing, sanding and shearing it. I found several who did individual processes, but not one who could do it all. I even went to Mexico in search of someone with the skill to do it, but except for the fresh tacos we ate walking along Tijuana's main drag, it was a wasted trip.

Back in LA, I found a small company practically in my own backyard. It was Mechanical Metal in Gardena, a family owned business that specialized in metal works. I met the father/owner, and his son Sol who was a few years older than me. Great people who'd been in business over twenty years. I explained what I wanted. No problem, they said. That was their business. They would sand, shear, burnish, and cut a bendable steel product, give it a shiny or satin finish, and cut it in three-quarter widths, and two lengths, one for men and one for women.

I designed a two-inch decal in my AFRO colors and found a company in the City of Industry that would make the decal out of mylar, a thin plastic, but stronger, and could be applied to the steel. Along with the AFRO decal, I had one made in red, white, and blue for USA, and one in red, green and white that said MEXICO. The influx of Latinos was already beginning to show in LA and Compton.

I created a smooth rounded mold out of wood, mounted it to my work bench in the garage, and used it to shape the sheared strips of steel into a cuff bracelet in two precise moves. From the time I began working with Sol, it took about six weeks before I had my first batch of 1000 bracelets ready to hit the streets. It was a process that ultimately required working with four different small companies to get the finished product.

Record stores, liquor stores, and head shops were my target markets. There were at least 50 head shops in Compton, small little hole-in-the-wall stores that sold Rasta and African clothing, Kinte cloth knock-offs, oils and incense, African artifacts, and drug paraphernalia. There were at least that many liquor stores on the streets of Compton, and the number of record shops was on the rise.

My 5 a.m. to 1 p.m. Marshal shift was perfect. I'd change out of my uniform after work, slip into civilian clothes, and for my first foray as a salesman, I set out in Old Blue with 200 bracelets and a receipt book in a cardboard steal box. A liquor store was my first stop. I was a little nervous, winging it, feeling my way, talking up the item with enthusiasm to the clerk behind the counter, but trying not to sound pushy or worse, desperate.

Some stores bought a dozen outright, while others took them on consignment. To those clerks, I'd give a free bracelet to wear. Free advertisement with the hope customers would notice and ask about it. This was a Catch 22 situation. Clerks were reluctant to buy something new because it wasn't popular, but how could it become popular if nobody saw it. Someone had to start the trend.

Another idea came to me. Every morning on my way to work at 4:30, I'd throw about a dozen bracelets onto the lawn of Compton High School. Kids would have to see them during gym class. It worked better than I imagined. Students found them, wore them and showed them to their friends. A record shop owner near the school bought two dozen and told me kids were coming in asking for them.

Sales took off.

I began hitting stores every day after work. In some shops the bracelets were hung on a string behind the counter. Some put them inside a glass display case. One store clerk suggested I needed a better display. A print shop in Carson helped me design a standup card, eight by twelve inches, in iridescent orange and yellow with slots to hold a dozen bracelets. A display card with a dozen bracelets cost the store $13, they sold them for $2, my cost was .25 per bracelet. Consignment cards were selling out. Calls for reorders were coming in almost faster than I could meet them. I stopped the consignments, went to Cash Only. My answering machine was full every few days with messages. "I need more Mexico." "I need two dozen." "When can you come by with more bracelets?"

I took the business to the outskirts of Compton, hired a high school neighbor kid to come after school and for $10 bucks he'd work in the garage for two hours shaping the bracelets on the mold. Bev affixed the labels.

For three hours a day, I was a one-man sales force, and sales were booming. I couldn't help smiling the first time I saw a man standing at the counter in the Marshal's office sporting an AFRO bracelet, unaware that he was standing across from the person who created it. It was a secret I didn't mind keeping, but it wasn't a secret very long. Deputy Durkin, AKA big John noticed a couple of bracelets on defendants in court, and even a judge noticed one from his perch on the bench. He called me over. "Isn't that one of your bracelets?" he said.

I had become good friends with Sol of Mechanical Metal, and briefly re-visited the Wax Stax guys. They told me of an upcoming three-day gift show at the LA Convention center. I told Sol, and we agreed to split the cost of renting a booth. He had two products to showcase, an aerodynamic ice cream scoop and a turtle ashtray with a shell that opened and closed. Bev came up with the name for our bracelets, Wrist-A-Craft, and designed a plaque to sit on the table in front of the display.

We managed our "Artisan Entrepreneur" booth

for eight hours. I took bracelet orders from several shop owners, hob-nobbed with other entrepreneurs, walked around like a potential buyer checking out items and even found the Wax Stax guys who had upped their game and were displaying even more items than I'd seen at their shop. The whole day was a great learning experience. By the time the show ended, I realized my "brand" needed more variety. Clerks at some of my shops had asked if I had zodiac bracelets. Astrological signs were hot. "What's your sign?" had become the new boy-girl opening line.

I immediately jumped onto that pony. I had labels made in silver and black for the twelve Zodiac signs, inscribing the symbols next to the words. Singer Al Green was hitting his stride on the rhythm and blues charts, so without a thought to possible copyright infringement, I had labels made with the title of one of his most popular songs, "Love and Happiness." I added new labels that said Ski, Peace, Homeboy, and Keep on Truckin, and all of them became winners. From those titles I had bumper and window stickers made. I added a necklace to my inventory made of large wooden beads in the Afro colors, strung on a soft piece of twine. I made dozens of them myself, each one slightly different, and they sold.

My goal was to make $200 a day and I usually hit that goal in three hours or less. I met other salesmen selling caps, stockings, headbands, scarves, paraphernalia, and various other items to the same stores. They began calling to add my items to their inventory.

I became a distributor. While it cut down on my legwork, and my profits slightly, it allowed more time for production which increased to about 2000 pieces per week.

I tried selling out of state. I networked the old-fashioned way by contacting the phone company. They would give free phonebooks, up to five per month to anyone who asked for them for any place in the country. I requested books for Atlanta, Chicago, Houston, and Oakland. I had a catalog sheet printed with pictures and the names, prices and quantity discounts of all my pieces. I mailed them out and waited. I contacted the main office of Thrifty Drug Store. They asked for a batch of 10,000 bracelets to be sent ASAP for a trial run, with payment to be made in 60 days. I had to draw the line. That was not doable.

The expansion efforts didn't explode like I'd hoped, but the investment did pay for itself. If I had been available to make the sales pitches in person, it might have gone better. But all was not lost. Wrist-A-Craft Sales were still good on the home front, enough that I could indulge myself once again.

## ~ Whose Bentley? ~

Bracelet money wasn't what I'd call disposable, but it was over and above marshal money which was "house money" to cover personal obligations, and entertainment. In a way, bracelet money was "fun" money, similar to what L'Arthur and I got when we went to the docks with dad, although that money was free. I was hustling with Wrist-A-Craft, so the return was hardly free, but it was from my own efforts. I had created it, I enjoyed being in the field selling my "wares" motivating myself. It was fun, and it didn't seem like work. Made me think of times when I was a kid on 84th, scuffling, and there were things I wanted but couldn't have. I became that kid again, and there were a lot of things l wanted. Now l was able to purchase some of those "toys."

l had the Porsche, l had my horse, and l hadn't forgotten the sight of those beautiful cars passing by the office on Burton Way. Every Sunday l'd check the auto section of the classified ads in the newspaper, just in case something of interest caught my eye.

l saw the ad for the 1960 Bentley and circled it, then continued looking at the rest of the ads. Nothing came close. A 1960 Bentley Silver Cloud 2 was on its way to becoming a classic. l drove to 39th and Arlington to check it out. The car was parked at the end of a driveway, and the car was beautiful.

The seller and l stood there admiring the creamy silver exterior, the plush red leather seats, the right-side drive. Behind the front seats were fold-down trays for the back-seat passengers, just like the trays in an airplane except these were mahogany, as was the dash and side door panels. He offered me a test drive. l told him right-side driving was all new to me. "Just keep your eyes to the right," he said. "Don't worry about the left, you'll be fine." Easier said than done, but l got the hang of it after a couple of blocks. The ride was like floating on a cloud, and l loved it. The seller wanted a quick sale. He was asking $7000 but he accepted my offer of $6000. l paid him with bracelet money.

l still had Old Blue, my work car keeping me honest. Plus, a Porsche in the garage, and now a Bentley right alongside it. That caused a stir in the neighborhood. My neighbor across the street eyed it from his driveway and came over to get a closer look.

l drove the Bentley to the Beverly Hills office and

Sgt. Pattison came out of the office to see it. "You said you were going to get one, and you really did," he said. On my drive home through the streets of Beverly Hills a driver in a similar car waved at me and signaled for me to pull over. It was the actor who played Artemis Gordon on the tv show *Wild Wild West*. I recognized him immediately but couldn't think of his name. He asked if I was an actor. I decided against trying to BS a real actor. I said no, and for a few minutes we just talked about cars. As he drove away, I remembered his name. Ross Martin.

The day I drove it to work to show Jay and Don, Judge Schaefer parked his Rolls Royce next to the Bentley. He was the presiding superior court judge in Compton, and he drove his Rolls to work every day. He came into the marshal's office pointing his thumb back at the parking lot. "Who's driving the Bentley?" he said.

## ~ Moving Again ~

By 1975 nearly four years after moving in, our Carson neighborhood had changed. The house across the street from us was burglarized in the middle of the day while our neighbors were at work. A body was found in a nearby vacant lot and was described as a possible gang-related murder. Other incidents of local crimes began making the news.

What had begun as a racially diverse neighborhood of Blacks, Caucasians, and Filipinos who'd had to qualify for a loan and make a 10% down payment, had become a predominantly black neighborhood whose new residents had moved in with no money down, as requirements for becoming a homeowner had changed.

It bothered me that I recognized some of the new faces in the area because I had evicted them from their homes in Compton for non-payment of rent. Compton was in close proximity to Carson, only about six miles away, something I hadn't considered before we bought the house. Another troubling sign of the increase in crime was the building of a new sheriff's station at 213th and Avalon. This may have been good news for residents, but it was bad news to me. I did not want to be living around people I might end up seeing in the lockup. The writing was on the wall. I wasn't happy about it, but I didn't bite my tongue. I told Bev it was time for us to move.

She didn't like what she was seeing and hearing in the neighborhood, but she didn't want to leave. We had poured our hearts into this house, she said. How could I so easily want to leave it? Pragmatism was needed here, not emotion. I went into "gotta convince her" mode. Gradually she began to reconsider.

We house-hunted for months and finally made an offer on one in Altadena. But there was a contingency. We had to sell Belshaw in seven days or our offer was off the table. Bev's stand against moving had changed slightly, but she wasn't quite sure that the Altadena house was "the one." For her, the contingency provided a ray of hope. Sell Belshaw in seven days? No way.

Not only was there a way, it wasn't even difficult. Belshaw sold in four days at our asking price, $36,000. We couldn't believe it. Bev's brief stint selling real estate provided enough expertise that she worked directly with the escrow company, handled much of the paperwork without a realtor, and closed escrow in 30 days. We saved the commission and cleared just over $8000.

I had been so busy with Wrist-A-Craft, that I had neglected Yago. The move would make it more difficult to keep my horse. Sol, my Mechanical Metal partner had ridden him and brought his teenage daughter who loved horses. Sol offered to buy Yago, but I didn't want Sol's money. I knew he and his daughter would take good care of Yago, so after having Yago for about three years, I gave my horse to Sol for him and his daughter to enjoy.

Bev was still sad about leaving Belshaw, but the packing had begun. Days before the move, with boxes cluttering the family room, I came out of the house at 4:30 a.m. to go to work. I usually parked Old Blue on the street, and Bev parked her VW in the driveway. But the driveway was empty. I looked up and down the street in disbelief, just an automatic response, but the VW was gone. Her Bug had been stolen right out of our driveway. I came back inside and called the police. Bev heard me talking on the phone and went outside to look. She came back inside, crying and angry. That was the last straw. It was time to move.

Her car was found later, stripped. A total loss. On our way home from the insurance office after depositing the insurance settlement draft, we couldn't believe our eyes. Parked on someone's front lawn with a FOR SALE sign on it, was a red 1971 VW Bug. No kidding! The mileage was low, there were no dents, the ride was like Bev's bug, and it was the right price. Such a lucky break. So, we bought it.

# ~ Skywood 1975 ~

Bev and I were on our own on the Sunday we found our new house, without our exuberant Italian realtor Franco, whose idea of "beeeutifole prrrroperties" in Altadena did not always agree with ours. We had come to Altadena in the first place on the suggestion of a friend, Greg Vital, who knew that Altadena was beautiful and had horse properties, but didn't know I no longer had Yago.

We really knew nothing about Altadena. Specifically, we were unaware that there was an east and west Altadena and that in "west" Altadena, in the areas that Franco showed us, the houses were older, and most residents were black, compared to "east" Altadena where the homes we saw looked nicer and its residents were predominantly white. That Sunday, unaware that we had ventured into "east" Altadena, we were like explorers following open house signs when we came across the sign on Skywood Circle.

We had already looky-looed at seven homes, most in the fifty to seventy thousand price range. My favorite of those cost $69,000 and had a tennis court. I thought it was doable, but Bev got a headache just guesstimating the payment. Skywood Circle was a cul-de-sac with five houses. The house for sale was a Spanish style and the only single-story home. Bev saw the words "Plus Guest-house" on the sign, and thinking this was way out of our budget, she shook her head. She was ready to go home.

I forged ahead pulling her by the hand. Once inside, it took about two minutes and I was sold. Well, maybe five minutes. It was the back yard that did it. In full view from the living room window was a huge yard, a giant oak tree and wall to wall greenery. The yard was on two levels, with a mountain view from the top, and the lower level was like a park, big enough for a pool. There were dry ponds just waiting for a water fall, shrubs and trees and gardens that needed some TLC, and I was anxious to give it to them. And then there was that guest house, a full separate unit like a bachelor pad. The main house had authentic historic amenities, said the realtor, like the Spanish tile around the fireplace, built-in bookshelves, the hard-wood floor, and the pantry.

They were asking $52,000. We offered $49,000, and they accepted it without making a counteroffer. I kicked myself for not offering less. Of course, Bev went into panic mode as she did on every major purchase, and some that weren't major. After we'd met the contingency by selling Belshaw so quickly, she spent the entire escrow period anxious. She would tell me later, that she was hoping the Skywood sale would fall through. But it didn't. In June 1975, we left Carson and moved to our new home in Altadena.

I told my liquor store buyers that I wouldn't be around as much with my merchandise and referred them to the independent vendors. One owner I'd become friendly with, who really took care of his three liquor store locations was Virgil Grant, a brother who had quit his high school teaching job to become his own boss. I told him I wouldn't be seeing him as often because I was moving to Altadena. He asked what street. When I told him he said, "Man, you're just a few blocks away from me. We're going to be neighbors." He too lived in "east" Altadena.

# ~ LANCE ~

Part of my job as a marshal was evicting people from their homes, sometimes whole families. I'd gone into homes and seen single mothers on welfare living in squalor with more kids than they could handle. I saw foster parents with too many children, abusing the system that was paying them to care for abandoned kids who were not their own. I saw kids sleeping on the floor in their day clothes in filthy homes, with no food or father in the house, and I was having to do the job of moving them out. I knew I couldn't help them all, but maybe I could help one.

Bev and I talked it over, had many discussions, and finally decided we would adopt a child. The more we talked about it, the more we wanted to do it, and it felt like a good thing to do. The subject came up while talking with a co-worker who told me he was adopted, and to quote him, "I turned out okay." Bev learned that her supervisor had two adopted children, and he suggested we go to the Children's Home Society. After a background check, we waited five months before receiving the name and photograph of a boy eleven months old with dark brown hair and big brown eyes who was in his third foster home.

Three months later, we were invited to an agency in northern California to meet him. Bev, Jon and I waited in a room for the case worker. There were toys on a table. The door opened, she walked in with a little boy, and walked him to the table as she introduced us. He played with the toys first then he looked at us. Bev reached out to him and he came to her with no hesitation. That's how we met our boy Lance for the first time. Each of us hugged him and held him and told him he was going to come live with us and be our little boy. He wasn't shy. He didn't resist us at all and there were no tears. He was smiling and happy. We brought him home to Altadena, and we never looked back. The adoption was finalized six months later. Jon now had a little brother, we were a family of four, and when my sister-in-law Vicky saw Lance for the first time, she said finally someone in the family looked like her.

## ~Max Burgers ~

By the end of 1975, Wrist-A-Craft was doing mostly repeat business and had saturated its immediate demographic. I realized the success of an artisan-based business relied heavily on creating another "hot new item" which I had done. The stickers and necklaces sold well, but not as well as my number one item, the bracelets. Something else had dawned on me by then: having a product to sell was good, but providing a service was better. I didn't immediately consider food as the service I wanted to provide, but an opportunity fell in my lap.

Max Burgers at Hoover and Florence made a good burger. The liquor store next door was one of my best bracelet customers. I'd gotten to know the Salvadoran lady, Elicia, who managed the stand and I had given her a bracelet of her zodiac sign. One day she asked if I'd like to buy the stand. "You could run this business. My boss hasn't paid his rent in three months. I would work for you."

My first reaction was, are you kidding? She explained the operation, the hours, the cost of supplies, and she knew the bottom line—the profit—after showing me her sales records.

Delving into the food business had not occurred to me, not even in my dreams. I was still a marshal. I was still manufacturing and selling Wrist-A-Craft. The prospect of a third "job" seemed loaded with potential, both good and bad.

The landlord wanted only his back rent and Elicia's boss just wanted out. I paid the back rent, signed a month to month, and I was in the burger business. Seriously, that's how simple it was.

My schedule became this: Five in the morning to one in the afternoon, I was a marshal. Midday I sold bracelets and filled orders, stopped by Max's to see how Elicia and her helper were doing before going downtown for produce, and on weekends, I was making burgers and fries, and a little profit too.

My father-in-law came by one day. I made him a burger and between bites he shook his head smiling. "Howie, you have got more stuff goin' on. Never known anybody with so many irons in the fire."

Days at the stand were slow but picked up at lunch time. Nights were different, and weekends especially were very busy. With the increase in sales came the increase in locos who liked to hang out and had to be asked to vacate. Along with making burgers, I was charged with that as well. My buddy Ramon came to work for me at the stand and took over some of the weekend shifts for a while. The months rolled by.

Working an eviction months after taking over Max's, my partner Jay Zuanich, and I were with a landlord who insisted on entering his rental to inspect the premises though he didn't have a key and hadn't called a locksmith.

The tenant was out.

"You want us to kick it in?" we asked. He said, "Yeah. It's my house. Kick it in." Jay gave it a kick, but it didn't open. "Let me give it a try," I said. I moved in front of Jay, and kicked it, my leg fully extended. The door swung wide, but at the same time, something snapped in my back.

By the end of the shift, the minor jostling in the car was sending spasms down my lower back. I ended up at Dominguez Valley hospital with a severe back sprain. I was given a six-week injury leave of absence, put on a schedule of ultra sound treatments, therapy three times a week, and a support belt.

Therapy really helped and being off from the marshal's office was great. On therapy days, I'd sell bracelets and work the stand. I still made trips downtown for produce, and I was able to lift the crates and load up Old Blue without much discomfort, but I was doing it looking over my shoulder. I was on paid injury leave. Workers Compensation would not look kindly on someone with a back injury tossing crates of produce.

I began feeling guilty, and a little paranoid. When the six weeks were up, I went back to work feeling better, and by then, I had decided to let the burger stand go. I'd hung in with it for about a year. Elicia's niece had been working the stand after her aunt returned to El Salvador. I knew I'd be able to sell my interest if the right buyer came along.

My ad in the paper got a quick response from a young Asian anxious to get into business. I sold him the "right to do business plus Good Will." From the experience I netted $10,000 and a year's worth of wisdom in the burger business. I was primed to get into something else.

# ~ The Six Year Itch ~

Nearing the end of 1976, Bev and I had been married seven years. We were pretty much settled in at Skywood Circle and our boys, Jon and Lance were active and fun, and getting along well. Bev was working at California Thrift in Covina after the company moved from their office on Wilshire Blvd., and after six years as a marshal, still working out of the Compton office, my feeling about the job was: *is this it? Will I be doing this for the next 25 years?*

My brother and I both were chomping at the bit to get into something else, but I just didn't know what. L'Arthur was leaning toward a liquor store and wanted me to go in with him. He hadn't made a move yet because we had also considered buying a McDonald's franchise which cost about $25,000. We got the bright idea that maybe we could talk Flora Bell into taking out a loan on her house. It was free and clear and worth about $100,000. We would repay her with interest and avoid a big debt going in.

She wasn't going for it. "Your daddy would turn over in his grave if I lost this house on your McDonald's pipe dream." We backed off immediately. We weren't surprised she said no. The last thing we wanted was Muhtha worrying about losing her house. Besides, my heart wasn't into running a McDonald's. More burgers?

Time passed. L'Arthur found his store, Danny's Liquor on Santa Monica Blvd. at La Cienega. It had been on the market for several months. He bought the store, leased the land, and quietly resigned from the Marshal's Department after nine years. He had wanted me to go in with him on the liquor store, but I didn't know how that would work. We both had families and kids. Would one store sustain us? I didn't like the idea of having to open and close, work the late hours, especially on weekends in an area like Hollywood, where nights would be the busiest hours of the day. He went for it alone and was happy about his decision. I was happy for him.

How is it that sometimes when you're looking for something, even when you're not sure what it is, it somehow finds you. I had begun noticing self-service car washes. They had always been there in Compton, LA and even Pasadena, but now I was suddenly seeing them. I passed a couple nearly everyday while serving papers, and somebody was always washing their car. Mornings, midday, late afternoons, people were in there washing. What I didn't see was an owner or manager. The washes were open 24 hours, seven days a week. I'd drive by hoping to see someone working, or see the equipment room door open, but the doors were always closed.

When Bev and I lived in the apartment on 6th Avenue, there was a coin-op car wash down the block near Pico Blvd. Every Saturday morning I'd take the cars, first Bev's then mine to that little car wash. It cost a quarter to wash and a dime to vacuum. I never saw anyone working then either, but almost always someone was washing.

I had finished my shift and was leaving for the day when Lt. Trout called me into his office. The lieutenant wasn't a bad guy, but the less the "brass" had to say to me, the better I liked it. He was in his chair holding my most recent performance report completed by Sgt. Carter, who always had my back.

"Outstanding evaluation" Trout said, "no negative remarks. Why haven't you put in an application to take the sergeant's exam? Every qualified deputy has aready applied. Why not you Higginson?"

I didn't want to tell him the whole truth, that Poltash and I had recently overheard two deputies in the locker room talking about going to the home of a certain superior officer to see a copy of the test before taking the exam. Something was rotten there. It seemed to me that the deck was slightly stacked before I'd gotten into the game. I had decided I didn't want to be in the game. I told him what had been on my mind for a while.

I said, "If I get an increase in salary here, it'll be harder for me to walk away from this job. And I don't want to be doing this for the next thirty years. I don't want my most productive years to be spent as a marshal. I don't want to lose the desire I'm feeling right now to do something more with my life."

What I was thinking was, I didn't want the regimentation of an eight to five job. What I envisioned for myself was going for runs in the morning, going out to breakfast, working out, being home with my family during the week, not just on weekends, making my own schedule, being my own boss, having more freedom. I wanted it sooner rather than later, without the politics I'd seen going on in this very office. That was my dream. It might not come about as easily as I envisioned it, but I'd be making my own decisions, and that's what I wanted.

One final thought came out of my mouth. "I want to make what *THE* Marshal makes," I said. I didn't know exactly what that was, but it had to be about $125,000 a year. I was smiling when I said it and the lieutenant smiled too. He thought I was joking. I was dead serious.

## ~ Hub City Wash ~

I had a first-time paper to serve at a liquor store on Holly Street. On the same lot with the store was a gas station that had been converted to a three-stall car wash. A man on a ladder was in one of the wash stalls working at something in the ceiling. I was known to start conversations with strangers, so I walked over to him and asked if he was the owner. He said he was the maintenance man and that he was removing the equipment for the out-of-state owner who was closing the wash down. Above the three stalls was the name Hurricane Car Wash.

There it was again. Opportunity staring me in the face. I looked around at the equipment that had not been removed and asked him to see the equipment room. I looked at the money slots in the bays and the old vacuums. The guy was agreeable. He let me look. Finally, I asked him for the owner's phone number and he gave it to me.

Over the phone the owner ran everything down to me. The car wash and liquor store were both his. The rent was $250 a month total, split between the store and the wash. The car wash equipment including the motors, pumps, booms, and money slides was old, but intact and functional. He wanted $1600 for it. I agreed. I would need to get a business license and have the electricity and water put in my name. When he returned to Los Angeles a few days later, we met at the car wash and finalized the deal.

After he'd gone, I sat in my car with the engine

running. I needed a little time to think about what I had just done. It was a leap, the start of my life in the car wash business.

It's funny how memories come back to you. I had all but forgotten that when I was about nine, my dad dreamed of having a place of his own where he could wash cars. He called it a "wash rack." He'd gotten the idea from a man named Johnny Washington who owned and operated a two-pump 76 gas station at 74th and Avalon. It was the fifties and rare for a black man to own a business, especially one that was legitimate. Dad bought his gas there. It was always a couple of pennies below the competition. He was proud to patronize a Negro-owned business. To the back of the station were two stalls, a sink and a faucet. Dad made a deal with Johnny Washington to rent that space on weekends to wash cars. L'Arthur and I were his "employees." It didn't last long but for a few months in the summer I was nine, we washed cars at Dad's wash rack.

There weren't many hoops to jump through to reopen the three-bay wash. Mostly legwork, making appointments, and waiting for service people. The existing water line was approved and reconnected through Compton's independent water department, and electricity was changed over into my name. Both utilities required deposits.

I signed the rental agreement, a month to month, and put a coat of paint on the old equipment. With my business license tacked to the wall of the 10x10 equipment room, and with a hand-painted "Open for Business" sign propped on the sidewalk, Hurricane Car Wash reopened. My entrance into car washing began, right there on Compton Blvd. and Holly in the hub city of Compton.

My first day's collection was memorable, not only

because of how much "jingle" I brought home in a jumbo-sized coffee can, but for the shear energy, excitement and thrill of stepping into what felt like new territory. Becoming a business person on a bigger scale than my bracelets or the hamburger stand. I was building a source of income apart from my regular job. Hearing the clink of those quarters was like the first time I gambled. I didn't know what the outcome would be, but my heart was so filled with hope and confidence, there was no room to feel that I might lose.

But there was another reason to remember that day. I brought the coffee can into the bedroom and spread a towel on the floor. Bev was as excited as I was. As I dumped the coins onto the towel, her smile disappeared. She knelt down and looked more closely at the coins. Some of the quarters weren't quarters. They were quarter imposters. Pieces of dull gray steel the exact size of a quarter that fit perfectly into the meter slots in the wash bays. How had I not noticed that? Bev picked a couple out of the pile. "This isn't even steel," she said. "It's linoleum!" They were slugs. But not the kind that eat flowers. They ate profits. This was a problem I had not anticipated.

Every day after leaving the Marshal's office, I went straight to the car wash. Business picked up day by day. I breathed a sigh of relief that after about two weeks, no more slugs turned up in the collection. I was hoping that since the business had reopened that people would see it was a going concern and maybe the culprits feared getting caught and decided to change their ways. But I didn't worry about that. Each day that I drove by in my marshal's unit, my pulse quickened a little seeing someone in the stall washing. As the business increased, my thoughts moved on to the next thing.

## ~ Vermont ~

Before stumbling onto the three-bay in Compton, I had been on the lookout for a vacant lot where I could build my own car wash. My vision was focused, my intentions undeterred. I was going to be in the car wash business for the long haul.

The lot at El Segundo and Vermont, a busy intersection on the border of Los Angeles and Gardena, had been vacant for six months and had a For Rent sign on it. I don't know how I'd missed seeing it for so long, but suddenly there it was.

An agent answered my call. I was told that the lot was owned by a West LA widow named Kendall who was not interested in selling but would consider a lease.

At the time, my building and design plans were all in my head. I didn't know anything about constructing a car wash, but I knew what I wanted. Six stalls of slab brick on asphalt, and if constructed on this piece of property, I wanted it to face Vermont.

I contacted two people, Jimmy Bell, owner of Bell Manufacturing, a builder and supplier of car wash equipment, and a second builder/architect named Palmer. Both could supply the equipment I needed but cost was a factor. I compared prices. Palmers were less. Based solely on that, I went with him. I hired him to draw my plans, submit them and pull the required permits.

Basic equipment for a six-bay wash included six of each: motors, pumps, booms, vacuums, wands, meters, and three holding tanks for the chemicals. The equipment cost alone was $20,000. It was either a refinance of the house or a second mortgage that got me $75,000 for construction costs. The equipment loan was separate and obtained through Bank of America. My head was spinning, but I forged ahead.

I mailed copies of the plans and my personal information to the widow's agent. He reported that she was impressed by my "entrepreneurial spirit." Her agent and I began discussing the terms of a lease. I suggested keeping the rental at $250, the same as the previous tenant, a gas station, and that I wanted a ten-year lease, and six months to build. They countered with a graduated lease for fifteen years starting at $300 per month, with a $50 increase every five years, and they agreed to the building time. I had nothing to compare with their offer, and no consultant, attorney or agent to guide me. I had to go with my gut feeling. I thought it was a good deal, and fifteen years seemed so far in the future. We signed the lease. The entire process was done through her agent, over the phone and through the mail. I wouldn't meet the widow Kendall until 1993.

I was on record with the building department as owner/builder. Palmer recommended a builder named Rodney. I would work with him on the construction.

We broke ground after Christmas, 1977. Rodney was a good builder, but not reliable. He was often late, and his crew wasn't very motivated unless he was there. I was still handling my marshal's duties and checking and collecting Compton. At Vermont we were making headway. Concrete was laid for the bays, the slab walls were up and by the end of February, work on the roof had begun. And then it started to rain. March was wet every day it seemed, and if it wasn't raining, there was too much moisture to lay concrete. It was a major delay, and discouraging, but hey, all I could do was keep on keeping on, and take care of matters that I could control. After all, it wasn't going to rain forever.

In April, I'd gotten personally involved with the building by mixing mortar, laying brick, even pouring some of the asphalt. I could honestly say I'd built the business from the ground up. Everything was done by the end of May including six industrial vacuums mounted on concrete stands. At a point where I could see that the end was near, I mixed a small amount of concrete and made a plaque on the ground just outside my equipment room door. In the wet concrete, I scratched in my initials, the names of my boys, and the date, June 1978.

We opened on a Saturday with streamers flying, and a banner over the equipment room door, that said "Howard's 50cent Quickie." Fifty cents to wash, a quarter to vacuum. At the time, that was the going rate. Cars began coming in, more than I expected. By mid-day it hadn't slowed down. The bays stayed full. Suddenly, I wasn't just the happy new owner overseeing the first day's business. I was a traffic cop directing cars in and out, a teacher, moving from stall to stall demonstrating the equipment, and a human change machine, turning singles and fives into quarters.

I stayed all day that first Saturday, waving people in, moving between the bays, helping female customers, observing the flow, making mental notes about necessary changes. Day one was hectic but exhilarating. I could feel it in my bones. This was going to work.

In November, to celebrate five-years with her company, Bev's boss Lou invited us to have dinner at Lawry's on La Cienega with him and his wife. By then, six months after opening, Vermont's monthly average was $2400, more than three times Bev's salary. She still liked her job after five years, but resigning was on her mind in order to do what she really wanted to do. Stay home and take care of the boys. She planned to tell Lou after Christmas.

We hadn't been to Lawry's since 1968, after we'd gotten engaged. On that night, ten years ago, I had dressed up in a suit and tie to take my fiancée to a classy restaurant. The dinner was great. Prime rib, baked potato, the creamiest corn I'd ever eaten, and Yorkshire pudding, whatever that was. What the heck. I ate it. We had ordered dessert, something chocolaty with two spoons. So romantic. Nothing would spoil this evening. Until the check came. The numbers were jumping out at me, like my heart. Uh oh. Seventy-eight dollars was the total, and that didn't include the tip. I knew exactly what was in my wallet. Not enough. Bev looked at my face and knew something was wrong.

"I'm short," I said. She started laughing. "What if we have to do the dishes?" she whispered. This was no joke. She opened her purse and pulled out a few dollars and loose change to go with my seventy-five. It was just enough to cover the tab. We left it on the table and headed for the door, holding our breath.

That's what we were laughing about the night we were on our way in the Porsche to meet her boss. We were stopped at a red light on Melrose when a string of motorcycles roared by going the opposite direction, and then BAM! We were rear-ended. On impact the Porsche was jammed into the car in front of us. Bev was thrown forward. When she pulled herself up to sitting again, blood was running down the side of her nose from a gash above her eye.

The Porsche was crumpled front and rear, but I was able to drive it. The police came. The senior citizen who had hit us was apoplectic when he saw Bev bleeding. He blamed the motorcycle gang for distracting him.

We drove to Kaiser Sunset, and after two hours in the emergency room, and a third call to Lou, who by that time was on his third martini, we walked through the door of Lawry's holding hands. I didn't think Bev would want to go, but there we were. Her boss was two sheets to the wind by then, but he was so happy to see us, he gave us both a bear hug. Bev wasn't in pain, but she had six stiches in her forehead, a hunk of gauze above her nose, and the beginnings of a black eye. Aside from a stiff neck, I was fine. Lou insisted Bev stay home from work for a couple of days, and she assured him she would. I stopped thinking about my smashed car when dinner arrived. I finally let go of Bev's hand which I was still holding under the table. I realized I was hungry. I dug into my prime rib and didn't give a thought to the check. The next morning I felt real pain when I looked at my smashed Porsche in the light of day.

In December, fully recovered, Bev gave her 30-day notice. Her co-workers gave her a party on her last day in January, and Lou promised that if she got bored, she could always return.

Repairs to the Porsche with the addition of a tail fin were paid by the insurance company of the man who'd hit us. We didn't get anything extra out of the settlement.

That was a sign of the times. Our fender bender with an injury didn't immediately prompt a call to an attorney. We healed, and the Porsche again looked like new.

*My buddies at Vandenburg, l-r, Elam, me, Johnson and Goodridge,*
*before I left for Vietnam. Elam went to Thailand, Goodridge to the*
*Philippines. The three of us are still in touch.*
*Johnson passed away some years ago.*

*L'Arthur and Lynn on their wedding day, 1966, with Dad, Muhtha,*
*Gwen and Lizzie. I was at Vandenburg unable to get a pass.*

*Vietnam, Da Nang Air Base with Watson. I'm wearing the helmet.*
*Sleeping barracks are on the right, re-fortified barracks on the left.*

*Da Nang Air Base, another outpost, a distance from the barracks*

*Security Policeman Higginson with partner Airman Finney
in glasses, DaNang*

*Da Nang Air Base, long shot of where the people lived*

*Good morning Vietnam!*

*Working the arms room; behind me are M-16s*

*At George AFB, Victorville, CA*
*young airman getting a commendation*

1968 Chevelle

*With my SS 396, home at last. I raced my car at Lions Drag*
*racing track and punched it up to 100 mph.*
*Over the loudspeaker the announcement was:*
*"Another crowd pleasing run by the black Chevelle."*

*Bev and her mom Etta, a youthful 48*
*(soon to be my Mom-in-law) parked at Bev's*

*Our wedding photo, Aug 30th, 1969. Next to the bride, her sister*
*Vicky, Sheila, Bettye, sister Sherry, Lizzie, Barbara; Next to groom,*
*L'Arthur, Gerald, Alvin, Ramon, Gary, Errol*

*Wedding day - Bev's parents, Duke and Etta, left,
Flora and Arthur on the right*

*Visiting the vacant lot in Carson
where our first home would be built.*

*The completed house, 20239 Belshaw Ave, June 1971;*
*Bev's VW in the driveway*

*Academy Graduation Day, Muhtha on the left, mom-in-law on the*
*right, the day I became a deputy marshal, officially*

*Wrist A Craft display card with bracelets, my "one hot item"*

*Jon and Lance, my boys, happy together*

*The boys again, after a ride in the Thing, Skywood Circle*

*On our way to church – Lance's first Communion*

*The Bentley, purchased with Wrist A Craft funds.*

*The Jaguar in the driveway at Skywood,*
*1958 Mark 8, right-hand drive*

*My 1968 Porsche, my pride and joy that I still have today.*

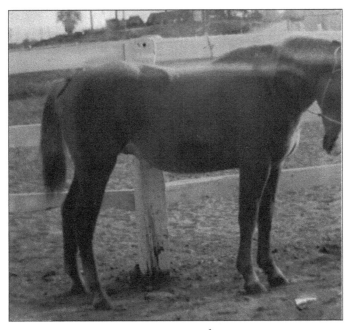

*Yago, my quarter horse*

*Early counting days on the bedroom floor with Jon.*
*1979*

*Long shot of Manchester Car Wash, midday*

*Working with my Doberman, Jaime*

*With Jon at the Manchester location, and Bev on the right, 1993*

*New sign at San Pedro location, 1998*

*My location at El Segundo and Vermont, after converting one stall into a takeout stand, Howard's Car Wash/4 Amigos*

*Jon and Lance, Jon's graduation from middle school*

*In Gorman, CA with our ATV's, Lance, Jon & I. Bev took this photo.
I bought 3 Honda ATV's for Bev and the boys, I got a Suzuki,
and had a trailer made. What fun.*

*Going through Needles, CA, with a stop at Mickey D's*

*We drydocked this Bayliner at Skywood for a brief time,
then at the cabin in Crestline, and finally at a drydock in Hesperia
not far from Silverwood Lake.*

*"Nice guy" head shot from my "acting" days.*

*This was my "tough guy" head shot, 1990*

*~ with Beverly Higginson ~*

On the SS Azure Seas, our first cruise (Bev took the photo)

The cabin at Crestline at Christmas, before the snow

*Maui, 1993, our 24th Anniversary*

*Catch of a 220 lb Blue Marlin in Cabo, 1999. I tousled with it for an hour. I couldn't straighten my arms for 6 hours!*

*The marlin's release*

*On the set of Devil in a Blue Dress*

*At the Dodger game with Lizzie and Julious*

*Bearded L'Arthur & family at eldest son Jeffrey's HS graduation
with Muhtha, left, sons Jason and Chris behind Jeff,
wife Lynn next to L'Arthur, daughter Sara in front*

*~ with Beverly Higginson ~*

*Bev and I with Kris & Jon, 2003*

*The Prowler the day it was delivered to Arbolada*

*Bev & I with Gary and wife Joan, having a Margarita,*
*still friends after 60 years*

*Bev & I leaving Lizzie's in the Nissan 300ZX. I designed*
*the side graphics on this red car to make it one of a kind,*
*and personalized the license to Znique.*
*I've had the Nissan now for 27 years!*

*Lance & daughter Lauryn, Jon & Kris and sons
l-r, Jordan, Jayden, JoVan*

*Lance and daughter Lauryn, around 2006*

*The family, l-r: JoVan, Jay, Bev, Lance (top) Jordan, Lauryn,
Howard, Kris, Jon*

*The grandkids in their cowboy/cowgirl outfits.
I searched high and low for those boots.*

*Bev and I with the grandkids, Christmas 2016*

*40th Anniversary Party, August 30, 2009*

*With Jon & Lance at our 40th Anniversary party*

*Celebrating MLK Day @ Pinks with Jon & the boys*

*Proud dad Lance with Lauryn, now a Sophomore, UCSD*

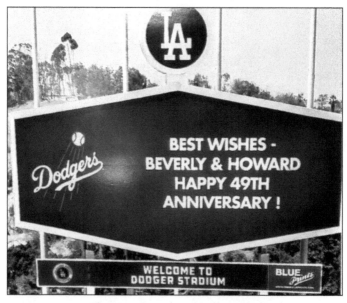

*Aug 2018   The Fan Board at Dodger Stadium for our*
*49th Anniversary*

*Aerobics Classmates at Ballys, when I was still agile, 2010*

# PART THREE

## 1979 - Present

## Down to Business

# ~ Switching Gears ~

March of 1979, two months after Bev resigned from her job, I pulled the plug on mine. No one was happy about my decision. Muhtha especially couldn't understand why I would want to quit such a good job, and even though Bev and I had talked about me leaving the department, she had a few shaky moments too, especially since it was the tail end of winter, rainy season, and maybe not the best time of the year for such a move.

March 31st was my last day, three weeks after my 32nd birthday. My retirement plus sick pay and vacation amounted to $15,000 which I was able to take with me. I got handshakes from some deputies who said in essence, 'gutsy move' and slow-shaking heads from others who were sure I'd regret this decision. Leaving the office that last day, the ground did quake a little under my feet, but in my mind like always, there was no going back. I was aware that reinstatement into the department was an option, but I was certain that for me, the marshal's door was closed for good.

I'd been a marshal for nine years. It seemed both a short time and an eternity. Now I had a mortgage, a car note, a commercial loan and a fifteen-year lease on a new business. The boys were still young, Bev was a full-time mom. She volunteered at their school, did the books for the business, and delivered meals on wheels in her Volkswagen with the boys as helpers. They called the VW her "Bo-wagon."

Even though I was busy, I was on my own schedule, not punching a clock, and I had the free time I'd dreamed about. Not having to be out of the house at 4:30

in the morning, I started running again on the streets of Altadena, realizing how much I had missed it. I alternated running and going to the gym in the afternoon, carrying on a workout routine I'd started while in the service. Bev and I had breakfasts out, I had time to work in my yard. Overall, I felt more in control of my life, didn't have to meet anyone's expectations but my own, and I had a good routine going with the two washes, Vermont and Compton, which were making nearly double our combined 8-5 salaries.

About seven months after leaving the marshal's department, Jimmy Bell, the car wash equipment supplier, contacted me about a four-bay wash on Western and 76th, formerly a Lerner gas station. I knew about it. It was in better shape than Compton, fully equipped, a going concern, and it was for sale. Was I interested Jimmy wanted to know? "Absolutely," I said.

I met with the young Korean owner at the wash and after an inspection, I agreed to his price of $10,000. We made the deal a few days later. I gave him a cashier's check for $8000 from my retirement money, and the balance in two canvas bags of quarters, $1000 each. His voice rose an octave when he saw the bags. "You give me quarters?" he said. But he took them. I half expected him to protest, but instead, he accepted the two bags of coin, we signed a bill of sale to close the deal, and the young Korean went straight to his bank.

In those days, the buying and selling of coin-op car washes that were going concerns was not only common, it was a simple, uncomplicated process. The transactions were done with minimal paperwork, without the use of agents, and often without the need of bank loans primarily because coin-ops in the small business category of "vending" were not that costly. Depending on the city, some did not require permits, and new owners had only to contract with landlords if applicable, and the utility departments to continue operating. Just as it had been when I obtained Compton, obtaining Western was just as smooth, especially since I had the cash.

## ~ Taco Truck #1 ~

By the summer, 1979, Vermont had been open one year and was doing well. One afternoon a Latino man introduced himself as Luna and told me he owned a food truck selling tacos and burritos to "the lunch crowd" mostly Mexican gardeners and construction workers. He asked my permission to park his truck on Vermont's busy corner, not only to create new business for himself, but to provide quick food service to customers washing their cars. He promised his business would not interfere with mine. His crew, he said, would watch the car wash during those hours that I wasn't there. He would provide a trash can for his patrons, and for use of the space he offered to pay me $300 a month. It sounded like a perfect arrangement. His rental payment would pay my car wash rent, a win win. As an added perk, I could eat off the truck for free. This seemed like a good deal, and Luna seemed honest. I had nothing to lose. It would be month to month, and if it didn't work out as designed, I'd have him move his truck. We shook hands on it. I loved doing business this way. No banks, no reams of paper to sign. A simple agreement based on a verbal contract and trust. This was my introduction to the taco truck business.

Luna provided his crew of two workers with everything they needed to sell tacos, burritos and sandwiches Mexican style, called tortas. Car wash customers became food truck customers and vice versa. The food was good, business increased, and the truck was there seven days a week. After four months, Luna had paid his rent on time every month. The agreement was working out well and I had no complaints.

## ~ Azusa ~

As 1980 rolled around, I had three self service, coin operated car washes, Vermont, Compton, and Western. All were doing well. Plus, there was a bonus! A taco truck tenant. I was moving in on my goal of making what the marshal made, but I wasn't there yet.

Then in the space of a month, I learned of three coin-op car washes that were for sale. One in El Monte, one in Irwindale, and one in Azusa. At the same time, I became aware of a vacant lot on Manchester Avenue, my old stomping grounds, across the street from ABC market where Gwen, L'Arthur and I had worked as teens, me only briefly. Posted on the lot was a for sale sign.

Only the four-stall car wash in Azusa had potential. It was on Foothill Blvd, a main drag, and was situated in the middle of a busy strip mall. The big money tenant was one of the oldest McDonald's in the San Gabriel valley.

The wash was called Foothill Car Wash. It was open but barely functioning. The owner had moved to Northern California for his job, leaving his wife temporarily to maintain the wash, and she was having a hard time. I met her there for an inspection. Inside the equipment room, the pumps and motors looked to be in good shape. I started one of the bays while making mental notes of what changes needed to be made.

I offered $20,000 to his $22,000 asking price with $5000 down. He accepted. We signed a note to finance the balance over eighteen months and negotiated a lease assignment with the landlord for an additional eight years.

I took Bev with me one night to see the place. Azusa was seventeen miles from Altadena, and she had passed it every day driving the 210 freeway when she worked in Covina. Azusa would be her car wash. She'd be learning my side of the business now. I won't say she jumped up and down and hugged me for this new addition to her CFO duties (chief financial officer) but she was game to help and become more involved with the business.

Over the next month, while keeping the business open, we painted walls, installed booms, replaced wands, put new motors in the two vacuums. I showed Bev how the soap and wax mechanisms worked, how to unjam a meter, how to collect, how to change a vacuum motor and repair a busted hose. Customers trickled in while we worked, and I got my handyman welder Lee, to work with me after hours, sometimes until eleven at night when no one was washing.

By April, Foothill Car Wash was looking good. People noticed, and surprisingly, it didn't take long for business to pick up. Bev made her own schedule, worked it a few hours every day and was home for the boys in the afternoon. Before long, we were swapping stories about our exciting days at the wash.

## ~ The Thing ~

I put a sign on my Ford, trusty Old Blue, and someone bought it. I took that cash and added some to it and bought a bright yellow car that was built like a Jeep. It was called a Thing and made by Volkswagen. The tops and windows came completely out. It was perfect for work and play, and this particular "Thing" had a history. It had been used in the Nancy Drew television series.

Our first trip in it was to the campgrounds in Sequoia, cruising up through the middle of California, listening to John Denver's *Rocky Mountain High* on the cassette player. Jon and Lance loved being in the Thing, tops out and wide open.

I had already sold the Bentley and made a modest profit of $1000. It was a beautiful car but caused a little too much attention. Still, I wasn't done with the exotic car market. I had my Porsche looking like new, and still perused the car ads in the paper. That's where I found the for-sale ad on the Jaguar Mark VIII and made a call to the seller.

Bev and I drove to the seller's home in Chapman Woods. He was the owner of Lamb Funeral Homes in Pasadena. He invited us into his elaborate, winding-stair-case-chandeliered-mini-mansion. He told us he had ordered this car from England and was planning to restore it, but his messy divorce had gotten in the way of that plan. Regrettably, he needed to sell it. The improvements needed were cosmetic. I looked at it as a project I could work on, to make the car as gorgeous as it must have been when it was new. I added to the profit from the sale of the Bentley, and for $3000, we made the deal on the Jag.

The next year was a good one for recreating. In February, we took a few days off and took Jon and Lance on their first plane trip up to San Francisco. Jon was nine, Lance was six. We rented a car, drove over the bay bridge to Oakland to visit Don and Albert, two brothers I'd known since high school. We took the boys on a trolley car ride, and got to experience the hills, the chills, and the foggy nights of Frisco.

In the spring we drove down to San Diego, and spent a few days at Sea World, the zoo, and the beach, and then in the summer, we took one of our first camping trips to Silverwood Lake in the Thing.

During the year, I took my time beautifying the Jag—I removed the wood dash and back seat trays, sanded them, varnished them, I ordered chrome wire wheels, and had the car painted white.  It wasn't quite the attention getter as the Bentley, but it was close.

On a fluke, I acquired another good dog. I had driven my Thing to the shop where work was being done on the Porsche. While I was waiting, a black Doberman pinscher jumped into the back seat of the Thing and made himself comfortable. I was hesitant about getting back in the car. As I said, this was a Doberman, not a poodle, and he looked fierce. One of the shop owners, Jaime, told me a customer had left the dog two weeks ago as collateral for the work done on his car and never came back to get him.

"He's yours if you want him," he said. "He doesn't bite. He's a smart dog." I looked at the steely-eyed dog. He reminded me of my old greyhound Cocomo.

I wasn't one to look a gift dog in the mouth. Despite his intimidating look, he was friendly. "What's his name?" I asked. Jaime threw up his hands. "Okay. I'm calling him Jaime," I said.

The dog rode in the back seat all the way home, and not until I got there, did I wonder if the Doberman would get along with our snow white female shepherd named Windy. Not only did they get along, they quickly mated. Six black puppies were the result, a litter of baby Jaimes. Jon and Lance wanted to keep all six.

I hadn't planned to get a guard dog, but I was dealing with a lot of cash. With training, Jaime would easily fill the bill. I took him to a center in Hacienda Heights and had him trained. Canine protection was a good idea, and few dogs were more intimidating than a Doberman. Jaime made his presence known. Leaping from the car at my call, customers would see him walk with me into the equipment room. I took him with me every day.

## ~ Manchester ~

Meanwhile, from the Hall of Records, I learned the vacant lot on Manchester was owned by a widow named Katz. I began to think I was destined to deal with widows whose last name began with K. Anyway, the lot was five minutes from 84th Place where I was raised and where Muhtha still lived. The lot was 200 feet wide, 120 feet deep. Asking price was $80,000, costly for the area but not for the size. I had no real insight into its potential, and Bev had even less. Once again, she freaked out. "80,000? More than we paid for our house. No no no." It wasn't easy, but I calmed her down.

I would have to get a loan, our largest debt to date, a hundred fifty thousand for construction, twenty-five thousand for equipment, plus a 20% down payment. I spoke directly with Mrs. Katz, told her my plans, and we arranged to get something on paper.

Manchester would be my biggest car wash. Eight stalls, eight vacuums, two bill changers, six vending machines, built on my own land. We would own this one, eventually, and it would be our retirement. This is what I had to impress on Bev, something my cautious wife hadn't considered. We still had twelve years on Vermont's lease, but who knew what changes might happen in twelve years, not that I was worried about that. It was still a long way off at a time when the years didn't pass quite so quickly. And I was nothing if not positive.

"But why eight stalls?" Bev asked, thinking of the note we'd have to pay. "Couldn't we save a little if we only built six stalls?" The answer was yes, a little, but I wanted this wash to accommodate every customer with little delay on its busiest days, or at the very least, make waiting times shorter. Vermont with six bays was my example. On busy days, some people didn't want to wait. They would leave. Manchester had to be eight bays and fully equipped.

I applied to the Small Business Administration, (the SBA) and was lucky to get loan officer Esther Jones, who happened to be a southern black woman who had worked for the SBA for twenty-five years. We were soon on a first name basis. She bemoaned the fact that there weren't more young black men like me with an idea and a vision, taking advantage of money available to go into business.

I contacted Mrs. Katz, the owner of the Manchester property. She was easy to reach and I applied for a permit, and had plans drawn. SBA required completion of a lengthy complicated loan application, a financial statement, bank statements, tax returns, personal histories, and most troublesome, estimates of what the business would gross called income projections. Esther helped me through some of it, but there was only so much she could do.

Our dining room table was cluttered for weeks as Bev and I worked into the night getting the information down. She was familiar with some of the forms, but the income projections? How were they supposed to look? What was the format? She couldn't Google for help.

Ultimately, we created our own format. We based our numbers on what Vermont had done, and my hopeful expectations. We submitted the package—over thirty pages of documentation plus two years of tax returns. We spent hours making sure everything was correct. It was such a relief to get the package completed and put it in Esther's hands. I never considered the possibility that it might be turned down, but it was. Bottom line, we didn't have enough assets, and had not been in business long enough. Esther was as disappointed as I was.

Months passed before I heard from her again. This time she called with good news. President Reagan had advised that the SBA had revenue in the amount of $200 million dollars reserved for small business loans. If the money was not allocated by December 31, 1981, it would be withdrawn from the SBA's coffers and distributed to other government agencies.

She asked if I was still interested in getting the loan. I said yes, that I was still hot to get it. She advised me to get a written commitment from the seller.

I contacted Mrs. Katz directly, no middle man.

The lot was still for sale, and she was happy to sell it to me.

At the time, real estate in the area was depressed—location, location—sadly a residual effect of the riot in 1965, sixteen years ago. But I wasn't discouraged. Even at $80,000 this lot was affordable, big, and Manchester was a busy street. I went for it.

I got back to Esther who sent me some additional paperwork to be completed, and along with the commitment letter from Mrs. Katz, I mailed everything to her. She would put a special recommendation on the package and resubmit. If approved, notification would come before the end of the year, but proceeds would not be distributed until sometime later.

Not until the spring of 1982 were we notified that the loan had been approved. I hired an architect to draw Manchester's plans.

Plan approval is usually met with delays. I couldn't do anything about that. Fortunately, delays were sometimes good. As summer approached, we made plans for a camping trip to Sequoia.

Bev and I and the boys, my two sisters and their families all caravanned up to the redwoods. We each had our own cabins and shared a cooking grill. We hiked the trails, had campfires, and enjoyed the rushing waters and giant trees of Kings Canyon again. It was one of the most fun and relaxing vacations we ever had. Later that summer, we'd had such a good time at Silverwood Lake the first time, all of us drove there together and rented a boat for the day, sailed on the lake, and fished off the side of the boat.

By the spring of 1983 construction was about to

begin on Manchester. At the same time, my sister Gwen had become an assistant travel agent and booked a week's vacation for her family on Waikiki with her travel assistant discount. She invited Lizzie and her two daughters, Bev and the boys, and Muhtha. The ten of them left the first week in May with my blessing. I turned my attention to breaking ground at Manchester.

When they returned a week later with a camera full of photos and Waikiki souvenirs, I was knee deep into the construction. For this, my largest car wash, I was listed as owner builder, but this time I had no general contractor. I got referrals from Jimmy Bell, hired block masons, roofing and framing contractors, and an electrician. I decided to have concrete laid for the ground for permanence rather than asphalt which is what I had at Vermont. I contacted my Uncle Joe, Dad's half-brother who had poured concrete for twenty years. He got a couple of guys that he knew to help with the job, and between the four of us, we concreted the entire lot, which was 200 by 120 feet. I never worked so hard in my life, but my uncle saved me a lot of money. I already had open accounts with suppliers like Kleenrite and Windtrax for vending and inventory, and this time I installed Jimmy Bell's superior equipment, including the pumps and motors. Construction moved along and each completed section had to be approved by the city.

At some point as we were nearing the end, I realized I needed $10,000 more. I called Esther. She suggested an additional $25,000 instead. The extra fifteen thousand could be used as operating capital. The money would be given to me incrementally as needed, and she would have no problem getting the additional money approved.

My payment which began in June, was interest only for the first eight months which minimized my costs during construction and gave me some breathing room prior to opening.

In November 1983, Howard's Car Wash on Manchester opened for business.

## ~ Slow Going ~

The first week of any business is too soon to make a judgement call, although, I had done that at Vermont on the first day, and the call was right. Vermont had taken off. Not so with Manchester. We opened at seventy-five cents to wash, a quarter to vacuum. The early going fell far below my expectations, even with the one bay I had dedicated to hand washing, which I did myself, alone, until one day, a guy named Charles rode up on his bicycle. He didn't know me and I didn't know him but he offered to help with the hand car washing. He called himself "the detail man." He was a nice guy, who lived in the projects and we were about the same age. He wasn't asking for a hand-out. He wanted to work. Together for some months, Charles the detail man and I did hand car washing in that bay. In an effort to get more cars in, I ran specials—senior citizen day, half price on Tuesdays. I dropped the price to 50-cents on Tuesdays during the fruit fly infestation, when the pesticide used to kill the pesky flies covered cars with a sticky residue.

The specials didn't help. Nor the fact that it was winter, and the days shorter. I couldn't figure it out. Cars just weren't coming in. I was more frustrated than worried.

Everything was new, the equipment was working. I had customers but not nearly enough.

I stuck to the belief that time was on my side. In time, Manchester's potential would be realized. I had to be patient and stay optimistic. I was banking on good service, word of mouth, and the steady income of my other three car washes. Fortunately, I had reserves in the bank. Manchester would turn around, I was sure of it. But in the meantime, I had some extra time on my hands. I got busy with a couple of temporary diversions, and even made a little money.

I'd helped my cousin Howard years ago land a security job at Sears. He'd recovered from an injury during TET and made it home from Vietnam before I did. He was now working as a courier for a small new start-up company, a mobile service for quick delivery of escrow documents, business correspondence, and small packages that needed to arrive same day or overnight. He asked me if I'd like to give it a try. It could put an extra $60-$75 dollars in my pocket for three to four hours of work. I said why not. All I needed was a car and a pager, and I had both.

Once calls for pick-ups began coming through on my pager, I had to laugh at myself. Here I was driving and delivering again, a glorified mailman on call from LA to Hollywood, to the beach cities and back again. It was the period of the refinance boom when lenders, escrow companies and realtors needed paperwork moved quickly and couldn't rely on something that had not been created yet— email. And a time when traffic on the Harbor freeway at 2:30 in the afternoon could actually move at 55 miles per hour. For a few months I made quite a few deliveries even into downtown LA, at a time when bumper to bumper traffic hardly existed.

l kept the courier job until the weather began to change and Manchester's business picked up. A couple of years later my attention was diverted again. l was offered an opportunity to be in a television show.

Bev had reconnected with her best friend from high school who was married to the producer of the popular television show *Silver Spoons*. Bev had been in their wedding, and the four of us had met for dinner. They invited us to the NBC studio to see a live taping of the show, and to bring Jon and Lance. It was exciting and fun for the boys who after the taping got to meet the star Ricky Schroeder who was a year older than Jon. Before we left, the producer asked if I'd like to do a bit part on the show, and he was serious.

Would l turn that down? No. Would l have been available to do it if l were a marshal? No.

As a "bit" player, l was part of the background in a malt shop scene. l had no lines, but l was on screen long enough to be recognized. One thing led to another, including hiring an agent, and becoming a member of Central Casting.

For several months l drove to Hollywood, Santa Monica, and Abbot Kinney in Venice for interviews and auditions, pictures and promotions. l went to a class to learn how to "cold read." l went on location calls where l had to report before dawn, and l worked on a couple of movies that kept us until after nine at night. l started calling myself an actor and spouting the phrase "actors act." It was exciting being on a set and seeing how a show came together from the inside out, but also boring at times, a lot of waiting around, and too much available catered food, primarily donuts, my weakness, on every set. In between, of course, I was taking care of my washes.

If I were to write up my performance resume, it would show that I did two episodes of *Silver Spoons* and one episode of *The Jeffersons,* where I had the pleasure of meeting Sherman Hemsley and Rosie Greer. I did two truck commercials and a construction commercial. I was an "extra" in the movies *Drop Zone* starring Wesley Snipes, Junior, starring Danny DeVito and Arnold Schwarzenegger, where I played an airline pilot, and Denzel Washington's *Devil in a Blue Dress* where I got to drive a 1941 classic roadster. Denzel was on the set and he spoke to all the extras. I did one commercial for a brand new company just starting out called Direct TV. For some reason it only aired in Chicago, but it paid me residuals for over a year.

Not all my auditions panned out. For some I was too young to play a Grampa, and too old to be the young stud. I auditioned for an Aflac commercial, and a Toyota truck commercial featuring a grizzly bear, but I didn't get either one. I had stopped being an early morning person when I left the marshal's department, so five a.m. calls were never fun, and sitting around waiting for the director to say "action" soon got old. After my episodes aired, it was fun seeing myself on television, and even getting recognized a couple of times at my car wash. But I had to face reality. I would never be the next Denzel Washington. I let my equity card lapse and told my agent to call only if I was requested. (Haha) For me, it was back to the car washes.

# ~ Taco Truck #2 ~

The taco truck was still doing great business at my Vermont location when Luna, the owner told me he was returning to Mexico and had a buyer for the truck. He told the potential buyer that he was paying me $500 a month for the space, which would be a $200 increase to me if I allowed the potential buyer to continue parking there.

I had become well acquainted with Luna's crew, Morales and Santos, and the food on the truck. I asked Luna how much the truck was making. He told me about $2000 per week after costs.

"You're kidding," I said. It was hard to believe, but I couldn't deny the number of people I saw during the week lined up to buy food from the truck. On Saturday and Sunday mornings, the crew would describe the crowd of people from the night before, waiting in line to buy their tacos and burritos, sometimes until midnight.

The potential buyer had his own crew which was a problem. If he were to purchase the truck, Santos and Morales might be out of a job. They wanted me to buy the truck which didn't sound like a bad idea. When I approached Luna about buying the truck, he smiled and nodded his head. "Yes. Of course you can."

Over the next few weeks, Luna and the crew let me watch the operation up close showing me what they were making and how they made it. From the produce purchases to the number of tortillas in a pack. They taught me the recipes, and where to get the best deals on the meats, all the necessary supplies, and how much the workers were paid. The crew was excited. I would become the new "patron."

The truck was a 1974 GMC converted to a food

truck. It was an older truck, but all the cooking equipment worked. I paid Luna his asking price of $7000 and felt confident I was getting a good deal. He wished me luck and days later, returned to Mexico.

From day one we were making money, and inside of three months, I had made back the cost of the truck, plus. It was hard to believe, but it was true. The truck was making more money than the car wash. Who knew? I started thinking that if one truck was good, two would be better. At the time there were very few taco trucks on the streets doing business compared to now, where "food" trucks seem to be on every other corner.

I bought a second truck a few months later, a 1976 GMC truck from A&A Catering, a large company that specialized in buying, selling, and converting large vehicles to food trucks. I parked the newer truck at Vermont and moved the '74 truck to Barron Liquor's lot at 159th between Avalon & San Pedro, right near JB's BBQ. It was an excellent location, near several factories, and there was a great lunch and night time crowd.

The truck, the crew and I were in a groove. I kept the trucks supplied with everything they needed, all the meats including asada, cabeza, pollo, carnitas, and chivo to make the birria soup which made me think of my neighbor Mrs. Alvarez from when I was a kid. Packs of tortillas, torta bread, produce, shrimp for the cocktails, all their paper goods, and sodas. They kept the orders filled, and kept their portable radio playing the best of Juan Gabriel's Mexican love songs.

The trucks were parked overnight at Torres Market at 135th and Crenshaw, an arrangement Luna made with Torres before he left for Mexico.

Torres Market had a huge parking area behind the

store. The arrangement initially cost me $150 a month for electricity and the use of his kitchen, but when I added a second truck, Torres upped the rent to $225. When I mentioned I might be getting a third truck, he said the rent would be $300 per month. Then out of the blue, he offered to sell me his store. "You're making enough money," he said. "You should buy it."

It was a taunt, not really an offer to sell. I didn't need a store, but I did need some other place to park, and a place to prep the food. The Health Department had begun citing catering trucks that weren't parked at a commissary overnight. Torres' lot was large and convenient, but it wasn't a commissary.

I mentioned this to Vahey, the owner of A&A Catering, and he arranged for me to get a letter from the owner of a commissary on Slauson Avenue much farther away than Torres Market. Besides the distance, parking the trucks at the Slauson commissary overnight would cost me $600 a month, but to get a letter *saying* I was parking there, cost a one-time "courtesy" fee of $400.

Vahey arranged for me to meet with the owner of the Slauson commissary. I walked into a red and gold business office and was invited to sit in a plush leather seat. I felt like I'd entered a scene from the *Godfather*. The owner seated behind a big desk was like "the Don." He was cordial and spoke to me like we were old acquaintances. He had a letter prepared that said my trucks were parked at his commissary for x amount of dollars. I thanked him for the letter and paid him $400. It was like a mafioso hook-up, and it bugged me. I left hoping I'd never see him again.

I made copies of the letter, put one on each truck,

and got back to a plan that had come to me in a dream. I'd hire the contract workers who had built the carwash to construct a small building at the northeast end of Manchester's lot, leaving plenty of room for the trucks to park, and consisting of a kitchen, a walk-in freezer, an office, a bathroom, and an order window for the tacos, burritos, and burgers we'd be making and selling. This didn't come to me all at once, but once I reconnected with my architect Neil, the visual all came together. It would be my own commissary.

The thought of dealing with the building department again, and permits, plans, inspections and construction was disheartening, to say the least. But I believed in the long run this last improvement would make perfect sense.

In the process, I bought a third newer truck, top of the line GMC, parked it at Vermont, and moved the '76 truck to La Brea and Arbor Vitae. There weren't many taco trucks in the area, but this location was no longer in the city of LA. La Brea and Arbor Vitae was in Inglewood. The city ordinance stated taco trucks could park no longer than one hour at the same location. It was a great spot for a few months, but after one ticket, the crew had to move. We found a spot on the street near an Arco station at Main and El Segundo and parked from 10-6 in the evening and did good business.

Once Manchester's restaurant was completed, I had a propane tank installed to supply the trucks with gas. By the end of 1986 the restaurant was certified as a commissary, and my fleet of three taco trucks had a new home.

I never had difficulty finding people to man the trucks. Santos and Morales introduced me to several young guys just up from Mexico. Guys looking for work would approach and ask for a job. Most weren't legal, some spoke very little English, but they were all eager to work and learn, and once given an opportunity, most, not all, but most of them were diligent, and did a good job. The woman who ended up running the restaurant stand at Manchester was someone who just walked in off the street one day and ended up working for me for 15 years. Hard working Mexican people with easy dispositions, and I was lucky to know them, work with them, and gain their loyalty.

I was glad I no longer needed the letter from "the Don." My sense of him was correct. Mafioso connections that ended badly. About five years later, according to Vahey, at A&A Catering, "the Don" was shot dead in his own driveway. No kidding.

## ~ Movin' and Shakin' Weathering Storms ~

1985-1990, were busy years. Vermont's income and Azusa's had increased every year since opening, and Azusa's paid-in-full note helped increase its bottom line. Manchester's slow start was virtually erased by how much its monthly income had grown. Supplying all three taco trucks, especially Vermont's kept me moving and all three were making profits. We were rolling.

Compton's income had held steady but not increased over the years, so when the owner of the property told me of a buyer for Compton's equipment, I was ready to let it go. When the potential buyer asked the price, I suggested he check on replacement costs, and when he did, and learned replacement of my equipment would cost about $12,000, he backed out of the deal not wanting to pay even $3000 for mine. He claimed he didn't really need the equipment, that his plan for the space was a used car lot. Because the equipment was vintage, I suspected he thought I would leave it. If I had, I suspected his plan of a "just a used car lot" might change. He didn't know me very well. I removed my equipment and it wasn't easy. But I took every piece. Vacuums, pumps, motors, booms, wands, hoses, light fixtures, meters, and the electrical wiring. My Compton Car Wash was done.

One of my last conversations with Esther the loan officer at the SBA was that if I ever decided to sell my car wash business on Western, I should give her a call. She lived only blocks away from the wash and wanted to purchase it for her 22-year old son to get him started in business. We agreed on the price of $10,000 to be paid in two installments. Her son and I signed a note drawn up by Bev and approved by Esther. Divesting myself of Compton and Western reduced my overhead and income, but freed up some time.

Besides Sequoia and Silverwood Lake, Bev and I and the boys packed our tent, sleeping bags and hibachi into Bev's Subaru and camped out at Lake Isabella, about 150 miles northeast of Los Angeles. On another excursion, we rented a fully equipped motor home for four days to see if one of those elaborate travel units on wheels might be in my future. We hitched our bicycles to it, and motored up the coast to Solvang, Pismo Beach, Morro Bay, and San Simeon for a tour of the Hearst Castle. As much fun as we had, even when we nearly ran out of gas, I had finally seen and driven a vehicle I'd probably never want to own, and Bev was glad to hear it.

Our 16th anniversary party was a scavenger hunt through downtown LA starting at the Bonaventure Hotel with ten invited couples. The hunt continued north on the 110 freeway and ended in Pasadena at a restaurant for dinner where everyone was presented with a trophy.

We bought four 4-wheel all-terrain vehicles, ATV's, after risking life and limb on three-wheeler bikes that we'd rented first to see if we'd like them. We jumped on those motorized three-wheelers and rode them through Azusa Canyon, all four of us, Jon was 12, Lance 9, with no lessons and no safety tips! After that first outing, we liked them so much, that I bought four quads, one for each of us. I had a trailer made to transport them, and we rode them in Azusa Canyon, in El Mirage in San Bernardino, and Gorman near Mountain High where we also went skiing.

One spring we drove up the 118 into the mountain community of Crestline. It was quaint and rustic, had cute little shops, a great market, and was built around Lake Gregory where you could rent canoes and go rowing.

I got to thinking how great it would be to have a cabin up there, to get away from the heat in the summer, and see the snow in the winter. We got a realtor to show us some cabins for rent. Cabins for sale as low as $20,000 were listed in the newspaper, which seemed too good to be true even for a "fixer-upper." Of course, it *was* too good to be true. The only fixing up for those "fixer-uppers" was to tear them down and start all over.

We went to the office of an architect/builder named Averill who not only showed us cabins he had designed and built in Crestline and Rim of the World, a community adjacent to Crestline, he showed us plans for a cabin he could build for us, and an available vacant lot. The total cost, $65,000. Bev pinched my thigh under the table to get my attention. I could see it in her eyes that quiver, that squint of doubt.

Mr. Averill gave us time to discuss and think it over, but it didn't take long. It was doable. We filled out initial paperwork right then and over the next few months, we watched the cabin being built. By June of 1986, the cabin, our "hideaway" was complete.

I'd been watching the newspapers for Housing and Redevelopment (HUD) homes that had been repossessed. I was thinking about making another real estate investment. A year later, on one of our visits, Bev and the boys stayed at the cabin while I drove five miles beyond Crestline to a rustic woodsy community called Twin Peaks in search of the cabin I'd seen listed in the paper as a HUD repo.

Around one last curve, I saw the cabin. It was set high above the road with a bunch of steps. I counted more than twenty as I climbed up to the front door. Taped inside the window was a HUD repo notice. I wrote down the id number. Looking through the glass I could see the cabin was empty, could see the kitchen, and the stairs leading up to the second floor. It looked to be in good shape. I went back down the hill, found a phone booth, and called Willie, a real estate agent, and the man that I'd formed a partnership with on a 4-unit complex in LA. I asked him to put in a bid for me. I wanted to buy it and rent it out.

It was a gamble to bid on a house that I hadn't inspected, and when no one else bid on it, I wondered why. Without a competing bid, the house was mine. I signed paperwork to assume the loan and paid only closing costs to finalize the assumption of the loan.

Two years after buying the cabins in Crestline and Twin Peaks, we remodeled our one story home on Skywood Circle into a two story by adding a living room to the front of the house, and above it, a master bedroom and bath, making our home on par with the others in the cul de sac, and increasing its value.

Fortunately, no major defects were found in the Twin Peaks rental. But the good fortune didn't hold. Renting it and keeping it rented turned out to be a nightmare. I learned that some of the people who seek the mountains and remote back woods areas to live, aren't doing it just because they're nature lovers. Some of them are wolves in very convincing sheep's clothing, hiding from bill collectors, bad debts and non-payment of rent. We had a couple of tenants who fit that description. I was forced to return to marshal mode, and begin eviction proceedings.

## ~ Sinnreit ~

Enterprise Car Wash, at El Segundo and San Pedro, was two miles south of my Vermont location and had opened a few months before I opened Vermont. Enterprise was my closest competitor.

The owner, Leo Sinnreit was an older Jewish man, a longtime friend of Jimmy Bell and had heard from Jimmy of how well his new competitor, Howard's Car Wash was doing. Jimmy called me on behalf of Sinnreit who wanted to meet with me. Networking again, and I wasn't even trying.

I met with Mr. Sinnreit at his favorite deli, Cantor's in West LA. He and his wife Betty lived in Beverly Hills. In the forties, her father had owned Scotchman's dairy, two blocks from where Enterprise CW was now located, and coincidentally, the dairy where L'Arthur and I had bought our calf when we were boys. Mr. Sinnreit confessed he was getting too old to maintain his car wash alone, but he wasn't ready to sell it. Instead, he proposed a partnership with me, a 60/40 split after expenses. For my 40%, I would oversee the maintenance of his wash, make the collections, and deposit the money to his Security Pacific Bank account.

His unexpected proposal was extraordinary and a complete surprise. This man didn't know me. But based on the success of Vermont, and a good word from Jimmy Bell, he was willing to trust me with his cash and his bank account number. I was interested in the proposal and flattered by his trust. But flattery alone didn't move me to accept his proposal. It was my hope that at some time in the future, Enterprise Car Wash, which I passed every day on my way to Vermont, would one day be mine.

A signed one-page contract sealed the deal, along with a handshake. I went with him to his Security Pacific bank and met his favorite teller who would be seeing me on a monthly basis.

Every month I met with Leo and his wife at the Hustler Casino on Redondo Beach Blvd. where he would treat me to lunch. My 40% averaged about $1500 a month, and Leo would hand it to me before the meal with a thank you for keeping things ship shape. "Get the business out the way," he'd say. I often wondered as I sat across from them eating their Reuben sandwiches, what other patrons might be thinking seeing the three of us sitting there, this Jewish couple in their eighties, and their young black friend, chatting about the state of the world and car washes. Leo and I had a good relationship that lasted about three years until ill health forced him to sell.

But did he sell the car wash to me? No.

At the east end of Leo's property not connected to the car wash was a drive-through dairy. It was leased to a Korean, one of three brothers who owned four other drive-through dairies in the city. They offered to buy the dairy and the car wash. Leo agreed. I was out.

Initially I was disappointed. But the more I thought about it, taking ownership of another car wash at that time may have been spreading myself too thin.

I was ankle deep into the taco truck business with three trucks working three locations, and a fledgling Mexican food stand working out of Manchester's kitchen. I called this off-shoot of Howard's Car Wash "El Mexicano" and had the title painted on each truck with my unofficial logo, a black-curled-at-the-tips mustache.

Every morning inside my little restaurant was a three-ring circus starting at seven a.m. Eight workers scrambling, speaking Spanish, in and out the open door, cleaning the trucks, washing pots and pans, scouring the grills, three female workers chopping produce, slicing meats. Spanish music poured out of a radio, my introduction to Los Bukis, along with the silky voice of Juan Gabriel, the premier messenger of Mexican romance songs. Sizzling on the grill would be carne asada, the aroma filling up the kitchen. Beans would be cooking on the stove's back burner, and on the front burner, tortillas warming over the open flame because along with preparing the first batches for the trucks, the guys had to eat. The sound of ice being made from the industrial sized ice-maker could be heard at regular intervals, and in the back office, I would be totaling receipts from the night before and stocking the cash tills for the day's business. It was hectic, busy, a high energy operation with enthusiastic workers, money being made, and thankfully, crews that were working together like a family.

My father-in-law Duke had always shown an interest in my various money-making enterprises. He called me Howie, and anytime he phoned or came by, he'd ask, "What are you kids up to?" He was good at dropping by one of the car washes to wash his car, unannounced, or coming to the house for a quick visit. Bev and I came home one afternoon and found him swimming laps in our pool. He waved to us and swam a few more laps before coming out.

Before he died in 1990, he came to Manchester one morning during the height of our preparation. He watched as the three trucks were being cleaned and loaded, and he stood in the middle of the kitchen looking left and right as the guys worked around him, doing whatever needed to be done. He came into the office laughing and amazed. "Howie, you got some operation going on here."

I hadn't given up on Enterprise Car Wash, and my interest increased every time the Korean brothers asked me for help or advice. I gave them referrals for supplies, even did a few minor repairs for them. Language and inexperience were proving a problem for them at the dairy and at the car wash. I helped as much as I could, but I couldn't prevent a tragedy. While closing one of their Compton dairies late one evening, the elder Korean brother was robbed and killed. He was 30.

The two remaining brothers struggled after the death of their brother. After a couple of months, they were ready to sell and offered the wash and the land to me. They recommended a Korean loan broker who quickly and efficiently prepared my loan package and submitted it to the SBA through a Korean bank. It was a big loan, $274,000, but I had a twelve-year track record in the car wash business by then. They took a chance on me and approved the loan.

In 15 years, after moving from Carson, the market value of our home on Skywood Circle had increased more than six times over what we paid for it in 1975. Carson's market values were far less. When we moved to Skywood, we were one of only two black families in the neighborhood for six years, and our neighbors hadn't changed over that period. By comparison, in four short years, our Carson neighborhood had changed by more than 60%. The ethnic diversity had all but disappeared. Only one race of people was moving in, and some, I'm sorry to say, were questionable. I didn't see this as progress, and being in law enforcement, I never wanted to live in the same area where I worked. Carson had been great for a starter home, but after three years I no longer wanted to live in a tract home. I wanted a house not quite so close to my neighbors, with a little more room, a little more privacy. I had learned that a home is also an investment. If it's possible to buy in a desirable area where anyone financially able can purchase a home, do it. Make that down payment. Buy "up" where the note might be a bit of a struggle in the beginning, but not impossible. Had we stayed in Carson, I would not have been able to pull

$150,000 out in equity, which I did by refinancing Skywood.

With the refinance, I had enough to make the down payment on Enterprise Car Wash, make necessary improvements, and deposit the balance into savings.

We re-opened for business in February 1992. We kept the name Enterprise, though we'd gotten into the habit of calling it San Pedro, which was the closest major cross street. With the help of Jimmy Bell's main equipment installer Miguel, we added a bill changer, new safes, and built vacuum stands for the vacuums. Lance was a junior in high school, and Jon who had graduated the year before and was a student at Pasadena City College, began working with me on weekends and learning the CW business.

We were now four car washes strong, Vermont, Manchester, Azusa, whose lease had been renewed for another five years, and San Pedro. Add to that three taco trucks, Manchester's take-out restaurant, a cabin and two rentals, (a 4-unit apartment building and Twin Peaks, which I still owned in 1992) my plate was full. I had debts, that's the truth, but that goes along with business. All of my obligations were being paid on time, and we had money in the bank.

## ~ Riot ~

The Rodney King riot in April of 1992 was more destructive, violent, and widespread than the Watts riot in 1965. The hotspot of the eruption at Normandie and Florence was about two miles from Manchester, and about three miles from my Vermont and San Pedro locations.

On the day of the riot, I was gone from the car washes at my usual time and was on the freeway around three thirty when the not guilty verdicts were announced for the police officers who'd beaten Rodney King. By the time I pulled into my driveway, the rioting was just beginning. It was still light outside. The police had not yet begun to move in. The news was taken over by coverage of the uprising, and people were warned not to go into the area. The scenes on television made LA look like a war zone. Some of the images were interspersed with replays of the video beating of Rodney King.

I was on the phone, two phone calls, one to a friend, also a customer who told me the Vermont location had been hit, even though my nephew Keown who lived less than a half mile away in Gardena had written "black owned" on the back wall. In 1965, the words "soul brother" written on the front of a business saved a few from being burned or vandalized. Not so in 1992. Within an hour the overview pictures on television showed hundreds of people in the streets, smoke and flames rising up from businesses on fire. It was chaos. My alarms at San Pedro and Vermont had gone off and the alarm company dispatchers called me to say the city was in crisis and the police would not be coming. The rampage went on all night.

The next day I went to Manchester first, despite the warnings from the media to stay out of the area. I had to find out how bad it was. The street was full of debris, smoke was in the air, but not many people were around as I unlocked the gate and let myself in. ABC market across the street was still being looted.

My crews had brought the trucks in early the day

before, parked them, locked the gates and went onto the roof of the building. Two of my guys had shotguns. They showed me how they had fired them into the air and kept the rioters from coming over the gate. They couldn't stop talking about how they kept out the bad guys.

I left them at Manchester got back on the freeway and went to Vermont. I pulled up slowly in front of my equipment room. Nobody was around. The window had been broken out and the door rammed open. The bill changer looked like someone had used a crowbar to open it. The money was gone, and the door of the changer was so dented and bent it couldn't be closed. I walked the bays and saw where they had tried to rip the meters off the walls. All the vacuum doors were open and twisted half off their hinges. I closed all the vacuums as best I could, taped them or put on temporary locks, up-righted turned-over trash cans, and secured the front door. Then I left to inspect San Pedro.

Driving down El Segundo two miles to get to San Pedro, the streets were cluttered with debris scattered everywhere, people looking desperate darting in and out of doorways, families still looting, coming out of small stores, even little kids carrying whatever they could hold.

I got to San Pedro and had my heart broken again. My newest car wash had only been open a couple of months. I drove onto the lot, looking around as I got out of my truck. The damage was the same as Vermont's. The steel door was rammed, the bill changer broken into, the equipment room ransacked. Trash cans were overturned, vacuums and vending machines dented and pried open. A chain link fence separated the car wash from the east end of the lot, occupied by the dairy which again was owned by a Korean. Walking toward the fence, I stopped in my tracks. The dairy was burned to the ground. As angry as I was for what had been done to my car washes, my buildings were still standing, and my damage could be repaired. I felt for the Korean. His business was destroyed.

Over the next couple of weeks, after considering how the damage to my washes could have been worse, I gritted my teeth and got busy with repairs. My focus was to resume the business of my business. Howard's Car Wash remained open.

## ~ Long Neck Long Shot (1993) ~

The "new beef." That was the topic of the article in the in-flight shopper magazine I'd read during the flight home from a car wash convention at Caesar's Palace in Las Vegas. We'd been there two days, enjoyed a little room service, saw the newest in CW equipment, and placed orders at discount for a couple of new products.

Once we got home, I went straight to the business section of the LA Times which still held interest for me though the stock market was not my focus. I wanted to invest in something unconventional, get in on the ground floor of "a hot new item" and maybe make a small killing, figuratively speaking, of course.

A trending food item reported to be leaner, lower in cholesterol, but more expensive than beef, was making a splash on the market. It was Ostrich meat and it was dubbed "the new beef."

I began looking for articles in magazines and newspapers, doing my homework. I found info on ostrich farms, the eggs and gestation, and investment opportunities, hoping to find something local that I could personally investigate. The closest I got was in Argyle, Texas, a bona fide ostrich ranch, called Longneck Enterprises. They'd been in business more than ten years, breeding the birds, hatching the eggs, and selling the meat to market.

After contacting the owner by phone, he sent me a video. I watched a red-faced farmer with a thick drawl and huge Stetson hat walk and talk me through the ins and outs of raising ostriches. By the end of the short sales pitch, complete with two gawky birds grazing in the back ground, I was very excited. The investment part sounded easy and lucrative. I was gung-ho, ready to proceed. Bev put up the roadblock, like I knew she would.

I explained the whole operation. We'd be buying our own birds, a male and a female, and each couple comprised one "share." All eggs produced by them would be ours to sell and one share cost $3000. I wanted to purchase six shares, $18,000.

Bev quietly hit the roof. She didn't want any part of it. She tried reasoning with me, being logical, sensible, and cautious. "Let's start with two shares," she said, even though six thousand was more than she wanted to risk. But if that worked like Farmer in the Dell promised (her name for the Texan) we could always buy more. "Doesn't that make sense?" she said.

Of course, it did, but I didn't listen. Farmer in the Dell sent us a contract. We signed it and I sent him $18,000, straight out of the bank. I waited expectantly for the photos of birds or eggs that were promised within the first 30 days. We received one picture of an ostrich and a brief note that everything was going along on schedule.

Six months passed without another word. No photos of birds came, no updates on eggs laid, no response to letters, and three phone calls went unanswered. We sent a certified letter demanding the return of our money along with a copy of the contract highlighting in bright yellow the guarantee of a refund if we wanted to cancel within a twelve-month period. Again, no response.

Bev and I didn't talk about it. We couldn't. She was fuming and I was in denial. I couldn't believe I'd been taken. I tried to stay cool, not panic, and that response triggered her action.

She took the contract, and copies of our letters to an attorney who had helped me years before with the resolution of a partnership. Mr. Montgomery was a rarity—an honest old-school lawyer. Bev poured out the whole miserable story to his sympathetic ear.

He called Longneck as our representative, got right through to the owner or someone posing as the owner and that person promised to send us our refund within seven days. He didn't charge us for the time or the long-distance phone call. He wasn't licensed to practice law in Texas, so the best he could do was give us a referral to a Texas attorney and wish us good luck.

Our luck had run out. The refund was never sent.

I wound up in Argyle, Texas at a hearing where I was the only black plaintiff in a court room filled with jilted investors, many of them Texans, all of them white. The judge ruled in our favor, but the judgement amounted to hot air. We got zero.

I was about 280 miles from Waco, not around the corner from my cousins, but I was in no mood to stay in Texas any longer than I had to. I paid the attorney, and flew back to LA.

It was hard to break the news to Bev, but I didn't sugar coat it. I told her flat out, we got nothing. The case was done. We had no recourse. It was a hard pill to swallow and an expensive lesson. Bottom line loss, $23,000. It pained me for a while, had me gritting my teeth in anger for being taken in, but I couldn't dwell on it.

Farmer in the Dell died shortly thereafter, his death verified by an obituary in the local newspaper and sent to me by the Texas attorney. Any assets that remained when his ranch went belly-up were sucked up by banks and creditors. At the hearing we were told no ostriches or eggs were recovered. According to the attorney, no plaintiffs were paid.

As an outsider, I had no choice but to believe the attorney. But that was Texas. I couldn't be sure that anything I was told was the truth. I'd been the victim of a "pigeon drop" to use my father-in law's terminology, and I'd gotten burned.

Bev forgave me. No divorce, though talk of it was in the air. (Just kidding, sort of.) We put it behind us and moved on.

You might think I wouldn't want any reminders of that costly scam, but a few years later, I bought a Cockatiel, a cute gray tweeter the size of my fist. Casting around my memories for a name, I decided on Argyle, the city in Texas where my biggest gamble on a bird didn't pay off.

# ~ Hacienda Days ~

The Hacienda Real was a huge dance club/bar/ restaurant in downtown LA. It catered to the young, Spanish speaking ever-growing Latino population, ages 20-30. I had become friends with Greg, the son of the owner of the club. We'd met at Nautilus gym (later Bally's and even later, LA Fitness) where I have maintained a $100 a year membership since 1974. I couldn't let that deal lapse.

We had become drinking buddies and fast friends, Greg and I, heading out most of the time to the Sawmill in Pasadena after our workouts. I told him about my car washes, my taco trucks and my family. He was a single guy, nine years younger than me, also born in March, and like me, had an older brother.

He told me how his father had bought several commercial properties in downtown LA in the 1950's after WW2, and that he had a ranch in Fallbrook, but seldom went there. And while his dad was quite wealthy, he was also eccentric and a non-conformist who lived in a one bedroom apartment in Pasadena, and had never bought a house. He dressed and looked like a homeless person, according to Greg, and in a rebellious move against auto safety standards, had cut the seat belts out of his car.

Aside from managing the club as a favor for his dad, Greg had a footwear business and was a gambler who almost never lost. He had a bookie who placed bets for him on horses and football games. He showed me how to parlay a $50 bet into a $300 win on a Joe Montana or Troy Aikman football game. I told him my dad never bet on football, but that he liked betting on those ponies.

One thing Greg didn't have was a girlfriend and he

needed one. I usually stayed away from playing matchmaker, but in the step aerobics class that we did every Friday afternoon was a young pretty Japanese woman who was a regular in the class. He liked her but always had some excuse for not speaking to her. I'd spoken to her a few times but then, I spoke to everyone.

Without really thinking about it, I invited her to the Sawmill that night, and to my surprise, she showed up. I introduced the two of them, and after a few months they were living together, and shortly after that, they got married! Bev and I flew to Hawaii for their wedding, and a year later we vacationed with them in Cancun. On many Sunday evenings the four of us dined at Monty's, our favorite steak house in Pasadena, and drank way more than we should have.

But before most of that happened, he had a little problem at the club that he thought I might be able to solve.

According to the Alcohol Beverage Control board, in order to keep the club and the bar open on those late weekend nights and make a grip of money, the very large kitchen, one that Puck himself would be proud to run, was required to serve food in the restaurant. The previous chef had prepared upscale, high-priced full entree fare that no one was buying. As a result, he couldn't pay the rent. The type of food needed for this weekend clientele to accompany the tequila shots and margaritas, was tacos, burritos, and nachos, street food at easy prices.

The deal Greg offered was, I would buy the supplies, create the menu, set the prices, and bring in a couple of helpers. Because we were friends, and the bar did enormous money on a weekend, he'd charge me no rent, and the profit after costs would be mine. Was I interested?

What else would I say but yes.

The club was on Broadway, underground, entered via a stairway from the sidewalk, and it was huge. More than 10,000 square feet, with a capacity of one thousand. The decor was all red, dimly lit with frosted glass sconces. Walls and seats were button-tucked, bull horns and massive wood sculptures hung on the walls. The red carpet was emblazoned with images of toreadors and bulls, and in every direction, mirrors made walls appear to go to infinity, and ceilings appear twenty feet high. A live band performed deafening salsa music until three in the morning, and every weekend the parquet floor would be packed with caballeros in cowboy hats, and leather boots, and senoritas in short skirts and stilettos. Members of my crew had been there once and were anxious to go again.

After two months of serving our regular truck fare to over a hundred people per night, Greg told me of the upcoming Christmas parties to be held there, the first one for 400 employees of a sewing factory. The reservation was already made. Could I handle it?

Never say die, that was my motto.

The cost was $48 per person, paid in advance to the company's personnel manager who was a college buddy of Greg's. I bought all the supplies and hired Tomaletta, a tamale maker supreme. She made dozens of tamales to go along with steak piccado, Spanish rice, refried beans, chicken enchiladas, quesadillas, nachos, a huge green salad and flan, all to be served buffet style. Most of the food was prepared by Stelle, my cook from the Manchester stand, and me, wearing my chef's hat and apron.

Once the food was prepared, we kept it hot, and rotated empty pans with fresh filled pans. In addition to my three crew members, two waitresses that I knew from a Mexican restaurant in Pasadena had never seen the Hacienda and offered to be hostesses just for tips. My crew wore crisp white aprons, the waitresses dressed in black. We looked professional and it was a big evening that turned into a long night. After all costs including paying my help overtime, I cleared about $8000.

We did two parties that year, and two the following year that turned out to be the last parties we would host. I never got to meet Greg's dad, but in a horrible accident he was killed one night in a car crash on the freeway. No other car was involved, and there was no determination on whether a seatbelt would have saved his life. Greg had been running the club as a favor for his dad. After the accident, he leased the club for a year, and soon after, put it on the market for a quick sale.

## ~Weathering Storms ~

After fourteen years being the "patron" for the trucks, I decided to sell them. I'd worked hard during those years, and there is something about hard work that you choose to do that makes it seem not so much like work. Besides that, the car washes were doing great business. I had a routine, and a schedule, but if the schedule got bent, if each small personal deadline wasn't met, I had no one to answer to but myself. That made a big difference. Besides that, I had surpassed my goal of making what *the* marshal made.

By 1993, my crew felt they could handle the trucks themselves, and I was willing to let them do that by selling the trucks to them. They knew better than anyone the income they generated, so we worked out a deal, a payment they could live with.

I gave them full access to Manchester's kitchen, and they continued parking the trucks there overnight. It seemed like a good plan at the time. For the next four months, I barely thought about the business of taco trucks though I was seeing them every day.

My cook at the Manchester stand, Stelle was seeing them every day as well, and she advised me of what was happening. Not having a regulator overseeing and keeping tabs on the operation, the business was declining after five months. The two crew members in charge were cutting corners, buying cheaper cuts of meat, and not getting out on time. The breaking point came when they fired four of the workers. One of those disgruntled workers complained to his sister who worked for the state department. She became their advisor. Before I knew exactly what had happened, the fired workers filed a suit against me. They blamed me for the loss of their jobs by selling the trucks. The two new "bosses" who fired them had no assets. I did.

Legal papers were served on me one week before Bev and I flew to Hawaii for our 24th anniversary. I didn't tell her about the suit. If you think that was a hard secret to keep, you're right. I managed to keep it to myself so we could enjoy walking on the beach, taking in a luau, and sipping Mai Tais from our deck. All things considered, we had a fantastic time in Maui.

When I returned there were hearings, depositions, and testimony to be given in court. It was nerve-wracking, time consuming, and costly. The judgement was in favor of the four workers, who wouldn't make eye contact with me when all of us were in the room. It resulted in a payout to them in four installments, $20,000 total.

I chalked it up as the cost of doing business, and once again as I had in the past, I pushed through, snapped back, and went on to the next crisis. Taking back my trucks. My two-man crew, and several new workers were not making it happen. They happily returned control to me, and we got back to better business.

A year later, with the court hearing finished, and the trucks working well again, Bev and I took our first Caribbean Cruise for our 25th anniversary. It was the maiden voyage of the Fantasia, Carnival cruise lines. We heard a few not so funny jokes about the tragic maiden voyage of the Titanic, but we weren't deterred. We flew to Florida, and had stops in Puerto Rico, the Virgin Islands, a day on the island of Grenada, a walking tour of Caracas, Venezuela, and snorkeling off the side of a boat in clear-water Aruba. It was all great, especially Aruba. We swore we'd go back, but the best intentions don't always pan out.

## ~ Obstacles ~

In 1996 The Athens Homeowners Association, acting on behalf of the residents in the neighborhoods bordered by Normandie at El Segundo and Hoover and 120th Street, petitioned the city council to prohibit fast food trucks from parking for more than one hour at any one location. To lead the charge, they enlisted the aid of city councilwoman, Yvonne Brathwaite Burke.

The initial intent of the petition escalated into a movement to prohibit taco trucks from parking on streets altogether unless the truck was servicing one business at a specific location for a specified amount of time. Ninety minutes was the maximum.

Those residents, most of them black, were interfering with my livelihood and that of my workers. My crews worked eight-hour shifts, but the trucks were there all day, and Vermont's truck worked well into the night. It had been parked on my property for fifteen years. Why should anyone object to how long the truck stayed on MY property? Aside from their opinion that the truck was an eyesore, I'm not sure they knew who owned it. I like to think that had they known the truck was owned by a black businessman who'd been in the area since 1978, they may have refrained from initiating the complaint. To be fair, once the complaint gathered steam, my grievance against their action overruled good judgement. I failed to attend one of their HOA meetings where I would have had the opportunity to state my case.

For months my trucks ducked and dodged a newly formed special sheriff's unit whose job was patrolling the area for food trucks in violation of this new ban. Naturally, business suffered with all the moving around, but I've never been one to turn palms up in the face of a crisis. We continued the duck and dodge until a light bulb clicked on in my head. Again.

As Vermont's truck was my biggest money maker, why not duplicate what the truck was doing without the truck? Why not convert one car wash stall at Vermont into a fast food take-out stand like the stand built at Manchester and offer the same menu. Would it work? I didn't know, but I was determined to try.

We sent a letter to Councilwoman Burke's office

explaining my plan and asking for a moratorium on the enforcement to allow time to get the stand built without interruption of truck business. She agreed to a 90-day desist of the enforcement unit. I could keep the trucks working and start building.

## ~ Azusa Sale ~

Foothill Car Wash, aka Bev's car wash in Azusa had been flanked by small businesses when we purchased it in 1980. By 1996, those businesses had either closed or relocated. Even the McDonald's open since 1955, had turned off the lights of the golden arches for good. The sole survivor was the car wash, but it too would succumb to Azusa's redevelopment project.

The city planners had negotiated with the owner of the shopping center to buy the center for expansion of Azusa Pacifica College. The property owner, our landlord, had agreed to the sale. Negotiations dragged out for over two years. Bev had spoken with her landlord, attended meetings with the planners, and fought hard to keep the wash open. But it was a losing battle. Appraisals were done of the property and the equipment, and papers were being drawn up.

I had started the bay conversion at Vermont and was hoping to use some money from Azusa's settlement to get it completed. I mentioned this to Greg in conversation as we left the gym one afternoon, and without hesitating, he loaned me  $10,000 on a handshake. As added insurance, Bev's mom took a tour of the nearly finished conversion and was impressed enough to loan her son-in-law

$5000, just enough to finish the job.

We opened the Vermont stand in the spring of 1997. I called the new stand 4 Amigos, after the four guys who caused me grief the year before. That could have been a negative reminder, but I had read something years before that always stayed with me: "With every adversity comes the seed of an equivalent benefit." I liked that quote and thought of it as I looked at the fast food stand, the result of my latest adversity, and I was grateful that I've always tried to stay positive when facing something that could be considered a major problem.

I didn't realize that people in the area were waiting anxiously for the "open for business" sign to appear in the window. On that first day, customers were lined up. Temporarily, I kept the truck on location because I wanted customers to know the food on the truck and the food at the stand were the same, with one exception. Burgers and fries were added to the menu.

Bev wanted to know how the first day went. I minimized it. Told her it was "a little hectic." She'd met the two workers who would be running the stand. They spoke almost no English.

"Who's going to help them? Who's taking the orders? Do they even know how to make burgers? Someone should be there to show them what to do." These were the questions she threw at me. She felt a real stake in this from the beginning since her mom had pitched in with the loan.

By this time, Foothill car wash was closed. Bev was very sad about that. She missed going to her wash. For seventeen years she had taken care of it, and now all that remained of the negotiations was the payout which they promised in 30-60 days.

So, I made a suggestion. I said, "Bring yourself on down girlfriend, and help."

Bev began coming to 4 Amigos every day, mornings to mid-afternoon. She took most of the orders at the window and showed her helpers how to write them up and give numbers to customers waiting. She taught them how to make burgers, they showed her how to roll a burrito. She taught them a little English, and she learned basic food Spanish. Some of the Mexican people would speak to her in Spanish after she'd learned how to say "para aqui, o para llevar?" There were some stumbles, but for the most part, they did a good business. I continued in my role as procurer, providing everything needed to run the two fast food stands, while maintaining my three car washes.

The deal with the city of Azusa ended in the summer of '97. They bought us out for $65,000, based on the amount left on our lease and our average annual gross. We paid back Greg and mom, gave uncle Sam his cut and banked the rest. Two years later, Foothill Car Wash was no more, and Azusa Pacifica looked like a brand-new school.

## ~ L'Arthur ~

Just before Thanksgiving, my brother called with something important to tell me, and he wanted Bev to listen on the extension. Without any build up, he told us he'd been diagnosed with prostate cancer. His voice got even more serious when he said, "You need to get tested, Howard. You might have it too."

His words didn't register. I told him to hold on.

Back up. Wait a minute! I made him repeat everything because honestly, I didn't understand. He explained that he'd taken the PSA test and that his doctor had told him that the result, L'Arthur's number, was higher than any he'd ever seen. I knew nothing about prostate cancer, and what was a PSA test?

When I got my voice back, I told him he should get a second opinion because this had to be a mistake.

But there was no mistake. L'Arthur had prostate cancer. He would be seeing doctors for the next few months to discuss possible treatment. I hung up the phone still believing something would happen to make this bad news turnaround.

With Christmas approaching, I wanted it to be special, like Christmas of 1994. That year I had rented a limousine to bring my mother, Bev's mother Etta, and my sister Gwen and her two sons to our house for Christmas dinner. All family members came to our house that year. After a great dinner, the limo took all of us for a cruise of the neighborhood to see the Christmas lights. It had been a real treat going to the Balian house, the whole block crowded with cars full of onlookers to see their annual decorations, and to West Altadena's Christmas tree lane.

But Christmas of '97 strained to be special. Muhtha's declining health had kept her from coming. Bev's mom was there but needed help walking. L'Arthur was there looking thinner but with a big smile. It was hard to believe he was sick. As it happened, that was our last Christmas at Skywood Circle.

I'd learned more about the prostate and the PSA test. PSA stood for Prostate Specific Antigen. The test determined how much of the antigen was in the blood.

With this test, a high number did not make you a winner.

In January I went to Kaiser and was given the PSA test. A normal range was 3-5. My result was 12. After a second test, it had elevated to 13. Not good news. Two weeks later, after a painful biopsy where eight to twelve sample nips were taken from the gland, I asked my brother why he hadn't told me it hurt so much. He grinned at me and said, "I figured you could handle it lil' brother."

The day I got the result of the biopsy, Bev was at a Jazzercise taping in Fallbrook. Even though we had talked on the phone, I waited until she got home to tell her the result was positive. I had prostate cancer too. I held her close to me so I wouldn't see her cry.

The cancer diagnosis stunned me at the moment I heard it, made me blink, maybe stopped my heart for a split second. That's how those words affected me. I guess if I'd had symptoms, or if I'd had pain or discomfort, wasn't feeling well or healthy in any way, my reaction may have been different. I might have been expecting bad news. But because I felt strong, felt like myself, I did what I've always done in the face of bad news. I let it roll over me and move on. Having heard it, my next thought was, okay, what do we do about it?

At my next appointment the doctor explained that my cancer was different than my brother's. His was aggressive. It had already spread outside the gland and gone into his bones and one kidney. Mine had not spread. It was still inside the gland. For me, surgical removal of the prostate gland was strongly recommended by both doctors who had examined me. L'Arthur's cancer was untreatable. Surgery would not save him. He'd been given a year to live.

On April 15th, 1998, I sat in Kaiser's waiting room with an empty stomach and Bev holding my hand. I don't remember feeling afraid. Maybe I was just trying so hard to be brave and keep her from collapsing right there on the floor, that my own fear left me for a time. There were some fleeting thoughts of doom and a familiar connection to how I felt when I left for Vietnam, but I pushed those thoughts out of my head.

I thought about my doctor instead, how I had confidence in him, a cool guy who spelled his first name J-o-n, like our son. He made no guarantees, but he had performed over 1100 successful "nerve sparing" operations, and he was sure mine would be one more notch on his belt. I had to believe that. I had to believe I would pull through, that this was the best treatment for me, and that everything was going to be okay. I'd agreed to this surgery. There really was no other option.

They wheeled me into the operating room at six a.m. I don't remember anything after that until I was in the recovery room. I didn't know where I was, but the first voice I heard was L'Arthur's saying, "Your mustache looks just the same." My brother still had his crazy sense of humor. Bev was there watching me toss and turn, still under the effect of the anesthesia. The doctor had already told her the nerve-sparing surgery was a success. I'd be out of recovery and home in a few days.

## ~ Leaving Skywood ~

No one knew it, but I was in a bit of a financial crisis at the beginning of 1998. A preponderance of misfortune had descended on us, but mostly on me. The misfortune included the ostriches scam, the truck lawsuit, bad weather in the first three months of 1998, my surgery, the cost of building 4 Amigos, the absence of Azusa's income, and the second refinance on Skywood that had increased our mortgage payment to a whopping $4117 a month, not including property taxes. To top it off, we were behind one payment. Is that too much information? It hurt me to even think about selling Skywood, but it seemed like the only sure-thing solution to the current situation.

We had twenty-four years of memories at Skywood, of family Christmas dinners, summers in the pool, windstorms that thrashed the yard, 4th of July fireworks in the driveway, our huge backyard, our mountain view, neighborhood potlucks, nice neighbors. It was the only home Jon and Lance knew, so of course, it would be hard to leave it. But we had to go.

We had listed it with a realtor before my surgery, not knowing for sure what the outcome of the surgery would be. During my recovery at home, we allowed only serious buyers to view it. Strangers walking through the house was an inconvenience, but it couldn't be helped. Then one day, a familiar face came through. It was the actor Dennis Haysbert, the Allstate guy. He didn't buy Skywood, but shortly after his visit, someone did.

I was laid up for a month and I hated it. Every move had to be slow and deliberate to avoid disturbing the stitches below my belly and the catheter insertion. It was removed after ten days, an excruciating procedure. It was a tossup as to which was more painful, the catheter removal or the biopsy.

Bev assured me that she and Jon were handling

the restaurant and the washes. "No problem," she said. But I needed to see for myself. By the end of May, I felt well enough to return to work for a few hours and go to each car wash. I was happily surprised that everything was going smoothly. They'd done a great job.

We started house hunting again. As Skywood's escrow neared closing, we had to choose between an older house in east Pasadena or a townhouse in an area off the Pasadena Freeway called Monterey Hills. We chose the townhouse.

Two roll-off dumpsters were needed to haul away the accumulation of things stored and stashed over 24 years at Skywood. Why had we held on to so much stuff?

In June of 1998 we moved into a two-bedroom, two bath unit in the Marshall Villas complex in Monterey Hills. It had a tiny den with a built-in mahogany bar, and a bonus that we discovered after a couple of months. Views from our terrace of the setting sun that took our breath away. We wondered how we ever lived without such a view. I took so many pictures of sunsets I could have papered a wall. We were tenants again with a one-year lease. Without having to pay a gigantic house note, we saved $2400 a month.

Out of the blue on a night in August, as Bev and I watched tv, I felt an unmistakable undeniable stirring below my belt line for the first time in five months. Could it be? Yes, it was. Yippee kayay! Hooray for nerve-sparing surgery. I declared myself fully recovered. On my next checkup, the doctor gave me a thumbs up with one commitment. PSA tests every six months for ten years. I told him if the finger exam wasn't required, I'd be there.

On February 2, 1999, I made the 70-mile drive to L'Arthur's house in Lancaster asking myself why had my brother moved so far away. The distance kept us from seeing each other more often. He was busy, I was busy, but he'd call and kid me about my drinking. "Still drinking that gin?" he'd say joking. My brother, the liquor store owner who rarely took a drink. When I got to the house he was in bed and in pain. We talked about old stuff, things that happened when we were kids. He talked about his toddler grandson Tyler and wondered if the boy would remember him. He was glad that Bev and I had come out to see one of his properties, an old ranch here in Lancaster that he wanted to give to me. He asked if I had changed my mind about it. But he knew I hadn't. With a knowing smile he nodded at me as if to say he understood everything, and he told me he was ready to go. "Everything is everything" he used to say, and I'd say, "L'Arthur, what does that mean?" And he would just laugh.

Two days later my brother was gone.

I tried to make sense of why this had to happen to L'Arthur. He was one of the good guys. I know it's not right to judge, but every day I dealt with individuals far less worthy who were still a part of this world, abusers of the life still theirs to enjoy. People who created problems, people who made life difficult for others, who broke the law, and yet they were still around. I saw them when I was a marshal. I saw them at my car washes. They ate off my trucks, some were customers at the stand. They were still here, but my brother was gone. A husband, a father of four, who always had a smile and a good word to pass on, who worked too hard and should have had many more years ahead of him. A young man at heart and so proud of his family. Gone at the age of 54.

As he'd done so often from when we were boys, L'Arthur had come through for me again, this time in the biggest way possible. He had saved my life.

For some time after my recovery and L'Arthur's death, I reminded friends that if they hadn't gotten a PSA test to get one. Often there were no symptoms, so the test was important. My nephew Chris, L'Arthur's second son and an army vet himself advised me to take my case to the VA and get re-examined. If a connection was made to agent orange as the possible cause of the cancer, I would be eligible for disability benefits from Uncle Sam.

At the VA the counselor informed me that the VA benefit would be determined by the severity of health issues that may be a result of serving in Vietnam. They asked if I was having nightmares, headaches, skin rashes, insomnia, nervousness, anxiety, anything that could be described as PTSD. I told them no, I wasn't, and thankfully, the prostate surgery had not altered my quality of life. After my full recovery, I went back to feeling the way I felt prior to the surgery. I felt fine. All physical bodily functions were "go." I had returned to my business and business was good.

I probably talked myself out of a larger benefit, but I couldn't claim something that wasn't true. The VA's final decision was that I was entitled to $84 per month due to exposure to agent orange. I appreciated the compensation from Uncle Sam, but I was most grateful that I didn't need that benefit to be any more than it was.

# ~ Paris (2000 ) ~

After buying our first computer for Christmas, 1999, figuring out how to use it, and making some stock market purchases, I booked a trip using the world wide web. In May of 2000, Bev and I flew to Paris non-stop from LAX and honestly, I didn't enjoy the flight. Twelve hours in the air was rough. But once we landed, I could only hope the French to English dictionaries Bev brought would help us, and that the many French guards we saw in and around the terminal in drab green uniforms would not have to use the M16's they were carrying over their shoulders.

Our hotel was small, with a tiny view, but cozy. The concierge's English was enough to direct us to the closest Paris Metro stop which was only a few steps away. We walked tiny narrow cobble-stone streets, where two cars could not pass at the same time and passed one restaurant after another with outdoor eating. We ate baguettes still warm from the oven. We went into an all-night club where a three-piece rock band was singing American songs with French accents. They invited me, the only black guy, to join in for a session as they sang Chuck Berry and Little Richard songs, *Lucille* and *Johnny Be Good*. They took me for a "rocker," too, but I had to beg off.

We had one meal at a genuine French café, where the food was only so-so, but the Crème Brûlée served flaming with raspberries and blueberries was to die for.

We bought very cool looking red and black leather jackets, his and hers from two guys in a sportscar who flagged us down as we searched for the Latin arrondisse-ment. It was as if the word "tourist" was taped to my back the way they zeroed in on us. My gut was saying I probably shouldn't buy the jackets, but I did anyway. The minute they sped away with our money, now *their* money, I had a serious case of buyer's remorse. More like buyer's fear of getting caught with stolen merchandise. We gave up looking for the Latin section. We hustled back to our hotel and stuffed the jackets into our extra suitcase. Then we sat for a while, waiting, maybe for a knock on the door, the gendarmes perhaps. But no one came. We ventured out again.

We walked the Champs-Elysees, where street merchants tried to get us to buy something, anything. Well, mostly me. Bev said it was the fishing vest I was wearing. It pegged us as tourists for sure. We resisted.

At the Louvre, we snapped photos of the Mona Lisa and the statue of David and met a guy from Senegal selling souvenirs. We told him we were Americans. To prove he knew about America he repeatedly said the only words he knew. "Mike Tyson. Mike Tyson."

We took the RER train to the castle in Versailles where a festival was getting underway, complete with walking gargoyles nine feet tall, exotic classic cars, and a hot air balloon that was nearly blown away by a gusty wind that gave way to a warm rain that lasted just long enough to get everyone wet.

We figured out the money and how to ride the Metro from stop to stop, but never could pronounce the names of the stations.

In Montmartre, we saw the home of artist Toulouse Lautrec, had our portraits done in paper cut outs mounted and framed, and bought art off the street from two of the hundreds of artists that lined the marketplace.

Something about my mustache and my fisherman's vest got people's attention.

Every evening the Eiffel Tower was lighted with a thousand lights or more, and at one of the subway stops was an area of sidewalk a short distance from the tower, where we stood at a rail with other tourists and just stared at its brilliance. Earlier in the day Bev walked halfway up the first platform. I was more up for a nap.

That same night as we stepped off the subway, a nice French woman directed us to the Moulin Rouge. Once inside the club and seated at our table watching the Folies Bergere, I wasn't sure about what I was seeing. "Are they topless?" I said to Bev. Well of course they were. She had probably told me, but I had to see it to believe it. In France, nudity is no big deal. Their feathery skimpy costumes didn't cover much from the waist down, but the waist up of twenty gorgeous dancers was absolutely in full view.

Yup. It was a trip to remember. I was dreading the flight back, but after a week, I was happy to be going home. Paris would be remembered for many wonderful things, and one eventual decision. It was the last time I would get onto a plane.

## ~ Unit 534 ~

Townhouse living agreed with us. I almost felt guilty that I didn't miss Skywood more. I certainly didn't miss the cleanups we went through after those notorious windstorms. More important, the money we were saving was making us feel comfortable again, and the car wash income was steadily rising. I'd sold the taco trucks freeing up more time, so we walked almost every morning, and if we didn't walk, I'd hit the gym early. At 53, I was still pretty agile.

Nearby South Pasadena had a great farmers market on Tuesdays, and we bought fresh fruit and veggies. We caught early movies in Pasadena and bought old junk we didn't need from the Salvation Army and Goodwill stores and browsed at least once a week to check the shelves for new junk. Occasionally we'd find a piece worth having. This was the kind of stuff I'd always wanted to be able to do, and now I was doing it.

By the middle of 2001 we'd been leasing for three years. We wanted to purchase our unit, but our landlord did not want to sell.I'd had my eye on the end unit, #534, across from ours that we passed every morning on our walk. It didn't have the great view ours had, but it had a patio. I was ready to become an owner again. If it ever came up for sale, I'd jump on it.

Then over the summer we learned that the wife in unit #534 had passed away in hospice care after a long illness. We didn't know the couple, but we'd heard the husband wanted to sell the unit and move to Florida. We waited a few days, out of respect, before introducing ourselves, and told him we were interested in buying the unit. He was an easy going free-wheeling kind of guy who had owned a yacht catering business in Marina del Rey and was planning to start that business in Florida.

He knocked $10,000 off the asking price to save the commission, we met his lowered price, and by the end of August we started gathering boxes for the move. Nine days later, on September 11th, everything stopped.

That morning 1 was sitting on the edge of our unmade bed, watching the television. Boxes were scattered around because we had started packing for the move. Bev came into the bedroom. She looked at me, then the screen. We stared at the television, at the plane, the explosion, the smoke and then as if in slow motion, one of the twin towers in New York City began to topple.

It hardly seemed that four years had gone by since Bev started working the fast food stand at Vermont (4 Amigos), but that's when she decided to throw in the towel. The brothers finally did her in. They harassed her at the window, demanded extras for free, cursed at the help, and tried to pass bad money, or not pay at all. She tried to accommodate them, give in to them, but there were some bad dudes in the area. Nothing seemed to work. I'd been telling her from my experience at the wash, some black folks in the area had no respect for anything. She was seeing it live and in person.

She stayed on to help the two female workers who tried to keep it open, but even when two other workers were hired it was too much for them to handle. After being closed for a month, we leased it to a Latino man experienced in the food business and he started fresh. He's still our tenant.

## ~ To the Beach (2002) ~

At my Vermont location one day, 1 found a catalog of homes and condos in the beach cities that were for sale. It happened shortly after friends, Becky and Ronald purchased a home in Redondo Beach. We still had our cabin in Crestline but making the 75-mile drive had become a chore. Traffic on the ten freeway was a nightmare no matter what time of day we went. I had never considered buying a house at the beach until the catalog put the thought in my head.

A quick www. check online got me in touch with a realtor who had a condo for sale in Marina del Rey at the Marina City Club. I knew the club and the area from the three weeks that I worked in the Culver City marshal's office.

The realtor met us at the MCC, and after finding the right elevator, took us to the ninth floor. The condo was a one bedroom a mile from the beach. It had an ocean view, a city view, and on a clear day with binoculars, a view of the Hollywood sign. Our reaction? *Whoa! This is cool.*

Minimizing our enthusiasm, we thanked her for showing it to us, went back to our car, and drove out of the lot. A block away I asked Bev, "Did you like that?"

She said, "Yeah, did you? "

I said "Yeah."

She said "Then why are we leaving?"

I turned the car around and headed straight for the realtor's office. At last, after thirty plus years of marriage, Bev and I were on the same page at the same time.Earlier in the year we had sold the cabin in Twin Peaks. Though we probably held onto it for too long, we had banked about $30,000 from the sale, and no longer had that note. Which is why we both felt this condo was doable. The realtor contacted the seller by phone with our offer, and he accepted. A month later voila! We had ourselves a condo at the beach.

During a trip to our favorite Goodwill store, we

found a framed painting of a lighthouse and hung it on the condo wall. Lighthouses became our condo theme. We started going to the beach once a week.

The year I sold the Twin Peaks cabin, 2002, was the same year I sold the four-plex on Hoover Blvd. in LA, purchased in 1987 that I'd had as a rental for 15 years. Sweet payback for no longer having those two rentals, I had promised to buy myself a Prowler. Yes, another vehicle. It was made by Chrysler and styled like a roadster of the 1920's. I showed Bev a picture of it. She waved me off, as if it were a joke. Even after all these years, she thought I was kidding.

Online I found a Prowler in Kansas City in the burnt orange color I wanted. Coincidentally the father of our friend Cindy lived in Kansas City. What are the odds? She called her dad and as a favor, he checked it out for me and said it was beautiful.

Late in 2003, the Prowler arrived at our townhouse on Arbolada. It became the third in my fleet of "hobby" vehicles: the Porsche, the Nissan 300ZX, and the Prowler, my cruising motor cars.

## ~ Muhtha and Lizzie (2004) ~

My Manchester Car Wash was four blocks from 84th Place where I grew up. Muhtha still lived there and had come to see the wash when it was being built. She didn't understand why I wanted to build there, but she was impressed and proud when she saw it up and running.

Leaving the wash one day I stopped by the house

to see her. She looked at me for a long time and I realized with a sinking feeling, she didn't know who I was. This wasn't the first time. I bent down close to her and said, "Who am I? Do you know who I am?" She stared at me, in silence, and finally said, "Yes. You're Keown." Keown was one of her grandsons, Gwen's oldest son.

We had never told Muhtha about L'Arthur's death and she never missed seeing him. All of us realized by then that Muhtha was losing her memory. She tried to recognize us. It was painful to see her struggling to recall our names and know our faces. She'd had other health issues, but now she was slipping away from us and we could not save her. She spent time in the hospital in a special care unit because she couldn't feed herself. Soon after, she stopped talking altogether.

When Muhtha died on August 30<sup>th</sup>, 2004, she was 85. In the thirty-four years since dad died, she had pulled herself out of her grief and become a teacher's aid at South Park Elementary where the staff and the kids all knew "nice Miz Higginson." She had learned how to drive a car but was never comfortable behind the wheel and would hand over the keys to one of her kids to drive. She was the backbone of the family, beloved by her four children, and a loving grandma to ten grandkids who called her Gra-mommie.

A few months after Muhtha's death, I was elected "member at large" on the HOA board of our complex thanks to Bev. In that capacity I was made privy to the problems of other residents in the complex, problems I preferred not to know about. Besides that, now that we had grandkids we wanted more room.  So, after six years in a townhouse, we began house hunting again.

We had looked in Eagle Rock in 1998 before leaving Altadena so we went back to Eagle Rock in search of our last home. We made a bid on a house that we both liked just days before Bev left with girlfriends for two days at a health spa. She came back refreshed and alert, but I had to prompt her. "Aren't you going to ask about the house?" I said.

"Oh, what happened?" she asked. She had forgotten all about it. Must have been some spa treatment.

"We got it," I said.

"We did?" Hugs all around.

There'd been a bidding war on the house, but I fought to the "bidder" end and came out on top, literally.

In 2005 we moved from the townhouse in Monterey Hills to the hilltop of Round Top Drive. We had a one hundred-eighty-degree panoramic view of the sky-scrapers of downtown LA to the houses and lights that stud the Glendale Hills.

"Trendy" Eagle Rock, twelve minutes to Pasadena, ten minutes to Americana in Glendale, fifteen minutes to Dodger Stadium, and on a good day, twenty-five minutes to my car washes. It's not "The Manchester" but this was it. Home. That year, 2005, I sold the cabin in Crestline to my cousin, and after leasing the Monterey Hills townhouse for a year, we sold it as well.

Lizzie and her husband Julious came to visit after we moved to Round Top. Little did we know it was the only time she would see the house. Less than a month later, without us knowing how seriously ill she was, Lizzie went into the hospital for heart surgery intended to extend her life by fifteen years. Instead, something none of us ever considered might happen did happen. After the surgery, she never regained consciousness. She hemorrhaged internally without the doctors knowing it and died in the recovery room. She was 55.

Lizzie's unexpected death was strike three for me, and l was out. Out of my faith, out of the ability to believe in a just god. Dad gone at 57, L'Arthur at 54, and now Lizzie. Before the year was over, Bev's mother would be gone too. Both of our parents and half my siblings, gone. lt was a rough few years.

## ~Turning 60 ~

Moose McGillycuddy's was my "Cheers," the place where l hung out after my workouts at the gym. l won't say everybody knew my name, but the barkeeps and hostesses knew my tips, and that was always good for smiles and greetings and the occasional vodka rocks on the house.

As my 60th birthday approached, l decided to have a special party at Moose's not only for the fun of having a whole restaurant for a night to celebrate with friends, but to honor my family members who were gone.

Neither my brother, my younger sister, or my father had made it to the age of 60. l couldn't deny the reality of that painful fact and l thought about it a lot. They missed out on so much. Reaching this milestone humbled me like nothing else in my life.

March 11th was on a Sunday that year, the week before March madness. We invited 120 guests to the party. For entertainment we hired a DJ, a comedian, a belly dancer, a Tahitian dancer, and lookalikes of Jack Nicholson and Dolly Parton to give the party a little Hollywood flair.

A photographer slipped in and around the guests taking pictures like the paparazzi, and everyone wore Hawaiian attire decorated by the flower leis we passed out.

The party was in full swing when my buddy Sol sipped on his Tequila Sunrise and said, "I didn't know you could close down a whole restaurant for a private party. How much did this cost?"

We were good enough friends that talking money wasn't a problem. I told him $10,000 bucks. It was expensive. But when guests said it was the best party they'd ever been to, I felt it was worth it. You only turn 60 once, and besides you can't take it with you.

## ~ No Longer a Tenant ~

When the original 15-year lease on my Vermont car wash expired in June of 1993, my landlady, the kindly widow Kendall ignored my written offer to purchase the land. I doubt that it was her decision.

She had remarried in her old age and turned her business dealings over to her new husband, the landlord from hell. I met with them both in 1993 to discuss a new lease or a sale of the property. Her husband's superior attitude suggested that he believed the south would rise again and that black people should still be treated like share-croppers. I had to deal with him through three five-year lease renewals. I owned the business, but he owned the land, and he wouldn't let me forget it.

By the end of 2008, prior to another five-year renewal, I made my third offer to buy the property. I don't know for sure, but I suspect that the election of President

Obama had an impact on the landlord's change of heart. Perhaps he feared a potential shift in his personal foundation, in property values, in the stock market, possibly in the country itself. Whatever the reason, he finally agreed to sell the property to me. He wouldn't budge from his price that was more than my offer, and more than the middle appraised value. But I had learned something from Poltash about "averaging down" in regards to the stock market and property purchases. My cost for the Manchester property at $80,000 was way under value. My cost for San Pedro/Enterprise was close to market value at the time. So even though Vermont's asking price was over-valued, by averaging down, the values for each property came to $400,000. More important, Vermont was my first car wash. I built it from the ground up. The property was worth it to me, so we made the deal. The loan process took nearly six months but finally closed and funded in June 2009. All three of my car wash properties had increased in value, and I was free of a landlord forever. The car washes were doing great business, and I had reached that goal. I was making more than "The" Marshal.

Our upcoming anniversary in August was a time to celebrate. We reserved the restaurant at the Marina City Club for a 40th anniversary party, and while discussing ideas with the party planner, she asked for the name of the happy couple. "We're the happy couple!" we said. "The party is for us." Her jaw dropped.

Bev and I agreed. The look of surprise on her face was genuine. She thought the party was for our parents and couldn't believe we'd been married forty years. That earned her a big tip. Then again, maybe that was her plan.

The party, held on Sunday, August 30, 2009 was emotional and fun, made us feel happy, sad, nostalgic and joyful, all at the same time. It was probably the best party we ever had.

*My 70th Birthday, March 2018*

*~ with Beverly Higginson ~*

# ~ Epilogue ~

I opened Vermont in 1978 charging fifty cents to wash, twenty-five cents to vacuum. After an increase to seventy-five cents, and then to $1.25 a few years later, I ran a special in 1984, from November through Christmas. $1.00 to wash! Mine was the first car wash in the area to lower the price. The increase in business was immediate. I left the price at a dollar, and that's what it is today.

In '78 there were two competitors within a five-mile radius. Now there are at least six. Ninety percent of customers are Hispanic, and the number of cars has at least tripled. Every car wash in the area is busy. They don't all come to Howard's Car Wash, but I get my fair share. Mine is one of the few black-owned businesses in the area, and the only black-owned of my six competitors. I still occasionally get new customers, and some are surprised to learn that not only do I work here, but that I'm the owner.

I told Bev in the beginning when I stumbled onto the Compton wash, that coin-op car washes could be a great business. Open 24/7, no full-time employees, just cruise by a couple of times a week, and collect the money. In reality of course, it's more involved than that.

It's a low cost service business for the consumer, an absentee-owner business that can be run in a variety of ways. For me, keeping three locations supplied with the basics—soap, wax, vending, and change—keeping the equipment working, the grounds free of debris, and the utilities paid is what I'm charged with. I've always had good people for part-time help with maintenance and some customer service, usually retired people in the neighborhood. But there is nothing my help does that I don't do myself when I'm there. And I'm there for some part of every day, seven days a week.

It's not always smooth sailing. In the past I've dealt with attempted burglaries, vandalism, graffiti and gang bangers. I paint over their junk, make necessary repairs, ramp up security, and keep my operation rolling. It's all part of being in business. I don't let those easy fixes interfere with my self-prescribed routine, or the simple pleasures I enjoy in life. And while I'm enjoying taking a spin in the Prowler or catching a mid-day movie, people are washing their cars at Howard's Car Wash. My days start late and end early. I made a comeback after the set-backs of the late 90's, and now, since 2010, the business has increased every year. After forty-two years, it was a great decision and I'm still enjoying it to this day.

Someone once said, if you don't toot your own horn, it'll go un-tooted. So, I'm tooting.

I'm a Grampa with four bright grandkids. Lance's daughter Lauryn is a college student, and Jon and his wife Kris, who married in 2000, have three teenage boys, JoVan, Jayden, and Jordan. After 50 years of marriage, Bev is still the love of my life, and Jon and Lance are navigating the ups and downs of parenthood.

I've lived in five different sections of the same city, bought and sold eight pieces of property, lived in five of them, rented out a couple, and been fortunate enough to have two as "getaways."

I've served my country as a member of the USAF, survived Vietnam, the marshal's department and two LA riots. I've worked in the holds of ships in San Pedro, served legal papers to the rich and famous in Beverly Hills and unhappily, evicted undesirables in Compton. I've had the experience of running a hamburger stand, a taco truck business, building two fast food stands, being an "extra" in Hollywood movies, and an entrepreneur in South Central.

Being the captain of my speedboat on Silverwood Lake was family fun, riding ATV's through sand dunes and riverbeds risky fun, and driving around town in a Jaguar, a Bentley, and a Mercedes, at different times of course, attention-getting fun. While I no longer have those vehicles, I still have my Nissan, my Prowler and the Porsche. Some possessions are hard to divest.

I took the family to Mazatlan where we ate al pastor street tacos, and to Jamaica where we rode motor bikes through Negril. We've vacationed in San Francisco, Santa Barbara, San Diego and the Grand Canyon.We visited the London Bridge at Lake Havasu, Hearst Castle, the redwood trees in Kings Canyon, the campgrounds of Lake Isabella, and skied the runs at Mountain High.

I've sipped wine in Paris cafes with Bev, snorkeled in Maui, helicoptered along the beaches of Kauai, caught a marlin off the coast of Cabo San Lucas and toured ancient dwellings in Cancun.

We've cruised Mexico for a short run, and the Caribbean for the long run, both enjoyable unforgettable excursions. I wouldn't trade a minute of those experiences, and yet, I believe Dorothy had it right all along. There's no place like home.

I recovered from a cut that split open the palm of my right hand and required 18 stitches, and as recently as 2018, I drove myself to the hospital after accidentally slicing off the end of my ring finger. Really. Those accidents were minor inconveniences when compared to prostate cancer which ended my brother's life, and of which I am now a 20-year survivor.

After working out for 35 years, I still go the gym, though Susan's aerobics class is a thing of the past. Instead, I ride the bike even with bad knees, and after ten years of yoga classes, I do yoga stretches in my backyard with Bev. Not as agile as I was five years ago, so I only do three songs in the Zumba class. (smile)

I'm a hands-on entrepreneur. I don't know any other way. Lucky for me, son Jon—like my right hand—knows the business and comes four days a week to do the heavy lifting and sometimes brings my grandsons to pitch in. Being retired was never my plan. The washes keep me going.

My brother once called me a risk-taker and my mother used to call me Mr. Smarty. Over the years I've stuck my neck out, but always with a goal in mind, and the determination to make something positive happen. If there is a *constant* running through my decisions, **it's that I wasn't afraid.**

I can still walk onto my lot at Vermont where I started Howard's 50cent quickie, see that slab of concrete with my initials and the initials of my boys, and see the fulfillment of my dream, my version of freedom.

It is my hope that Howard's Car Wash will be my legacy and benefit my family long after I'm gone.